J I M M Y
WHITE
SECOND WIND
M Y   A U T O B I O G R A P H Y

Sport Media

To my late dad,
who was my best pal

Sport Media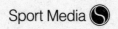

By Jimmy White
with Chris Brereton

© Jimmy White

Paperback Edition
Published in Great Britain in 2015.
Published and produced by: Trinity Mirror Sport Media, PO Box 48,
Old Hall Street, Liverpool L69 3EB.

Publishing Director: Steve Hanrahan
Commercial Director: Will Beedles
Executive Editor: Paul Dove
Executive Art Editor: Rick Cooke
Senior Sub Editor: Roy Gilfoyle
Senior Marketing Executive: Claire Brown
Sales and Marketing Manager: Elizabeth Morgan

ISBN: 978-1-910335123

Photographic acknowledgements:
Front cover image: Tony Woolliscroft.
Trinity Mirror, David Muscroft, PA Photos, Jimmy White collection.
With thanks to Simon Flavin and Jason Francis.

Thanks to Clive Everton.

Printed and bound by CPI Group (UK) Ltd, Croydon, CR0 4YY.

Contents

Thanks

All the people I care about in my life know I care about them. I'd like to thank them all for everything they've done for me. They know who they are.

I would also like to thank my publishers Trinity Mirror Sport Media, who have always been so enthusiastic about the book. One man has stood out. I'd like to thank Chris Brereton, who has done a fantastic job putting my story together. He's a first class writer and a top lad. Thanks for everything, mate.

I've been asked why I'm writing this book now, at this point in my life. It's simple, really. It's time to get the real story out there. I've written a book before but I held back. I wasn't ready to tell it like it really was. Now I am.

There are people in my career who have helped me along the way. I'd like them to know what it's meant to me, so I hope how I feel about them comes across in this book. There are also people who haven't helped me. They're part of the story too.

I've made mistakes in my life. I know that, but it's important to me that other people know. It's even more important that they learn from my mistakes. By telling my story, if I stop one person from taking one line of cocaine, then I will have achieved a goal. I call it the Devil's Dandruff. Be wary of it. It will destroy you, like it nearly did me.

My story is also, of course, about the wonderful game that I've been privileged to call my job. Snooker has been my life. When you start playing a sport, if you do it for enjoyment then you can keep it going as long as I have. I still feel the same magic now when I pick up a cue as I did when I was a young lad. I've got more to give. I'm not done yet.

It's been pretty emotional looking back. At times, it's been hard. I've been a very silly boy. I'm lucky to be talking to you now. I'm lucky to be given a second chance to tell my story.

Jimmy White, October, 2014

When it comes to (quite rightly) sharing the praise for this book around, firstly I'd like to mention Jimmy for his co-operation. Parts of this book will make for an unsettling and disappointing read for some of his fans but Jimmy was unflinching in his desire to paint an accurate picture of his life.

His hands are no longer tied and he wanted to unburden a lot of the secrets and stories that cost him so dearly in Sheffield and elsewhere.

Whatever anyone thinks of him after reading this autobiography, Jimmy can at least be confident in the knowledge that he told his version of events as thoroughly and as passionately as possible and you can ask no more of a man than that.

At Trinity Mirror Sport Media, I'd like to thank Steve Hanrahan, Paul Dove, Roy Gilfoyle, Rick Cooke, Will Beedles

ACKNOWLEDGEMENTS

and Elizabeth Morgan for their diligence, hard work and humour in making this book come to life. I've never once had cause to lack faith in their abilities, particularly the editorial talents of Paul, and this book has reaffirmed my admiration and belief in their skills, judgement and vision.

I'd also like to thank the friends and journalists who I hounded for their opinion on the early drafts and for their advice. Neil Goulding, Jamie Bowman, Robin Brown, Greg O'Keeffe and Jonathan Northcroft all pointed me in the right direction or provided a contact or tip that made the whole process easier. Mark Boyns was also on hand night and day to offer his own snooker expertise as was Clive Everton, a peerless snooker journalist, the editor of the brilliant and vital Snooker Scene magazine and someone who has earned every ounce of the esteem in which he has been held for some 40 years. Thank you chaps.

My dad, Stephen, mum, Mary, sister, Cassie, and brother-in-law, Daniel, all deserve recognition for their humour, support and love throughout an often punishing process – a process made inestimably easier by their advice and hospitality. I hope they are as proud of me as I am of them.

Finally, I'd like to dedicate my efforts in this book to James Kenyon and Alex Miller. Two young men, two fine men, and two friends, taken far too soon.

Chris Brereton, October, 2014

1

The Duke

I stand over the cushion, chalking my cue, buying myself some time, trying to breathe properly. Just look nice and calm Jimmy, nice and calm. I scan the table and there are only the colours left. I'm the skinniest, scruffiest kid in South London. But also the sharpest.

Put me on a snooker table and nothing is impossible but, for once, I'm in trouble. I'm stood in the back of New World Snooker Club in Wandsworth, on one of the tables close to the bar and I need the 27 points remaining if I'm to get out of here alive. I walk around the table, picking bits of imaginary fluff off the baize, trying to stop my legs from shaking, trying to control my cueing arm.

JIMMY WHITE

I'm playing a guy called Derek Rogers, for money. The same as always. The only problem is, he's a bodybuilder and I don't have a penny on me – what's coming in one pocket through the snooker is quickly going out the other in the pub or at the track. Being skint isn't an issue because I'll get the barman, a bloke nicknamed Enoch Powell, to stand my bets for me. He'll just give me the money out of the till to sort me out. Not a problem, or so I think. I take Derek's money off him all the time even though he's a very good player. But tonight is different. I've been outplayed and I'm getting done, good and proper.

I look around to the bar to get Enoch to stump up some cash and, shit, he's not there. "Where's Enoch?" I ask the new barmaid. "Sorry love, he's gone home," comes the reply. I try to ring his house phone but can't get hold of him anywhere. 10p after 10p goes in the club payphone with the dingy fag-stained receiver, but I'm getting nowhere.

I'm in the shit here, deep shit.

Luckily enough, I've played hundreds of these kinds of frames so I know I just have to hang in there. Keep taking your time Jimmy, wait for your chance and don't show any panic. If Derek knows you're worried then he's too good a player to let you off the hook. I've scraped through the frame this far and just about stayed in the match until, now, every colour is life or death.

I slowly start potting the colours, one by one, until I'm finally on the black. It has to roll in. Please let it roll in. If I don't win and can't pay, Derek will have the absolute right to batter me. And he will do. And he'll do it properly. I've had £240 a week off him for six weeks running and then the first time I lose I can't pay up? That's a big no-no and all those times I've beaten him will be coming in if I don't see him right.

THE DUKE

Now that's pressure. I will go on to win ranking tournaments and feel less nervous than I do right now. My left arm trembles slightly as I get into position but I hold my nerve and the black ball sinks into the top right-hand pocket, as safe as anything. Relief floods through me. Once again, I've made a few quid and escaped a beating.

Oh, and by the way, I'm 15.

Welcome to the mad, bad world of James Warren White.

•••••••

When I was a kid, the youngest of five, there was one time of the week that I looked forward to more than any other.

I was born in Balham in a prefab-style gaff on May 2, 1962 before Mum and Dad, Tom and Lillian, moved us all (me, my brothers Martin, Tommy, Tony and my sister, Jackie) to Topsham Road in Tooting, a lovely semi-detached council house where I – as the baby and as the spoilt one – shared a room with Tommy before I finally got a little box room of my own.

South London, then and now, was a great place; somewhere that was proud part of London but also a bit different to the rest of the place.

Maybe it's the way the River Thames cuts us off from the rest of the city that makes us feel special – a sort of 'them and us' feeling – but South London feels like each and every area has its own identity and culture and Tooting was no different.

Growing up there was interesting, to say the least. The towns and cities and places you grow up in shape you and I was no different.

Victor Yo, my next door neighbour, was my best mate. He was 12 months younger than me but we quickly became inseparable after meeting outside our house when we were barely out of nappies. We did what other young lads did back then when there was nothing else to do, no Facebook or any of that. We romped around in a gang, bunked off from Hillbrook Primary School, caused my mum, Lillian, and his nan, Bet, no end of trouble and generally did as we pleased.

Anyway, the favourite time of the week I was talking about was Friday afternoon, usually around 4pm.

My dad was a carpenter. He was a very proud man who always worked. He was my hero in a lot of ways and somebody I always respected, looked up to and loved very dearly.

When I got to be about nine, I used to go with him on the Friday after school to a pub called The Duke of Devonshire on Balham High Road, which is still there, halfway between Clapham South and Balham Tube stops.

I used to count down the minutes to those afternoons because it meant I got to spend time with just my dad. My mum was a cleaner in a hotel in Clapham at the time which meant she couldn't pick me up from school – not that I was ever really there anyhow...

Mum and Dad's relationship was very, very solid. They met in a coffee shop during the war in 1943, soon after Dad had been hospitalised after taking a terrible pounding on a French beach. Dad had been sent to a mental hospital up north somewhere but scarpered as soon as he could and ended up fixing lorries in the army as he waited to be medically discharged.

He got talking to mum in a coffee shop, one thing led to another and they ended up happily unmarried for 53 years before Mum died. Why did they never get wed? "We just never got round to it," used to come the mutual reply and who's to say they weren't on to something?

I know that me and my three brothers and one sister always felt wrapped up in a loving household – and the older you get, the more you look back on that kind of start in life with respect. Not that I recognised that at the time. I didn't recognise a lot of things at the time.

But we'll come to all that.

My dad used to meet some of his mates who worked for him in The Duke. Friday was payday so Dad always went along to sort them out. The Duke was a rough pub. In those days it had a public bar and a saloon bar and it badly needed a lick of paint, like many pubs did then and do now. It was your standard London working-class boozer. Patchy carpets, walls and ceilings stained with cigarette smoke and it always carried that feeling that anything could happen in there.

My dad had a red Ford Transit lorry which had an open back on it. I remember that it was a big event for us when he got it. My dad wasn't a good saver and generally enjoyed himself, so he probably bought the van 'on tick'. It was a lesson I picked up from him 20 years later. But mine was a Ferrari.

Anyway, at 4pm after school, I would be sat in the front of this truck with my dad, as happy as can be, my legs barely touching the floor of the cab, as we drove to The Duke, where I would then sit in the lorry while he went inside to pay his mates and have a little Friday afternoon drink, the same as millions of other blokes up and down the country.

I was sat in this truck one day, in my scruffy school uniform. (I never wore a tie – I was too bad a pupil to actually wear what

I was supposed to – and some days I would even be in shorts rather than trousers, that's how young I was). Then I spotted this pool table through the window of the pub.

It was just your standard pub pool table. Nothing fancy. Not in good shape, not in bad – just there for the punters to keep themselves entertained, keep them in the pub and keep them supping and spending.

I watched through the window of the Ford Transit and the streaky stained glass of the pub for about three months, completely uninterested in this pool table or the characters around it. Some days the rain would race down the windows of the Transit and my view would be ruined, but generally I got a pretty good look at the pool table and the blokes around it – all of them rough men but good men.

These men understood and upheld the code of honour of pubs, a code that you either understand straightaway or spend a life trying to get your head around. Trust me, I got to grips with it very early.

It was the same code that was in place where I grew up. I would think nothing of coming through the back door and seeing a couple of our neighbours in the lounge, waiting for my mum to come home. They would've used the key under the mat. That was just how it was back then, it was a completely different world to the one we live in now. If someone burgled someone's house and they heard about it, they either got sorted out by your own people or shopped to the police. And the pubs were the last place thieves or drug dealers would go as they wouldn't last five minutes. So, yeah, The Duke was edgy but it had its own code, its own way of doing things.

Eventually, after watching hundreds of frames of pool through the window, I'd had enough of being cooped up inside while my dad had all the fun. I remember sneaking out of the side of the truck, quietly closing the door so he couldn't see me, then inching towards the glass window to get a better look at what was going on inside.

I was so small I could barely see in through the windows and I had to stand on tiptoes just so I could look over the ledge, my grubby, snotty fingers clinging to the edge of the window frame, which was covered and scarred in bits of old paint and fag burns.

Eventually, Dad spotted me and let me come in with him. Finally, I was in the inner circle! He must've worked out that the language wasn't too bad and that I could hold my own with his mates. I was probably safer in the pub as well, rather than sitting outside in a van. It was fantastic to a young boy to see his dad taking pride of place in the middle of the pub with the conversation and drinks flowing. I don't know why but it fascinated me then. It fascinated me for a long time as well.

Again, maybe too long.

I didn't used to get home until maybe eight or nine o'clock. Some people might think that is bad parenting but to me it was anything but. Dad worked Saturdays as well as all week so this was my only real, proper time with him. Sundays were spent with all the family but this was my time; my dad, my hero and me, the baby of the family.

Eventually, sipping a soft drink, I was offered the chance to play pool. I can't remember who asked me but it was one of Dad's mates – the pub was full of working-class Irish lads, just normal blokes. The minute I picked up a cue for the first time it was like a chemical reaction in my head.

JIMMY WHITE

It was complete and total love at first sight, or first break. I played and played and played until I couldn't play any more. How could a bashed-up old pool table hold my attention so much? It was just one of those things, one of those times in your life that doesn't make sense; like when you know, you just know, your horse is going to come in, or the long pink you've taken on is going to go straight through the jaws and nestle in the pocket. Not everything can be explained rationally and my love of that pool table was one such thing. Teachers and scientists can't explain everything and I suppose I was just destined to become a snooker player. As simple as that.

After I began playing pool, those Friday afternoons became even more important to me. I was just a tiny kid and people let me win at first until I started showing some flair and talent for the game. Before you knew it, I was beating all-comers, left, right and centre and a taste for baize, pubs and adventure had been well and truly picked up.

This fixation with Fridays carried on for about two years until I got to about 11. By then I'd well and truly decided that school wasn't for me. I decided the best way to cope and survive my schooldays was by simply not going. Along with Victor, I wagged off constantly. I don't mean an hour here or a lesson there, I mean permanently. Days, weeks and months seemed to go by where I pretty much forgot what my teachers looked like and vice versa. I wasn't a rude pupil or a bully or anything bad; I just didn't want to go, didn't want to be there, didn't think that it was a useful way to spend my time.

I was a kid thirsty for excitement and action – and I always managed to find it, alongside Victor, the perfect partner in crime.

THE DUKE

We would roam the streets of London, looking for any mischief we could get into, jumping on and off the Tube without paying, dodging bus conductors if we decided to go to the West End.

If there was a blag or a prank involved, we were up for it.

We used to be starving hungry most of the time so we'd play the altar-boy act to an old shopkeeper who would take pity on us and give us whatever food she had spare in the back. My mum and Victor's nan always gave us dinner money but that had gone long before on fags and sweets. It was, looking back, a hell of a lot of fun, even if I'm glad my own kids have not followed my example.

They were innocent times and we never meant any harm by it, walking into these massive museums and libraries all over the city and shouting up or causing havoc, doing anything for the thrill of getting chased by someone, anyone, in an official-looking uniform. Boys will be boys I suppose.

•••••••

One day, while me and Victor should've been in maths or some-thing – who knows, I'd never stayed in school long enough to find out the timetable – it was pouring down with rain so we decided to duck into a snooker hall called Zan's, named after its owner, Ted Zanicelli, who also had another snooker hall in Morden. It was only around the corner from Topsham Road so I suppose it was only a matter of time before me and Victor found the place.

I don't know what Ted Zanicelli did for a living but he had a big yacht. He was a big fat fella and, when he came in, all the blokes we knew in there respected him.

Again, as I crossed from the street into that club, it was another crossroads moment in my young life.

I'll never forget it.

We pushed through the big heavy doors and we were confronted by these full-sized snooker tables. Just like in The Duke, it was like nothing else I'd ever experienced and if falling in love with pool was like a teenage crush, snooker was the love of my life.

Everything about Zan's fascinated me. The sound of the click and tinkling of balls being smoothly potted; the hacking, chesty laughs of the old blokes at the bar; the hushed, tense tones of those playing, usually for money; the smell of the place – a mixture of ashtray and beermat – and the people in there, as strange and as wonderful a mix of blokes as you could ever meet.

Zan's was rough. Now I mean seriously rough. There were all types of characters in this dimly lit, smoky room, full of tension. The place was dank and simmering constantly, as if the walls could sense that trouble was brewing and always around the corner. I adored it.

In Zan's, if you sat on the cushion, minding your own business, you got a right slap. If you whistled you got barred for a week. It was as uptight and as moody as anything.

Zan's had a minder/bouncer called Mad Ronnie Fryer and he scared the shit out of me. He scared the shit out of everybody. He'd come in twice a day and check that no liberties were being taken on the place. When he came through the doors, and I'm not making this up, you could literally hear people crashing and darting to get out of the way. Others wouldn't move. He'd walk in and look around and that was enough.

THE DUKE

He would slap you straight away if you crossed him and I saw him knock plenty out.

One day, Mad Ronnie Fryer came in to the club in a hurry and you just knew something was about to go down. I was only about 12 so what could I do? When it kicked off in there, I'd just pick up my cue, stand as close to the edge of the room as possible and let the heavies sort it out.

Ronnie flew down into the cellar with the police not far behind and this copper shouted out that they'd better send the dogs down to get him out. If this was meant to scare Ronnie, it didn't work. This massive Rottweiler dog went down the cellar steps and the next thing you know, there was this horrible, strangling noise and the dog, with a snapped neck, was thrown back up the stairs.

Ronnie had killed the poor thing with his bare hands.

They didn't have tasers in those days so God knows how they finally got him out. That was one of the scariest things I've ever seen. I was only a kid so what was that all about? How hard is that geezer down those stairs? I was learning fast, maybe too fast, that the real world, the one outside home and school, wasn't as cosy and as nice as I'd thought.

I was 12, going on 25.

Eventually Mad Ronnie Fryer committed suicide in prison after killing another Zan's punter. But it didn't put me off. Despite all that, it was becoming my kind of place.

Just like I'd understood with my dad in The Duke on those Friday afternoons, Zan's had its own laws.

People like Ronnie taught you respect, even if it was the hard way. For example, if someone ever came into the club and started boasting about burgling someone's house then they'd be sorted out in no time at all. They'd have to put it back or there'd be big trouble.

Saying all that though, at Christmas, the place was like a market stall. I'm not kidding. The first four tables in the club were piled high with stolen goods. Tellies, irons, hoovers, you name it. All sorts of punters would come through the doors, looking moody, wondering if they could pick up a new bike for their kid or a nice pair of earrings for the missus. There wasn't exactly much money floating around South London back then and it showed as Zan's turned into a Christmas market for those who had nowhere else to turn.

As with snooker halls around the world, the place was rammed with characters, chancers and one-offs.

There was this one guy called Jock. He was a really good snooker player who worked in a soap factory during the week but on a Friday night he would be in Zan's and up against all the best players around.

Jock and his mates would have table 16 on a Friday night. The table would be beautifully ironed and they would play, no word of a lie, until well into Saturday night. A full 24 hours of snooker. Crazy really, looking back. Four of them would play for big money and they let me play occasionally although in the end they wouldn't let me join in the fun because they knew I'd soon see their weekly wage off – even if I gave them a 40-point start.

I got friendly with Jock and used to ask him to lend me money when I was a bit short. There were plenty of people about who would lend you a few bob when you needed it. £100 on a Friday meant £110 when you paid them back in the week and everyone knew the rules. Jock would never lend me a penny in the club, though, and always insisted I visited his house. "Jock, I need a float," I'd say in the club. "No chance mate but come round to mine," he'd reply. I'd go round and he'd lend me a grand, on the spot, just like that. One time he gave me £5,000, no questions asked. He knew I was good for it and that I would pay him back from my snooker winnings.

It turned out that he owned about eight houses on one street and was seriously flush, he just didn't want to let people at the club know. Also, he had no need to play in Zan's for cash but he just loved snooker and the atmosphere in snooker clubs.

He was spot on – it's addictive. Like a lot of other things in life can be. The smell and scent of money, adrenaline, danger and success is a hard one to ignore. And, trust me, once it gets in your veins, you're a dead man.

One night, me and Lenny Cain (more of him in a bit) decided to do Jock over. We bought these joke shop explosives that you could put in the end of a cigarette. What was meant to happen was that Jock would smoke this cigarette and it would go 'BOOM!' and that would be that. We poked it in the end of the fag, sat back and waited.

Only problem was, Jock turned the cigarette around and started smoking it the wrong way round. It meant that all the explosives were now firmly stuck in his mouth.

Oh shit. 'What can I do?' I thought, 'I can hardly tell him now' and, sure enough, it didn't take long before these explosives went off right in his gob.

He knew straight away what had happened. "Lenny Cain, wait until I fucking catch you," he screamed, chasing Lenny around the tables, getting knackered in no time at all while the rest of us were crying laughing.

Jock is dead now but I'd still like to apologise to him. That's the first of a few apologies to be made in this book...

Another Zan's character was Flash Bob who also went by the name, 'The Calico Kid'. He was a really handsome guy, who had apparently been a male model. He was about five years older than me, stick-thin lean with jet black hair. He was a hustler in his own world but we never knew what he did. He used to live in a car and would grab a wash and a shave in Zan's itself – a brave thing to do if you'd seen the toilets. One minute he'd look like a tramp, a day later he'd have a fur coat over the top of a brand new three-piece suit, cash falling out of all of his pockets. He was just that kind of bloke, living on his wits, earning money doing God knows what, God knows where.

After going in the toilet with his toothbrush wedged in his mouth, he'd come out 10 minutes later, wish us all a fond farewell and he would be out of the door. That was the world we lived in – people disappeared for days at a time.

Nobody asked questions. Nobody wanted to know.

Later on in life, I was invited to a tournament in Thailand and I invited Flash Bob along. "Come on Bob, I think you'll like the place," I told him. Like the place? He stayed six years! He's calmed down now and lives in Portsmouth with a couple of kids but he always used to be good for a story and a laugh.

I remember he played in Zan's one night and he had no money to back himself. He told his opponent, "If you beat me, I'll shave all my hair off but if I win, you give me £40." Well, the match went ahead, Flash Bob gave this fella a 60-point headstart and Flash Bob lost. Next thing you know, the clippers are out and Bob's big dash of black hair is on the floor. He paid up, just as he promised.

THE DUKE

As I've said, that was one thing you always did; you never welshed on a bet. If you owed, you paid. And it was well known in and around Zan's and wherever else you played that if you owed and hadn't coughed up then you were in big trouble. It spread like wildfire. That's why paying your debts was so important.

The lunatics ran the Zan's asylum. There was this other guy called Lofty. He was absolutely massive and I used to do him for his money every Friday night. Week after week, he never learnt. One Friday I beat him and he'd had enough. "Fuck it, I'm not paying you," he said.

I didn't want to lose face, not in a place like Zan's because to show weakness in there would've been a fatal mistake so I tried to stand up for myself. "Lofty, mate," I said. "You knocking me isn't on. You knew this was coming, just pay up."

Well, that didn't go down too well did it? He lost his temper, chased me around Zan's, in and out, behind the bar and under the tables until he was totally knackered. Being so skinny did have its advantages after all. I bumped into him about 20 years later when I was a bit flush and gave him a few quid to tide him over and we had a good laugh about it. It had been nothing personal. Zan's was dog eat dog and if I hadn't taken his money someone would've done, that I can promise you.

As I got older, I left primary school and went to Ernest Bevin Comprehensive – supposedly anyway. My bunking off got even worse as I just couldn't stay away from Zan's. I'd wag school and then be in there all day, every day; learning how snooker worked, learning how the world worked.

I'll never forget the first time I actually played. It was table nine and my brother, Martin, could see me hiding in the shadows and decided to let me play with him. I was supposed to be in school so was expecting a bollocking but Martin knew how much I loved the game and I couldn't move quickly enough when he asked me if I wanted a frame.

After that I'd beg Martin to let me on table nine with him all the time. I'd do whatever it took to get into Zan's and onto a table. Every day, as soon as I got 'home' from 'school' my mum would force-feed me and I would then be in the snooker hall from 4pm until she would come out, screaming at me to get home.

Mum sometimes sent one of my brothers down to drag me out but I never wanted to leave. Why would I? Even then, as young as I was, I knew, without a shadow of a doubt, that snooker was what I wanted to – had to – do with my life.

I don't say that as if it was a sign from God or anything wacky. I was just very good at it naturally and I loved it, *loved it*. I would play anyone who would let me. Snooker was the last thing on my mind at night and the first thing on my mind in the morning – and that's not forgetting when I dreamt about it as well.

Most nights, when I could, I would let mum or someone drag me home then I would 'go to bed', escape through the window and shin down the drainpipe. I was that addicted to playing, nothing or nobody could stop me. Not mum, not school, nobody.

Most mates had posters of that girl showing her arse in a tennis outfit on their bedroom walls; I had a photo of Alex Higgins.

My style of play developed naturally through the hundreds of hours and hundreds of frames of snooker I'd played in Zan's. I learnt how the game was played on the baize and on my feet, not from a textbook, and it was the best education you could ask for. Using the rest, controlling the cue-ball, breaking into the pack, developing checkside, back and top spin, stunning the ball, screwing the ball – you name it, all those tricks and techniques were picked up from other players in Zan's and from doing nothing else but potting snooker balls for as long as possible, every single day.

All I wanted to do was pot balls. Pot, pot, pot. And I'd play in the dark when I couldn't afford the lights. Tony Drago reckons that the speed at which he plays is down to him running out of cash to pay for lights when he was a kid back in Malta. The quicker he cued, the more frames he could fit in and maybe there's something in that theory.

I was certainly lightning quick around the table and I could size up what shot needed to be played next before the cue-ball had stopped rolling.

Eventually, the endless practising and playing began to pay off – literally. I started to become so good that all the hounds of South London heard about me; the pale, skinny kid who could knock them in from the lampshades.

The party was about to get started.

•••••••

As my reputation grew in Zan's, geezers wanted to start playing me for money. It's hard to overestimate how insane this world was for a teenage boy. But it was my world. Snooker, gambling, playing for fast, hard cash in a fast, hard environment.

The scrapes and scenes – such as Mad Ronnie Fryer's antics – were unbelievable when I look back, especially as a man who's now settled right down and who has kids of his own, one of whom, Tommy, is the youngest – like me – and, at 15, is a lovely, educated, intelligent young man. He lives in a world about as far removed as it's possible to be from the one I operated in at his age.

I'll give you an example. Victor had four sisters, all of them Bunny Girls, so their house was alight at night. They'd sleep all day and then go to work, come home and then they'd need a few drinks to relax after working the clubs because they'd all be wired and would need to unwind a bit.

I'd be lying in bed next door, knowing that this world of parties and booze was happening just yards away and I'd be off through my bedroom window, down the drainpipe. I'd knock on Victor's door and get involved.

I often used to sneak out of our house at midnight and go and see Victor's nan, Bet.

"Bet, lend me a tenner," I'd plead.

She would do, reluctantly, and then I'd be off to Zan's with it.

Within two hours, I'd return to Bet's with £600 quid in my back pocket. She'd get that money back plus a few drinks and I'd leave a stash with her to look after for me.

That's how easy it was. That's how crazy it was. £600. That was a hell of a lot of money and I could earn that in less time than it takes most snooker players to win three frames. I was just that quick, that good and that comfortable in a world where money was so easy to come by.

After a night racing around London, especially when Victor's nan got a bit old, I'd knock on the door for him in the morning, before 'school', then we'd go round the back of the house, sneak back upstairs through the kitchen window, sleep all day in his room and be ready to go again that night. To me and Victor that was 'normal'. It was madness, really. A very strange environment. I wouldn't let any of my kids anywhere near it, even if it was a magical time when anything seemed possible.

Nothing was going to stop my snooker, not even a broken foot – an incident that has led to one of the best myths about me. Fair enough, I hold my hands up and admit that I've done nothing over the years to stop the legend from growing but I reckon now, at my age, I've got enough great stories that are true so I might as well burst the bubble on one that is false.

Me and Victor were masters at not paying a penny on the Tube or on the bus. Wherever we went, we went for free. We were that small and quick that no conductor could catch us and we could jump any Tube barrier with ease. All you had to do was take a deep breath, take a long run up and go for it. Dead easy. Too easy. I was getting bored of doing it without any risk involved so I started taking the piss one day, jumping over the barriers with no hands and basically being a dickhead.

This one time, me and Victor had been to the West End and were getting off at Tooting Bec station when my luck ran out. As I was mid-air, a Tube inspector nearly collared me and I hit the barrier, BANG, and then very quickly hit the deck. Fuck me, my foot! The pain was like nothing else but I was more scared of getting nicked than I was the agony I was in so I got up, grabbed Victor and we managed to scramble up the stairs and out of the way.

About 100 yards away from the station, around the corner, we lay on the pavement looking at my foot. It had this massive lump on it growing by the second. It looked bad and hurt even more.

"Jimmy, look at your foot," were the last (helpful) words I heard from 'Dr. Victor.' Next thing I knew, I was seeing stars and I passed out. I woke up in hospital with a doctor, a nurse and my mum and dad all surrounding me, wanting to know what had happened.

I didn't want any more broken bones so I made up some bullshit story about being tackled playing football in the street. I was given a cast and a crutch and although I could tell nobody believed me, I managed to get away with it.

Soon after (and this is where the legend gets destroyed) I was playing a match and I was hobbling around the table on my crutch, propping it up on the side of the table while I took my shot, before then switching back to the stick when I had to get around.

This break was going well so I started taking the piss and I decided to start using the crutch to pot the coloured balls. I got a tip and taped it to the end and off I went. Steve Davis, who was on a nearby table, walked over to see what all the fuss was about and was told by some wag watching my game that I'd used the crutch for the whole break, not just the colours. Davis fell for it hook, line and sinker and that was where the myth came from. Sorry Steve (and sorry fans!) but it's not true. Playing with a crutch was just me fucking around, acting up, loving life. And that's how the myth got created.

It just goes to show you; you shouldn't believe everything you hear about me. Well, not all of it anyway...

2

Tony & Dodgy Bob

Of all the people I met in Zan's, two in particular would have a huge impact on the next few years of my life. The first bloke was called Tony Meo, who was a few years older than me and who also went to Ernest Bevin. Like me, he was a boy wonder on the snooker table, but that's where the similarities ended, even though we became great mates.

I was this painfully rake-thin scruff, wearing whatever I could be arsed to put on and Tony was a chubby, beautifully dressed lad, an excellent dancer and an all-round fashion victim. His Sicilian father had died a few years earlier while his mum ran a clothes shop and restaurant and Tony made the most of both businesses.

We'd seen each other knocking about in Zan's and on the odd occasion we went to school and we ended up becoming mates. He was amazing at table tennis but even better at snooker. Me and him used to light Zan's up with the way we played. He was very quick, deadly accurate and always had a sharp and canny safety game to back himself up, so we ended up becoming partners. Between the two of us, we started winning plenty of cash from plenty of punters, none of whom thought they could possibly lose to two kids – basically two cocky urchins.

And where there's money, there's opportunity.

Me and Tony kept playing together, kept winning stacks of cash and kept having a good time and this eventually drew the attention of a black cab driver called Bob Davis – forever known locally as Dodgy Bob.

Dodgy Bob had spotted a gap in the market and he wanted to use me and Tony to make some serious money. And he meant serious *money.*

•••••••

We were in Zan's one day and me and Tony noticed that we were getting watched very closely by this old bloke. Getting an audience for our matches was nothing new but Dodgy Bob had something else on his mind. "Listen up you two," he started. "I've been watching you and you're very, very good. I'm semi-retired and I've got a black cab. I can drive you anywhere you want to go in the country, I'll put up the money and we could all win some cash."

It sounded too good to be true. At times, me and Tony were so skint we couldn't afford a cup of tea between us. In fact, we used to play for free at Zan's if we came in early to clean and brush the 16 tables in there. Me and Tony used to take eight each. We weren't allowed to hit a single cue-ball until that job was done, and they were all perfectly brushed and ready to go.

We'd get in there at about half-seven in the morning, do all the tables and then we were allowed to play from 11am-1pm as payment for our efforts. Trouble is, when we were ready to play, we'd put so much effort into cleaning the tables, the muscles in our arms had gone! We couldn't pot a thing until the strength came back later in the day. We did that every day for about two years. I might never have been in school but I was getting my own kind of education right there. I knew every hole and every roll on every table. I can still remember them to this day. Table 14 had a nick in the baize, halfway along the baulk cushion, table eight had a tiny tear in the cloth. I could go on and on.

So anyway, we were so skint that when Dodgy Bob offered us this deal, we were all ears. Of course, when something sounds too good to be true, it usually is. "I'll give you 10 per cent of any winnings," Bob said. That wasn't what we wanted to hear but Bob was smart. "Lads, lads," he said. "You don't have to pay for a thing. I will drive you everywhere and stand all the bets. I will just give you a percentage if you win and take the hit when you lose."

Don't forget, I was only 13 and a bit, about five stone wet through and I was basically a kid – although one that had grown up fast in a man's world.

Tony wasn't as keen as me to do it and with Dodgy Bob raking in 90 per cent of our hard work, I could understand why. But we went for it anyway, simply because it meant we had the chance to play more snooker.

Again, pot, pot, pot.

All I wanted to do was play different people in different areas and on different tables. That was all it was about, that was all the motivation we needed. If giving Dodgy Bob most of our winnings got us more frames and more matches then why not? Ten per cent was better than nothing and 10 per cent of Dodgy Bob's cash was better than the 10 per cent of fuck all we were currently getting paid. Plus, if we'd turned it down we would only have been playing in Zan's anyhow, so it made sense.

And so the fun really began.

We started off by going to a club in Neasden owned by a fantastic snooker player and coach called Ron Gross. Steve Davis used to play there and me, Tony and Dodgy Bob would regularly make the trip over as our 'partnership' got off the ground.

We'd be going across the river for about six months before Dodgy Bob wanted to spread his wings (and boost his bank account). Trips to Streatham soon became a reality and we went from there. My addiction to snooker was unbelievable. I was just so hooked. Pool got me interested but then when snooker came along it was something totally different. It was like going from playing six-a-side footy with your mates to playing 11-a-side at Wembley. Everything was so much better and we were now getting paid for it, admittedly not as much as Dodgy Bob but you can't have everything.

We kept travelling further and further afield and we were cleaning up wherever we went. Me and Tony were making mugs of players all over London. Everywhere we went, we left with money spilling out of Dodgy Bob's pockets.

We might have barely reached the table but there was nobody more feared than Jimmy White and Tony Meo. Tony was a more cautious player whereas I was an Alex Higgins-type who always played his shots and when the big money games got really hot, they would always pick me to play to try and scare the opposition away by attacking them.

I don't know where my urge to attack comes from. It's just natural. I can still do things with a cue-ball that others can't. Ronnie O'Sullivan is very similar in that respect. Sport nowadays is all about winning but when I started, it was just as much about what you could do with the ball. Sidespin, smashing into the pack, cue control, cue-ball control; these were the things that people looked out for and admired. We used to do all the flair stuff and I did it from the age of 13. It thrilled me doing it and it seemed to thrill the public too – I think that's why I had so much public support when I went professional.

I always, always went for my shots. I played the game from the heart and maybe that wasn't the winning way – especially not in the World Championship, we'll get to that later – but that was the way I played and still play now, as simple as that. It's harder to play that way and eventually you fall down. It has cost me untold numbers of tournaments but that's me, that's life. I'm a snooker fan as well as a player and I'd pay to watch me.

Back then, my style had the whole of the London snooker world, including Ronnie Gross, who really knew his stuff, talking. Everyone was taking an interest in me and Tony.

And that included my headmaster, Mr Beatty...

•••••••

Throughout all mine and Tony's success, ducking and diving (and winning) in snooker halls across London, my school attendance had got even worse (if that was possible). Things were coming to a head until Mr Beatty finally did a deal with my mum, prompted by me hitting my first century break.

He knew I hadn't been coming to school but I doubt he had much of a clue about just how good I was getting at snooker until he opened his newspaper one morning and saw my mug splashed across it.

That's right. Back then, if a 13-year-old was good enough to hit a century break, the news made it into the national press and I was in all the tabloids. Nowadays I meet 10-year-olds who can do it but it was big news back then and it made Mr Beatty sit up and take notice.

I'll never forget that century break for as long as I live. It was at table 16 in Zan's. That was the best table because it had about 20 seats around it and was well tucked away from the door. Zan's was like a fucking turnstile with people coming in and out but that table was nice and quiet so you could play for money and not be disturbed. The Old Bill never used to come around that bit, so it was well cut off. It was like the centre court of Zan's!

For the last couple of months I'd been getting loads of 95s, 96s and whatever else but I couldn't break the century. My style of play meant I could miss anything and I was doing. Zan's had a few 100-break men in there so they knew how important it was for me to finally do it.

As I approached the ton I was completely riddled with nerves. The brown wobbled on 80-odd, the blue was easy, as was the pink but the black rattled the pocket before finally dropping. It was such an incredible moment and when I did it I ran around Zan's about 10 times, screaming. It's probably like your first eagle at golf or your first proper hat-trick. It was against

Derek Alexander, the bloke I talked about who was nicknamed Enoch Powell. I remember he gave me a big cuddle – he was as delighted as me when I did it.

The black only just went down. You should pot a thousand out of a thousand of them but it's like penalties in football isn't it? The extra pressure makes you miss and sometimes you have to deal with it. I'd learn all about that one day. Making a ton was a massive turning point and my game exploded. Every time we went away to play for money, it was getting easier and I was getting faster.

It's fair to say, though, that Mr Beatty wasn't as happy about me finally breaking the century barrier. Phone calls and letters with home were exchanged until he finally had a meeting with mum and laid it out on the table.

"Look," he said. "Jimmy hasn't been showing up for months. But he has a real talent for this snooker. So, I'll do you a deal. If he comes in to school in the morning then I will give him the afternoon off to play snooker."

He even came down to Zan's and spelled out the same deal to me in person. I couldn't agree quick enough. School for a few hours and then snooker all day? You can't get much better than that! It was unheard of back then. If he did the same today he would be shot but it was an acceptance by school that I was a lost cause. Snooker was clearly the only subject I showed any flair for, so why not let me run with it and see what happened?

The freedom – and permission! – to wag school opened me, Tony and Dodgy Bob up to an entirely new level of playing and winning. As Dodgy Bob's confidence – and bank account – started to grow, we really started going for it.

Trips to Birmingham, Newcastle, Manchester and even

Scotland were soon on the cards. I can't get into a black cab nowadays without being transported back to those times; me and Tony in the back, lying flat out on the floor, our jackets rolled up under our heads, hearing the rattle of the diesel engine, as we try and get some shuteye on the floor with Dodgy Bob chauffeuring us home.

I used to walk back through the front door to screams and shouts from Mum, who was mortified that we were basically roaming around Britain's snooker halls, outclassing people two, three times older than us, leaving with all their cash and then legging it back to London.

It was so easy.

If we turned up in, say, Birmingham, Dodgy Bob would walk in the club and say, "Who's the best in here? There's £500 in it" and they couldn't get enough of it. My cue was the same size as me. Who wouldn't take that on? We didn't care what money was on the game. Me and Tony wanted to play so much that Dodgy Bob's bets meant nothing to us. Sure, we'd go back home with a fortune sometimes but who cared? It was the thrill of the game that got me hooked, not the money. Nothing changes.

That period taught me to watch my back in life. I'm a good spotter of someone who needs swerving. Rogues, or whatever you want to call them. I got an instinct for them. As for the game itself, I was just happy to be playing. I was never happier than when I was potting balls. Like Seve Ballesteros or someone like that who just used to practise for hours and days on end.

If you were the best player in an area – especially in pre-internet days when you couldn't do your research – and two snotty-nosed kids walked into a snooker hall, you would heavily back yourself and, crucially, so would all your mates. Thousands and thousands of pounds used to ride on these matches. The local legend against two kids. A no-brainer. And yet it was the two kids, along with their delighted 'manager', who would ride off into the sunset, the two best gunslingers in town having gunned down the sheriff on his own turf.

We would clean up and then they would be in so much shock that they would invite us back the following day. And we would clean up again! By the time I was 15 I had £10,000 saved up. That was a ridiculous amount of money, and certainly more than my mum and dad had ever got. But then I wasn't my mum and dad, as much as I loved them both dearly. I was learning to operate by my own rules.

If we lost, which did happen occasionally, we would simply come back the next day and win the money back. Of course, it didn't always go to plan and it didn't always end happily. The simple truth is that whenever unlicensed sport and gambling meet there is always one side-effect lurking around the corner.

Violence.

We played in a snooker hall one day in London, I don't want to say where, and we did this bloke all day long for every penny he had. He put his house on himself to beat us and we just kept destroying him. By the end of the day, me and Tony were quids in. Or maybe not. "Look," this fella grinned, cracking his knuckles. "If you three don't fuck off out of my sight, right this fucking second, I'll beat you [Tony] up, you [me] up and then you [Dodgy Bob] up."

"Fair enough, see ya, thanks mate," I said, and we were out of the door. I was too small, too young and too scared to say or do anything else.

Another time, after we had won £1500 in a club, we walked

back to the taxi and there were four lads standing there. They hadn't been in the club but word gets around.

"Alright lads," the biggest geezer said. "We know what you've won today, so I suggest you hand the fucking lot over."

Yep, no problem. Simple as that. None of us were willing to get beaten up for £1500. Not when that kind of money was always around the corner anyway. I can remember where that happened but I'm not telling; I don't want to put one town down – I've got mates everywhere!

Me and Tony used to have one motto: 'Anything but our cues'. Sure mate, mug me, pinch my day's earnings, threaten to beat the shit out of me – but you ain't having my cue. We didn't care about money but our cues were sacred.

We spent months polishing and shining them. I see the same in the kids today and I love it; you have to take care of your cue and take time to get to know it. It takes three months to get used to a cue's grain and weight and how the butt fits in your hand. A good all-round cue is something that is very precious and they need protecting. That is why John Higgins has struggled in recent times. His cue broke and they're not something that can be replaced very easily.

I remember one time I got the Tube to Neasden and these lads decided to mug me. I had 20p in my front right pocket so that I could pay from the last stop if I got busted and I would then have £4 stashed in my front left pocket for situations just like this.

My real stash, say about £500, was safely nestled in my back pocket. I'd start out giving the muggers the 20p, they would tell me to fuck off and look for more cash. The £4 would then disappear and that would be that. They never got to know that the real stash was in my back pocket. Again, that was a regular occurrence.

Dodgy Bob worked us so hard that sometimes we could barely keep our eyes open. We played hard but we played fair. And we never, ever hustled. We never had to. I've known hustlers and seen hustlers in action and we were never like that. A hustler works by sucking you into their game, letting you win a few frames and sucker-punching you later. We would never go in there and not give our best game. I've stood in bars in Thailand and seen some of the girls hustling the punters, letting them play and win for 500 baht. You come back an hour later and some bloke's done 20,000 baht. That was never our style.

One night I showed Mum and Dad just how easy it was for me to win big money.

I was playing in a match when all of a sudden, cash started pouring in. People were betting on me, left, right and centre. I legged it home and begged Dad to join in the fun. "Dad, please, lend me some money, anything, a fiver will do," I pleaded. He only had a 10-bob note on him and that would have to do. I even ironed it before I raced back to the club.

About three hours later, I returned home and Mum and Dad were sitting in the living room. "I've got something for you," I said. I'll never forget the look on Dad's face as I pulled note after note out of my pockets. I'd turned that 10-bob note into about £800 – a huge amount of money back then.

•••••••

When you're thrown into a world where a grand was as easy to come by as it was for me, then you're never going to get a proper grasp of what is considered 'normal' spending behaviour. If I could make a grand in two hours but then gambled £800 of it away in the next 60 minutes, was that stupid (of course it was, looking back) or was I still a hero for being £200 up (of course I was, at the time).

Money ebbed and flowed into my back pocket and whatever me and Tony won, we immediately threw it away, as fast as possible. Horses, cards, dogs – you name it. One night we won £1500 and by dawn the next morning we'd found a way of losing the lot. We should've gone home in a gold carriage but we didn't even have enough for a cab. We had to wait for the first Tube train and then hop off and jump the barrier.

If me and Tony were a bad enough influence on each other, I turned even madder when I used to hang out with a mate called Lenny Cain.

Unfortunately for me, and for Lenny, I liked a drink and he liked a drink so when we got together, we were always pissed and always gambling. That meant I wasn't giving my snooker game the attention I should've done either. As soon as we got cash, we'd be drinking and having a great time; it was only when I got skint that I would drift back into my other life – the life of practice and snooker. When I was flush I was on the piss, when I was skint I'd be on the table. Life was upside down!

In between going broke through the gambling and missing practising, I was spending my time as a lookout for Lenny who did fruit machines over with another bloke I only ever knew as 'Irish Frank'.

Lenny was a good snooker player and was eight years older than me. We met on the snooker circuit in London and he's still a pal now. We immediately clicked and I liked his outlook on life and his slang; he was sharp and funny and he used to reel jokes and stories off all the time. In that world, you get to meet so many different people, and characters, and Lenny was certainly one of them. When I got good in Zan's I got to know every rogue for about 10 miles.

We ended up as mates and even when I was going skint through gambling, it didn't matter because I could quickly recoup that on the tables or when we went out and did the fruit machines. We would attach a 10p or a 5p to some cotton thread, drop it into the slot, dot up loads of credits and then take the machine for all the money. I suppose it was theft in a way but it never felt like that because those machines used to mug people off all the time, so we were just getting our revenge on them. We just saw it as a laugh and another scrape, although that's no real excuse. Lenny and Frank were brilliant at dangling these bits of thread. They even used to do it with the cotton in their mouths so they could have both hands down by the gambling machine buttons and it looked like they were playing for real. We did that for years. We used to do hundreds of boozers and motorway service stations and thought we were far too clever to get caught.

One night, in Fulham, we did loads of machines and then decided to go for a drink, mainly because we wanted to change the money up. We were counting the money up, sipping vodka and orange – 'Screwdrivers', my favourite drink back then – and thinking how smart we were, when this Black Maria police van stormed out of nowhere and we were nicked. We had a table covered in silver coins right in front of us and coppers swarmed in from every angle, throwing us to the floor.

Eventually we got bundled off to the nick. The police reckoned we'd been around doing electricity meters. Of course, we only had coins on us so it made perfect sense from their point of view. They waited and waited to see if someone would report an electricity meter burglary but, of course, none had happened so they had to let us go. Mum arrived to pick me up and she was fuming. I knew what was coming. "Jimmy!" she shrieked, followed by a wallop across the back of my scrawny head.

That was in front of all the police who found it very funny but I knew Mum was trying to take the heat for me. She thought that by giving me a right slap in front of the coppers, that would be the end of it. We all went home on police bail.

"Come on Jimmy, who've you been robbing?" they'd keep asking and asking. I just smiled sweetly, my pockets brimming with two-bob coins and say, "We've been saving up and we broke the jar to come out for a drink." The coppers weren't laughing. They let us go after six or seven hours.

Me and Lenny were always getting into shit. We just couldn't help ourselves and loved practical jokes.

We never liked bookmakers, mainly because we used to hand over every fucking penny we ever made to them, so we used to go to the dog track and change a pound into a hundred pennies. I was that thin I could squeeze past those old, rounded cast-iron turnstiles at the dogs. I could turn sideways and nip through, easy as anything. Turns out that being able to sneak into a race track was about the only result I got there...

Once in, we'd pick a bookies about 25 feet away and aim these pennies at his head. We'd get that good at flicking pennies that we could land one on their foreheads from that distance. It used to crack us up because the bookies could never find us in the crowd and we'd get away with it.

TONY & DODGY BOB

Me and Lenny also used to tie a bit of string to a fiver or a tenner and leave it on the pavement and just wait to see what would happen. Sooner or later, someone would spot this note on the floor and you could see them think 'JACKPOT!'

They'd slyly try and pick the money up and we'd spring into action, tugging on the string and making the fiver dance in the air. People would go bright red with embarrassment. Me and Lenny would be lying on the floor going bright red with laughter. We were toerags but it was the time of our lives.

•••••••

If you're going to get some vices then you might as well do it properly. By the time I was doing the fruit machines with Lenny Cain and playing every decent snooker hall with Dodgy Bob and Tony Meo, I'd also picked up a huge thirst for booze.

My dad had always liked a drink. He didn't drink at home but he liked pubs and clubs and the atmosphere in both. I'd be with him in The Duke of Devonshire and then on a Sunday we would go to the Balham United Services Club. For the last 25 years of his life he was president of the club – they didn't even have a vote in the end because he won it every year. There was a snooker table in there and I used to play on that a lot, so I was always around drink. I was part of a world where drinking went with gambling and the pair of them went with snooker.

As me and Tony progressed at snooker we finally ended up playing proper matches, rather than just rinsing people for their week's earnings. We eventually drifted away from Dodgy Bob and ended up playing in the Harrow and District Snooker and Billiards League for a team managed by Ron Gross.

We used to play in the Fisher Snooker Centre in Acton. It had a little bar in it with a cracking looking barmaid. Me and Tony loved it and even though he didn't drink, he wanted to be in there to try and chat this barmaid up. We thought we were getting somewhere but we were absolutely clueless. We used to be sat in the bar stumbling through our shit chat-up lines, and I found a real taste for booze in there. I'd get a Screwdriver as soon as I sat down and I wouldn't move until I was called out for my match. I usually took the deciding frame if we played five-a-side because my attacking flair used to see us win more than we lost.

All the time in that bar meant that drinking became a completely normal part of my life, even when I should've still been in school and studying for exams or whatever else a 'normal' teenager gets up to.

I didn't start drinking to run away from anything or anyone or numb any pain or any of those 'deep' reasons. I'd had a swig or two of vodka at Victor's, I really liked it and I was up and running. I drank because it agreed with me and I agreed with it. Simple, really – and probably a bit of a let-down for anyone wanting to hear some pained story about how it helped me do this or that. I wasn't drinking to forget or for the taste of alcohol or because my life was full of strife or anything; I was boozing because it was fun. I was a very happy drunk. Simple as that.

Me and Tony had become really close because of our time on the road but I used to go out with Victor the most because Tony never touched the stuff. The pair of us loved to go out – but we also loved to go home too, especially his house, because then we could chat up the Playboy Bunny Girls.

They'd look after us and we'd think we stood a chance, when

First break: Me as a fresh-faced 17-year-old (above and right) competing at Wisbech Conservative Club in Cambridgeshire in 1979. I would be the world amateur champion within 12 months

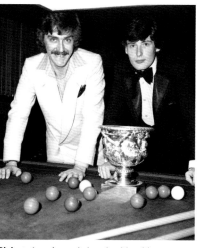

Rising star: An early brush with a big name. Me and Cliff Thorburn in 1980

That's my boy: My proud mum Lillian polishing a few of my trophies. After she agreed a little deal with my headmaster I was able to concentrate on my game even more

My hero: It all started on a Friday afternoon in The Duke with my dad. He was my biggest fan and very popular in snooker circles – becoming big mates with Bill Davis, Steve's dad

Hit for six: Patsy Houlihan, Tony Meo, Wally West, Flash Bob, me and Noel Miller-Cheevers at the Pot Black Snooker Centre, Battersea Rise. I'm fresh-faced but I was already living life to the full

Two of a kind: Sharing a joke with Tony Meo. We felt invincible travelling up and down the country in Dodgy Bob's taxi, our different styles made us a formidable partnership

Friends and rivals: Going head to head with the great Alex Higgins in 1982. Notice how I'm avoiding eye contact with him!

Chalk and cheese: Me and Steve Davis lining up before the 1984 World Championship final. We were completely different characters but I had great respect for the way he played. He was the toughest of the lot

The player: Concentrating hard and sporting a sharp-looking white waistcoat at the Masters at Wembley. Just look at my eyes – showing all the signs of a good night out

White wedding: With Maureen shortly after we'd tied the knot in a ceremony at Wandsworth Town Hall

Road to the top: Snooker was big in the '80s and as I started to make my name in the game, there were always opportunities that came my way

The new me: My manager tried to change my image to cash in on my success. Here I am trying to look cool in a manufactured photoshoot

Sealed with a kiss: Being congratulated by sister Jackie after I had beaten Terry Griffiths to win the Masters in 1984

Good company: With the great Ray Reardon and world champion Dennis Taylor at a charity event in 1985. Like the whole nation, I was glued to the TV watching Taylor's epic final with Davis

In demand: Me, Steve Davis, Stephen Hendry and Neal Foulds. We often travelled around the world to meet people and play special matches – it was always an adventure

The future's so bright... Living the life back in the day. I never went anywhere without my cue!

Matchroom boys: Joining the Barry Hearn stable. Pictured with me in 1986 are (left to right) Willie Thorne, Neal Foulds, Dennis Taylor, Hearn, Tony Meo, Terry Griffiths and Steve Davis

Sign of things to come: My first World Championship meeting with Stephen Hendry was in 1988 (above) and he wasn't happy when I won! I knew then he'd be a top player and he proved that by getting the better of me in the 1990 final

Highs and lows: Winning the World Masters in 1991 with victory over Tony Drago. Later that year there was heartache when I lost to John Parrott in the World Championship final (right)

in fact we were hopeless. There's me, a buck-toothed, scruffy little shit, trying it on with these worldly-wise girls, all of whom would flirt and humour us. All of a sudden the cards would be out, the poker would start, the booze would flow and it was 8am before you knew it.

From the age of 13, I was desperate to be out and about, in all sorts of places. Me, Victor, Lenny and another mate called John Malloy, or Peewee, just couldn't be stopped. Peewee was a boy wonder at snooker and could've been a top player but that went out of the window when he got married.

He was a good looking boy with long hair and a American car. All the birds loved him and although he was closer to my brothers in age, me, being a toerag, realised he had an American car and a shitload of birds after him so I started going around and boozing with him.

As we got older we drank in every pub in Tooting, getting totally smashed all the time. Everyone in Tooting knew me because I was in the paper all the time as the local whizzkid, I was like a mini-celebrity and I loved it, almost as much as I loved Screwdrivers.

I was just chasing the funny side of life – and the funny side of life just so happened to revolve around boozers. If I went to a lock-in and we were having a great laugh then I'd be the last to bed but if it went quiet or moody like it can then that was me off.

More often than not, though, the party would keep going and going and you can drink forever as a kid and get away with it because your mind, body and soul can take whatever punishment you want to hand out.

It's only years later that you start paying a price for it.

3

The Player

As well as catching the eye of Dodgy Bob, one day me and Tony Meo were in this takeaway kind of place close to where we lived and a girl walked in and, out of nowhere, asked for my autograph.

That all seemed a bit over the top to me and I thought that she was just taking the piss at first. This girl was best mates with Denise, Tony's girlfriend.

She'd seen me in the local paper and knew who I was, plus she'd gone to primary school with Tony and they lived on the same street, Brudenell Road, which was literally the next one on from my house in Topsham Road.

Her name was Maureen Mockler.

One day she would become Maureen White.

THE PLAYER

After first meeting each other in that takeaway, me and Maureen started bumping into each other quite a bit. There was a Catholic youth club up the road, me and Tony would go and she'd be in there with Denise. Tony was well into Denise and he always wanted the four of us to meet up and go out, plus Tony was the most fantastic dancer so he used to love all the attention in the club.

I was really shy and never used to say much but me and Maureen had a few awkward conversations until one day I gave her my phone number and plucked up the courage to ask her out.

"Fancy going to the cinema?" I said. "There's a new film on called The Omen."

I should've known then...

We were about 14 and we went to a cinema called The Classic in Tooting Bec. The Omen was an '18' film. We were well underage but we loved it and it all just went from there.

We started seeing each other regularly. She'd occasionally come on the road with me and Tony but I still wanted to spend most of my time in Zan's rather than being in a proper long-term relationship.

Soon after that cinema date, I decided I better take Maureen dancing at the church hall as well. I couldn't dance like Meo and I couldn't dress like Meo, mainly because any spare cash I won went straight on gambling or drinking. Fashion was for other people.

After asking Maureen out, I thought I'd better get some new clothes to try and impress her so went around to Tony's to beg for some of his offcuts. He wasn't having any of it. I remember shouting at him, "Come on, mate, just lend me some shoes" but he wouldn't help me out. Finally my temper got the better of me and as I went to storm out I slammed a glass door and cut my finger really badly. There was blood pissing out everywhere. It still didn't postpone our date. I took Maureen dancing with blood all over my shoes and trousers. She didn't seem to mind. Romantic, eh?

My dancing might've been terrible but my snooker just kept getting better and better. The older I got, the more I seemed to enjoy the attention, money and bit of fame that came with playing. I was fast around the table. People used to cram into whatever club I was playing in to watch me; I always wanted to entertain and I always played risky shots. This time it was safety that was for other people. I'd taken my inspiration from Alex Higgins and I wanted to play the same. Fast, furious and entertaining.

When Ron Gross spotted my talents, I ended up playing in more legitimate competitions and I just cleaned up. I was the youngest player on the London side that won the Inter Counties Championship; I became the Under-16 National Champion and then in 1979, I entered and won the England Amateur Championships, held in Cornwall, beating Dave Martin in the final, aged 16 years and 11 months.

To be honest, it barely even registered with me.

I had no idea it was that big a deal or that important. When you've spent most of your life getting chased out of clubs up and down the country and transported around in an old black cab, going to an important tournament and winning was no problem at all.

Mum came down to Cornwall to watch me in the final but she couldn't handle the nerves. There was a crowd of about 600 inside but she stood outside, unable to watch. I won 13-10 but didn't make it easy for myself, so maybe it was better that mum wasn't watching.

If you look at how I won – and if you look at my whole career – it was the same old story. I went flying out of the blocks, I was 9-3 up before I knew what had happened and then I switched off. I just totally lost concentration.

After those first two sessions, when I played unbelievably well, I should've just chilled out in the afternoon but even then I couldn't sit still, couldn't relax.

I went out running around the town and even popped into Marks and Spencer and picked up a new white shirt for the next session. John Virgo was there and couldn't believe it. There was me, in the biggest match of my life, wearing a shirt that still had the lines on it because it had come straight out of the packet!

The evening session came along, Dave hit back, and the score went from 9-3 to 10-8 in no time. Drastic measures were needed. So after Virgo made another comment about the shirt, I switched back to the first shirt and I was then back to my best, winning the three frames I needed to become the champion, making a break of 68 to seal the title.

Winning the English Amateur Championship really put me on the map – and it also caused one of the biggest regrets of my career. I don't regret much – life's too short – but after winning that, I could've turned professional on the spot. If I'd done that, I would've had two more cracks at the World Championship in Sheffield. If I'd entered as a professional in 1979, I reckon I could've won it but I held off because, back then, the fashion was to try and go on to win the World Amateur Championship. I wanted that on my CV, so I didn't take the plunge.

By the time I won in Cornwall I was a flash little git because I knew I could do something nobody else could do. I could win snooker games with ease and I could control the flair, turn it on and off, whenever I liked. I don't know how or why, it was as natural as breathing – or boozing. I could play whatever shot on the table I wanted to and the balls just used to disappear.

In between playing in 'proper' tournaments, Ron Gross made sure we had plenty of exhibitions and challenge matches.

Our line-up was just incredible. Me and Tony Meo; Noel Miller-Cheevers, who was a fantastic potter; Patsy Houlihan – one of the greatest players I've ever seen; Flash Bob and Eugene Hughes. You couldn't have dreamt of a better side than that.

We used to put notices in magazines challenging people to come and play us at the Pot Black Snooker Club in Battersea Rise. Contenders flocked from all over to try and win the £500 a match that was at stake but they never did. It was like walking into the lion's den. We never lost.

So by the time I'd won in Cornwall I was a proper Jack The Lad. I'd got a little bit of fame, unlimited amounts of cash thanks to the snooker – give or take the disastrous afternoons at the race track – and I was loving life. Maureen was still around but, to be honest, life was too short – and too fast – to be really concentrating on anything other than making mischief.

•••••••

My reputation as a serious player began to spread ever quicker and I finally caught the eye of a bloke called Henry West.

Henry managed John Virgo and Patsy Fagan. Patsy was the amazing Irish snooker player whose career was wrecked by the 'yips' following a car crash. Henry said that he wanted to manage me.

Now nobody messed with Mr Henry West.

He was as subtle as a sledgehammer, often walking into pubs that had pool and snooker tables and telling the landlord that, all of a sudden, he was their new table supplier and would they kindly mind getting rid of their current tables so he could replace them. For a fee, of course. "You'll be using my equipment from now on, you won't be needing those old tables now will you?" he'd say. As a former boxer, boxing promoter and a man who clearly knew how to handle himself, few landlords disagreed.

Henry was delighted with my English amateur win and did all the paperwork for me to take part in the World Amateur Championship that was being held in Tasmania in November, 1980. Before that, though, I had to go to Pontins in Prestatyn to represent England in the Home International Amateur Series. I was as cocky as anything and thought my plane journey to Tasmania was already booked. Henry told me I was wrong and sent me to Wales with a warning. "Jimmy, you need to behave up there. Don't drink too much and don't cause any trouble," he said. "You know they'd love to find any reason not to pick you."

Yeah, yeah, fuck that. Talk about falling on deaf ears.

I was so confident at the time that I thought I could just waltz up to Prestatyn and easily win the tournament, so I did what I always did back then. I got pissed and enjoyed myself. To be fair, this time it wasn't all my fault! What happened was this...

The England team manager was a Scouse copper called Bill Cottier who I felt never took a shine to me.

I got up to Prestatyn in good time and bumped into a mate called Joe O'Boye. Joe was a wonderful snooker player and he could also pack the booze away.

"Jimmy! How are you mate?" he said. "Great to see you, let's have a drink!" Well, what harm can half a lager do? "Okay mate, just a small one though."

We went to this dingy Pontins bar – they always looked the same – and stood there, catching up and chatting shit, and – crucially – nursing halves of lager. I wanted to play well for England that day and didn't want to mess things up.

Halfway through this lager, as I was waiting to be called up for my match, Cottier pounced on us at the bar and went crazy, as if we'd been on a right bender. We'd only had a half! "White, that's it, you're not playing today – I'm not putting you on when you're pissed. You should be ashamed of yourself, and you Joe. You can clear off."

Eh? "Fair enough Mr Cottier, whatever you say," I replied.

Cottier had just cleared my diary for the rest of the day and that meant only one thing. "Well Joe, if we're not playing now we might as well enjoy ourselves," I said. "Barman, can I have two of the biggest vodka and oranges you've ever poured please."

The chaos had begun. Me and Joe stood at the bar, knocked those first ones back and off we went. Catching up with a snooker mate is always fun and this day was no different. We were talking rubbish, laughing and knocking off vodka after vodka.

About 8pm that night, well and truly pissed, Bill Cottier came back over to me with some bad news.

"Jimmy, you're on table nine," he said. "Quick smart, they're waiting for you." I was totally gobsmacked and too pissed to do much about it.

"But I thought I wasn't playing today," I slurred.

"Well, you are now, you're playing Wales," Bill said.

"Okay." I said. "One more question though Bill, who's Wales? Do I know him?"

I practically crawled to table nine and got ready to play Steve Newbury. By now, the drink had really got hold of me and I was well gone.

I kept looking at the balls and then my cue, and then the balls again. My head was spinning like crazy. Miraculously I managed a half-decent break of 50-something and that made me think I could bluff my way through it. Everyone could surely tell I was pissed but I thought I could survive if I kept my head down. So far, so good.

I glued myself to the corners and the pockets on my way around the table, trying to stand straight, until, finally, the game was up.

I got into position to play a red, my eyes looking in different directions and I could feel myself going. 'Oh fuck,' was all I could think as I fell over, lying under the table with hundreds of people looking at me.

Screwdrivers had screwed me. It was a complete nightmare.

I think Bill didn't like me or Joe too much and he wanted a fellow Scouse lad to represent England at the World Amateur Championship rather than me, so he pulled a fast one on us but that doesn't excuse the fact that we were pissed playing for our country.

Steve went on to win that match 3-0 and that handed Wales the tournament. Whoops.

Bill was raging afterwards, threatening me with all sorts and trying to ban me from my trip to Australia. "As long as I've got any power, you aren't going," he kept screaming at me.

I staggered off back in the direction of my chalet, wondering if he meant it. He probably did. I suppose I'd have to get to Tasmania another way then, eh?

In the meantime, Bill went back to his office and delivered the bad news to Henry over the phone. "Henry, there's no way I'm taking Jimmy, he's a madman," he said.

Henry thought the best thing to do would be to get up to Prestatyn as quick as possible to sort it out with Bill in person – and kick my arse at the same time.

I stumbled back to my chalet and fell asleep until the game of cards going on in the front room woke me up. I had a few pals knocking around and I told them that Bill Cottier could fuck off. "I'm definitely going to Tasmania, he's not stopping me – no chance," I said, and with that I staggered off and ran a bath.

Henry finally arrived in Prestatyn at 2am, steaming mad with me, and he banged on every chalet door until he found mine.

"Right, where is the bastard?" he asked my mates and someone told him I was in the bath. He almost kicked the door in as he flew into the bathroom, about to give me the bollocking of my life. The door flew open and he never said a word, he was too stunned by what he saw.

Finally, he opened his mouth.

"Jimmy, what the HELL are you doing?"

"Oh hello Henry," I replied. "I'm rowing to Tasmania."

I was sat in the bath, water overflowing and drowning the place, still wearing my dickie-bow and dinner suit, using my cue as an oar. "Bill Cottier says I can't go to Tasmania with him so

THE PLAYER

I'm setting off now, otherwise I won't get there." Henry didn't know whether to laugh or drown me.

"Jimmy stop being a fucking idiot and get out," was all he eventually came out with. "Get some sleep, get these idiots out of here and let me try and get you out of this."

He kicked all my mates out, apart from Joe who I was sharing the chalet with, and off he went. On his way out he locked us in the room but I got out of the bath, dried off and then sneaked out of the window with Joe for more drinks at the bar.

Fuck staying in all night – rowing is thirsty work...

Henry worked his magic and I got away with it. I copped a fine – about £200 I think it was – and I was put on about my ninth final warning. Henry had persuaded Bill and his mates on the board that they had to take me to Tasmania – I was the English amateur champion and the best player in the country.

I got another bollocking from Henry, though, before we left. "Jimmy, straighten yourself out. You need to grow up."

The problem was, I really did not give a fuck about anything. I needed to mature but I just wanted to run riot all the time.

Henry came with me and Joe to Tasmania but decided to try and curb our boozing and gambling by giving us no money at all. But this was me he was talking to – I always found a way to get hold of cash. My Tooting street education saw to that.

As part of the trip to Australia, me and Joe were entitled to $1500 expenses each so as we sat on the plane, sipping a vodka, we decided to blag the money from Bill Cottier, who was my new best mate all of a sudden.

"Come on Bill, please, just give us the money up front, we won't blow it," I promised. Joe nodded his head as well, doing his best altar-boy act. Bill was meant to give us the cash bit by bit – a $50-a-day allowance – but we wanted it all and we wanted it now.

We landed in Australia and by now we'd done enough to break Bill down. He found a counter that would cash traveller's cheques and then started muttering to himself, "I shouldn't be doing this, I know this is a bad idea – I just know it."

We promised him we would behave and not waste a single penny of it. Scout's honour.

The minute the cash hit mine and Joe's hands, we were off. We didn't even wait to go to the hotel and check in. Our cases were ditched and we hit the road, in search of the races. We were two mad boys and it didn't take us long to find a racetrack with a meeting on.

In Australia they love the trot racing, where a horse has a harness on, and me and Joe went crazy, backing anything that moved. Unfortunately for us, if they moved at all, they only went backwards. You name it, me and Joe gambled on it. Just like in Zan's, it went in one pocket and out the other.

By the time we hitched a lift to the hotel, we didn't have a single cent on us. Not one. We were screwed and we had to work out a way of getting through the next 10 days with no way of eating, drinking or, the worst thing of all, having a good time.

There was only one thing for it – we threw ourselves at the mercy of anyone who would let us scrounge some food and a bed. In the end we were saved by a mate of mine from Northern Ireland called Larry Rooney.

Larry, who is still a good pal, took pity on us. He is a stocky little bloke, a plasterer these days, and we would've been totally lost without him.

THE PLAYER

Every day he fed and looked after us. We used to try and cram as much food from the tournament buffets in our mouths and jacket pockets as possible, anything to survive. I was supposed to be trying to win the amateur game's highest honour and there I was, more bothered about seeing if I could squeeze five cheese rolls into a tuxedo jacket.

We kept landing on our feet and even found a hotel that stupidly thought that just because we were English we were two nice gentlemen who would pay their bill every day. We soon put them straight. Our room looked like it had been burgled with clothes, mattresses and mouldy bits of food all over the place.

"Yes, don't worry about a thing," me and Joe would tell the concierge. "We will get you your money tomorrow." What money?

We'd never have survived without Larry who raised our spirits with loads of nice one-liners, just like most people from Belfast. "Fucking consistent me, fucking consistent," he would say after every match he played. "I lost 4-0 again. That's fucking consistent."

Somehow, I got through to the semi-final, despite days of living on scrounged food and drinks, and I came up against Paul Mifsud, a lad from Malta. This is when Larry really came good. I'd prepared for my match against Paul in my traditional way by drinking like a lunatic and it showed. Larry could see that my game was off, I wasn't clicking and that, if I wasn't very careful, Paul would beat me and my trip to Tasmania would've been pointless. I was shaking and had the proper booze withdrawals when your hands and brain aren't listening to each other.

Even through the haze of the drink and the gambling at that

time, I did still want to win the world amateur title, otherwise my two extra years as an amateur would've been a real waste.

Granted, I'd done nothing in the build-up to prove that desire or to give myself even a half-decent chance but back then I was so good and so fearless that I didn't care about preparing properly. It nearly cost me then.

It would cost me in the future...

So I was 6-4 down to Paul and it looked like I was slipping out of the semi-final. I couldn't get going, couldn't get any real rhythm and I knew I was on my way home. 'Well, you've fucked this up,' is all I could think when I returned to my seat after another missed red.

Fortunately, during one of the frames, Larry spotted the problem and soon sorted me out. He sneaked around the corner, shoved a large Southern Comfort and lemonade into my hand and whispered, "Drink this, it'll bring you around."

Well, yeah, you could say that.

I downed it, strictly following instructions of course, then made a century and won the other two frames I needed pretty comfortably to sneak into the final – so thanks again Larry!

In the final, I played local favourite Ron Atkins who'd had an easy route to the final. I was up against him in his own backyard but that didn't bother me at all as I blew him away, 10-2.

In the final frame, he missed a red to the top left cushion after a break of 32 left him 44 in front and I flew out of my chair, the balls nice and split, and I knew this was my chance.

The balls were perfectly placed and I began tucking into the blacks, comfortably closing the gap on Ron and inching my way towards the title.

However, I then missed an easy blue to the middle pocket.

THE PLAYER

It was just too simple and I was in the groove too much for it not to go in but it jawed and came out. Again, pressure can do anything to a player's arm at times like that.

I didn't have long to wait, though, as Ron potted the blue, went in off the pink and I rolled the pink in to win the title. It was an amazing feeling, one of the best I would ever experience.

I'd come to Tasmania, caused chaos, been constantly on the piss, scrounged a hotel room, begged and borrowed from everyone, not been to bed before 4am – and I'd still won the tournament.

That's how good I was at the time; that's how easy it was.

In fact, we'd been so confident I would win the tournament, we had the celebration party the night before the final!

Everybody crammed into a room and the booze flowed. Me and Joe enjoyed ourselves and I was congratulated on a job well done – and we hadn't even played the fucking match yet. That's how bulletproof we were. I knew before I even picked up my cue that Ron Atkins wouldn't cause me any grief. If only Bill Cottier could say the same about me and Joe...

Finally, after lifting the trophy, it was time to check out of the hotel. The owner had got wise to us by now and knew that we were going to try and scam him.

Our room needed condemning, not cleaning. We tried to do a runner but my suitcase broke as we were trying to get out of there. Nobody needed to see 10 days' worth of socks and shirts falling over the place but that was the last memory of Tasmania – our washing lying all over the street as me and Joe scarpered for the bus to the airport.

On the way back to England we stopped in India for the

Indian Amateur Championship and I had to buy a fresh set of clothes when we landed because most of mine were lying on the pavement about 4,000 miles away.

However, me and Joe didn't learn our lesson. We were again up to no good, staying in a beautiful hotel in Kolkata and turning it into another dump as we had food fights and stayed out all night.

When it came to the snooker, though, I couldn't put a foot wrong as about five days after becoming world amateur champion I'd added the Indian title to my silverware, beating Arvind 'Tornado Fats' Savur 9-7 in the final. You could say The Tornado was blown away by The Whirlwind and the snooker world seemed there for the taking.

India was something else when it came to poverty and the conditions that people lived in and although me and Joe might've cared more about being idiots, you couldn't help but notice how tough life was for most people.

Every street was surrounded with beggars and kids with an arm or a leg missing. That brought home to me how far from Tooting I was and how lucky I was as well. We used to get followed everywhere we went by loads of tiny, smiley kids, all just wanting to say hello. They had nothing, literally not even a shirt on their back, and we tried our best for them, giving them food and water and whatever else we could manage.

Me and Joe kept feeling worse about what we were seeing so he suggested we take a load of these street kids to a restaurant one night. That was a great idea, so we picked our spot and as we walked through the front door, the manager tried to smack these kids away, smiling and apologising to us for them being a nuisance. "Fuck this," I told Joe. "I'm not having that", and we turned around and took them all somewhere else. It doesn't matter where you come from in life, everybody deserves a break – that's the way I was brought up anyway.

We used to pay some kids to carry our cues and we'd give them whatever was in our pockets – I can't even remember how much it was but it wasn't a lot – and the look on their faces was something else. Me and Joe could burn $1500 dollars each in one afternoon whereas these kids looked at our spare change like their lives depended on it.

I can't honestly say though that it made me sit up and take notice or look after my money any better. If anything, I probably went out and gambled more than ever, knowing how lucky I was and how easy money was to come by.

●●●●●●●

If everything was going well on the table, life was moving pretty fast off it too.

As time had gone on, me and Maureen had got closer and before we both knew it, she was pregnant. We were only kids ourselves and both sets of parents were hardly over the moon about it all.

But pregnant she was and that was the end of it.

It knocked me over because I was just a kid, I was running around and kids having kids is just no good. I was 18, she was 19. I can't remember where I was when Maureen told me – it was just one of those things, and where I'm from, you stick by someone you've got pregnant.

There'd be no running from the situation for me, even if, as a teenage boy myself, there would of course have been some fears and doubts about everything. If you've not grown up yourself, how can you be expected to bring a kid up?

The pregnancy was fine but I wasn't there for the birth and that is something I still regret.

I was at bloody Brighton races with Lenny Cain, Peewee and another geezer called Gerry. I knew her due date was getting near but I didn't think too much of it so I rang the hospital from a payphone at the races at about 6pm just to see how she was doing and I got the shock of my life.

"Mr White, Maureen has been asking after you," this nurse said. "She's in labour."

Fuck. There's me in Brighton and there's Maureen in Clapham.

She was in the South London Hospital for Women and Children – it's a block of flats now – so I thought I'd better get there sharpish. Well, not sharpish as such, but I'd better get there at some point. At three in the morning to be precise.

After a long day at the races, I was more than ready to see my new daughter, even if the hospital staff were not having any of it.

"Sorry Mr White, it's the middle of the night," the nurse on the door said, trying to make herself sound as bossy as possible, but I had so much front, so much confidence and swagger from a life spent in snooker halls and boozers, that I soon charmed my way past her and into the ward where Maureen was with Lauren, the most beautiful thing I'd ever seen.

It was an amazing moment and I was smitten on the spot – the same as any other dad. To hold your own flesh and blood is just mind blowing. Until you've done it yourself you can't really explain what it's like. Feelings pour out that you didn't even know you had in you. It was wonderful. Me and Maureen looked at each other happily and she forgave me for being absent so I celebrated my new daughter's birth – and getting back into Maureen's good books – by going on the piss for a couple of days. Obviously, I'm not proud of it... but we didn't so much wet the baby's head as soak it.

Following Lauren's birth, we all moved into a block of flats in Battersea – and Maureen did a great job in making it a proper family home. The only problem was I was never there. I can't say becoming a father made me see the light or start behaving – in fact, I was probably out more than ever. There was no way I was not going to do the right thing by this new bundle we had. But, at the same time, I was still acting like an arsehole, out drinking and flying around London, playing the big-time boy. I thought as long as I paid the bills, there wouldn't be any screaming from Lauren or Maureen. You can imagine how that went down.

Off the table, life continued to take off and, to be honest, I lapped it up too much and my head went because I could now afford to go to the West End as well. I was well and truly in the big leagues now, or so I thought. I was just full of it – the same as most lads would've been at that age. I had talent, money, birds throwing themselves at me, you name it – it was there for me to take full advantage of.

Back then I used to have a bouncer/runner with me and he looked just like Bob Hoskins. I mean, he really, really looked like Bob Hoskins. If he walked in the room you would do a double take. When I was going round town with him, The Long Good Friday had just come out and we used to play on that, big-time. We used to walk up to the velvet rope at a club. I'd loudly call him "Bob" in front of the owners and we were inside, sipping champagne in the VIP lounge before you know it.

Until now I'd been well known in snooker circles and been in the odd newspaper story here and there but the wins in Tasmania and India meant it was now time to become a full-blown professional.

Snooker was now my job as well as my love and it was time to start doing battle with older, more experienced players who wouldn't let me get away with the shots and the tactics I'd used in the amateurs.

It was time to get used to being on the telly every five minutes, making front page headlines as often as back page ones and trying to cope with the huge changes I had on my plate – from becoming a dad to becoming a household name.

And, above all else, it was time to face the man who would cause me more problems in the 1980s than anyone else.

4

Sink Or Swim

A little while ago, I did an exhibition in Scunthorpe with Steve Davis. It had been a good night, we'd had a laugh, entertained the crowd and we were stood in the car park afterwards.

I was chatting to John Virgo, one of my oldest mates in the game, and as Steve got in his car to drive off, he turned round and went "See ya later Jim."

I turned to Virgo and said, "Well that wouldn't have happened 30 years ago would it?" and we both started laughing.

Steve Davis is a wonderful, wonderful snooker player and we've always had a lot of respect for each other. He is a gentleman, he is great for the game and if I rang him up and asked him to do something for charity – like an exhibition or a signed photograph or whatever – then I know he'd do it in an instant and vice versa.

But there's no point in pretending that we've got much in common or that we're alike in any way.

We are just two totally different blokes and that meant that during our heydays we were never close, at all. In fact, in the 1980s, it's fair to say that we had no relationship whatsoever. There was no animosity or aggression from either of us towards the other – neither of us are built that way – it's simply down to the fact that we're chalk and cheese.

Thinking about it now, Steve must've spent most of the 1980s rubbing his hands and laughing at the way I prepared for tournaments. He wasn't stupid and he knew I could beat anybody on my day if I prepared properly and looked after myself.

But me preparing properly and looking after myself was as alien to me as it would be for Steve to go out and sink 15 pints the night before a match. We were just two different animals and neither could have lived the life of the other, even if we wanted to – which we definitely didn't. Steve would happily sit in his room and play chess or a board game whereas I'd be out somewhere, causing murder. I liked to dabble, he liked to Scrabble.

When we played in tournaments, Steve never spoke to anybody and kept himself to himself. He had a bit of a smirk on him and I think that was more a tactic rather than because he was shy. It makes sense, in individual sports, because you always need to try and get one over on your opponent psychologically.

Snooker players back then used to stick together and travel together. We were always checking into the same hotels, the same airports, the same bars and the same clubs. You can't help but get close to people you're spending 80 per cent of your year with. However, Davis distanced himself from the group so we had very little to do with each other. There was never any dislike or distrust, we just hung around in different circles. Don't forget as well that I was almost always in the company of a Mr Alex Higgins, a man who despised Davis because he believed he played snooker in the wrong manner.

Higgins was wrong about that – Steve was entitled to play the game in whatever way he wanted and good luck to him for that. But me and him could never have got close because Higgins terrified Davis – like he did a lot of people – and so Steve was just protecting himself by avoiding Higgins and also avoiding me.

If I didn't really get to know Davis as a man, I certainly knew all about him as a snooker player. And what a player. He was granite. Without a shadow of a doubt, Davis was the hardest player to beat. I've played Steve at his peak and I've also faced Ronnie O'Sullivan and Stephen Hendry at their best and I can say that Steve was the toughest of the lot.

If you played four frames against Davis and it was 2-2 then, trust me, you'd had to climb two mountains. You had to play four fantastic shots to get in, have perfect safety and never give him a sniff. He grew from strength to strength and Steve was also very lucky to have Barry Hearn behind him. They were like brothers. Over the years, I'm sure Hearn has used Davis to open doors for him and also vice versa – the two of them are the closest of mates, they've been very successful in business and Barry has done amazing things with his Matchroom company that keeps going from strength to strength.

Steve had the support of Barry from a very early age. One

day in Romford in about 1974 or 1975, so the story goes, Barry was doing the accounts for the Lucania chain of snooker clubs and as he was sat there doing his sums, he looked through this one-way glass and saw this skinny ginger kid and couldn't believe how good he was. He watched him practise for six weeks, signed him up and the rest is history.

Steve gave you nothing when he played. Fuck all. Every pot, every frame, every minute of a match with him was a battle. His safety game was second to none, he could score when he got in and he had the perfect temperament. He was totally cocooned in his own world when he was under those lights.

I'd first met Davis when I was about 13 and we were playing in tournaments across London. He had just started to take the world by storm. Steve is a few years older than me and he kept himself to himself but the first time we met was at Ron Gross's club in Neasden.

I could tell straightaway that he was a devastating player; he just had this amazing cue action – the best I've seen along with Ronnie O'Sullivan – and he was potting balls that he had no right to do. He was really lanky with this fuzzy mop of ginger hair everywhere. Normally, someone would've taken the piss out of that but Davis soon shut them up when he got into the pack and showed everyone in Neasden what he was about.

After that we didn't really have much to do with each other over the years as we made our separate journeys into the snooker world. Davis did his thing and I did mine until we had our first real, proper dust-up in the first round of the 1981 World Championship. I was making my debut in the tourna-ment, along with Tony Knowles and Dave Martin.

After the first session I was 4-2 down to him and I looked in real trouble, especially as my tip was giving me all sorts of grief. I managed to repair it and stayed in the match until it was 9-8 to Steve. He just needed one frame to win. I felt like I had all the momentum after fighting back and I thought I could snatch the match. The crowd was with me, too. I desperately tried to claw my way back but I lost position and Steve finished me off. Davis went on to beat Alex Higgins in the next round before beating Terry Griffiths and defending champion Cliff Thorburn in the semi-final. He beat Doug Mountjoy 18-12 in the final to claim his first world title.

I always look back and think 'what might've been' about 1981 because I think I had a great chance to beat him. I was level par with him at the time and felt I was improving as he was improving. That first round match was the hardest Davis was pushed in that World Championship. At the Crucible that year, nobody else came within four frames of him.

After losing to Steve at the Crucible, I gained some kind of revenge over him when I went on a great winning streak, defeating him 6-5 on the way to winning the 1981 Scottish Masters before also beating him him 11-9 in the final of the Northern Ireland Classic.

The Lang's Scottish Masters (as it was then called) was my first professional tournament victory as I beat Ray Reardon, Davis and finally Cliff Thorburn in the final. Those three had all won the World Championship at some point so I felt like I'd really arrived and could also really threaten Davis. Plus the £8,000 prize money for winning the Lang's could certainly buy a few Screwdrivers and a half-decent night at the track or in the bookies.

That win over Ray was all the more special because I had a

court case looming at the time and the way it happened perfectly sums up the bedlam of how I was living – and why that gave Davis the edge.

It happened like this.

Me and Maureen were in a nightclub one time called Flickers in Tooting Bec when we heard there was a riot going on outside. There was trouble up and down the country in 1981 and it was always kicking off in South London.

We didn't know what was going on because we'd been on the dancefloor but at around 1am we decided to leave and it was chaos outside. "Jimmy, you can't go out there mate," the doorman, who knew me, said. "You'll get killed." "What are you talking about?" I asked. "My mum only lives across the road, we'll be fine."

The doorman tried to talk me out of it and told me that the police were just picking everyone and anyone up off the streets, whether they'd been causing trouble or not.

Outside, the police vans were everywhere, there was smoke and broken glass all over the pavement and I was walking along, really pissed, just chatting shit to Maureen, when we came across this shop with all its glass front smashed.

I just wanted a bit of fun so I crunched over this glass and picked up this shop dummy and started dancing with it. "Jimmy, put it down," Maureen said, laughing, but I was just taking the piss and messing about.

The next thing I knew, the Old Bill arrived from nowhere, grabbed me and Maureen and dragged us off to the nick at Amen Corner in Tooting.

When we got into the station, it was absolutely packed full of looters. You couldn't move for them.

SINK OR SWIM

The room was full of cigarette smoke, danger and adrenaline. There were rogues from top to bottom in the station and when I walked in, up went this massive cheer. I was getting a bit famous by now and the police started interviewing me in front of everyone. There was no room to do it in private and a bit of a crowd started gathering.

"Name?" this copper said.

"James Warren White," I replied.

"What's your job and how much do you earn a week?" he asked.

"I'm a snooker player and I earn about 50 times more than you do."

I probably shouldn't have said it but, fuck me, at the time, I'd done nothing wrong.

This copper wasn't happy and he jumped across the table to try and hit me before this massive sergeant stopped him. He totally lost his rag. I couldn't blame him because my cheek had sent the room into chaos. Everyone was laughing and cheering at what I'd said.

I eventually got put up in front of the judge at Battersea Magistrates Court and won the case but lost the costs.

The judge knew that I was guilty but the police had bungled the case. They'd claimed I'd come from the south but my lawyers argued that there was no way I could've done and still been nicked where I was, so I got off on a technicality.

The judge wasn't happy and made me pay up – he knew I'd been up to no good and was fuming that the police had messed it up.

•••••••

I genuinely believed I was as good a player as Davis and definitely easier on the eye because I tried to combine winning snooker with exciting snooker whereas he was happier to just grind it out. After winning the Scottish Masters, I said someting along those lines to the press who quoted me as saying that I wasn't scared of him and that he was just another player on the tour.

How did that go down? Well, put it like this, Steve responded by hammering me 9-0 in the UK Championship semi-final! I got a bit flash in that match, trying to show that I was the most exciting kid on the circuit and I took too many risks. Before I knew it, I was 4-0 down and Davis was cruising it. It was a tough lesson. When Davis got his hands around your throat, he almost never stopped squeezing.

He just played all round quality snooker. The public might've thought it was dull but as a fellow snooker player you couldn't help but admire him. He wasn't boring at all – he was like a machine that gave you nothing. If you just look at his trophies, prize money and reputation, you don't get that without being a great, great player.

I knew it wouldn't take long for our paths to cross in the World Championship final and I wasn't wrong. 1984 was a great season for me, including winning the Masters. I really wanted to do well in Sheffield and it was one of the World Championships that I did actually prepare properly for. On the way to the final I'd played some wonderful snooker, seeing off Rex Williams, Eddie Charlton and Cliff Thorburn, before edging out Kirk Stevens 16-14 in the last four. I was 22, I was fearless around the table and I thought it was my year.

Davis was quick off the mark, winning the first three frames.

SINK OR SWIM

I won one back but then he reeled off another five to leave me looking at an 8-1 deficit.

I recovered a bit to take three more frames but still found myself 12-4 down after the first session. Davis had annihilated me. I couldn't find my fluency, I couldn't get into the balls and hurt Davis – apart from one frame where I made a 137 – and I couldn't use my safety game because of the very simple fact I didn't have one at the time.

I was staring at a heavy defeat and the biggest humiliation of them all – losing a World Championship final with a session to spare. That is probably the worst feeling a snooker player could have; to be so close to being the best in the world and then be destroyed in no time at all. Just like in 1981, Davis was putting the squeeze on. The comparisons with that year didn't end there as, once again, I was having loads of trouble with the tip of my cue. It felt like history was repeating itself.

As the Crucible emptied after the first session, I just needed some time to think and to work out what I was going to do. This was my big chance of glory and it was going wrong. Something had to change.

Loads of pals had turned up in Sheffield when I made it to the semis, hoping I would go all the way and during the downtime between sessions I would normally have gone for a drink with them. Understandably, I wasn't in the mood this day.

I found my dad and told him what to do. "Dad, take the lads back to the hotel," I said. "I need to get some practice in and get my head straight."

I needed some space and I also received some crucial help from Jim Meadowcroft, who'd been knocked out that year in the last qualifying round by Neal Foulds.

I think Jim was doing some commentating and he saw me looking paler and skinnier than usual (which took some doing back then). "Jim," I said. "Feel this tip for me would you. Am I going mad or is it knackered?"

Jim took one look, twirled my cue in his hands for five or six seconds and then confirmed what I thought. "Jimmy, you've got to be kidding," he said. "You've been playing with that? Are you joking?"

Yes, it was as bad as I thought.

"It's rock hard," Jim said, before coming to the rescue. "Give it here and I'll fix it," and we sat in the Crucible while he got to work. There was just me and Jim sat in the auditorium, dusty and echoing, until finally we were spotted by this security guard who wanted us out. I slipped him £50 and stayed in there with Jim, talking about the match, sorting my tip out and getting some practice in.

Jim worked his magic and in the next session I was back in the match. I soon pegged Davis back from 12-4 to 12-7. I was then 39 in front with 51 left in the 20th frame when he doubled a red and cleared up.

Despite the setback, I wouldn't let him get away and I eventually won the session 7-1 to leave myself just two frames behind at 13-11. It was an incredible comeback and one I was proud of. But Davis was Davis – you couldn't afford to make a single mistake and the higher the stakes, the calmer he seemed to get. I kept throwing punch after punch at him but every time I got him in my sights, he pulled something out to win the frame.

I won three frames in a row at one stage in the final session, and the last three frames were incredibly tight. Davis edged one 59-55 before I hit back to win 65-60 and make it 17-16. I had

40 points on the board in the final frame but Davis eventually sank a pink into the middle pocket to fall over the line, 18-16.

It had been an epic final but it was another 'what if' moment. If my tip had been okay in the first session and it hadn't been such a disaster, I think I'd have had enough in the tank to beat Steve.

But that's life isn't it?

Afterwards, during the presentation ceremony, I felt sick. Take my word for it, whenever a sportsman or woman has lost a major final, shown around the world, the toughest thing is to stand there and paint a smile on and pretend it's not eating you up inside because part of you is gutted. I was no different but, just the same, there's no point moping about it for too long – it's only a sport.

I wanted to get out of the arena as fast as possible so I could get to my mates and to the bar and to get out of the spotlight for a bit. I wanted to have a drink and enjoy myself.

Back then we stayed in the Grosvenor House Hotel in Sheffield and I always took a suite on the top floor while my mates would stay in Bed and Breakfasts or even in the suite with me. After losing to Davis we hung around in Sheffield for a few days, staying up all night, drinking, playing poker and unwinding. Seventeen days' play at the Crucible knocks it out of you and I wanted to relax a bit, get pissed and laugh. Maureen wasn't there so we could get up to whatever we wanted – nobody wanted to check out and get back to the real world.

You get over these things and get on with life.

Davis had a little dip in the World Championship in 1985 and 1986 when he lost in the final both years, first to Dennis Taylor and then Joe Johnson. Even then though, I never thought he'd peaked or had stopped being my main rival. This was definitely his era. He was the greatest player in the world at the time, no question about it. He was invincible – when he lost, every other player couldn't believe it and it used to make all the news programmes. It takes a special kind of player to make the world stop, just because you've lost a snooker game. It goes to show you how big the game was back then, too.

I'll never forget the 1985 final – the same as everyone else.

I've played in some classic Crucible matches myself and that match is up there with the very best of all time. I couldn't believe what I was seeing. Everybody knows that the match went on for ages and it was well past midnight when Taylor finally won it. I was sitting at home, Lauren was asleep in bed and Maureen was sat on the couch with me. Like the rest of the country, I couldn't take my eyes off the telly. Dennis had been murdered 7-0 in the first session, he was 8-0 down after the first frame of the second session and I'd spent the best part of a day feeling sorry for him. Goodnight Vienna.

Davis was like a robot – nobody in the world could believe he would let it slip from there. If they had internet gambling back then you would've put a bet on Davis at 1000-1-on to win the tournament. £10,000 would've paid out a tenner but you know what, it would've been like printing money because, surely, there was no way that Dennis could pull the match back round. Dennis might be the only person on earth who thought he could still win. In fact, ring him, he'll let you know about it!

Slowly, he chipped away at the lead until that famous last few frames. Dennis was behind in the entire final until the last black of the last frame. Talk about timing. He'd not been in front once, not once, until that black went down.

SINK OR SWIM

I was so pleased for Dennis because Davis looked like losing nothing. If there were nine tournaments in a year, he looked a banker to win five of them. You had to play out of your mind to beat him.

The year after, Joe Johnson played phenomenal snooker to beat him. Joe played the match of a lifetime – a match that was beyond his wildest dreams and as he'd been a 150/1 shot at the start of the tournament nobody, not even Joe, had seen that coming.

Again though, it wasn't as if anyone on tour thought Davis was shot and he proved that in 1987 when he got his revenge on Joe by beating him in the final and that goes to show you what a great champion he was. To come back from two unexpected losses in the final – the most hurtful way to lose – and to then bounce back and win it again takes unbelievable skill, dedication and mental strength and Davis had that in buckets.

•••••••

Around the time Davis was regaining the world title, I'd joined Barry Hearn's Matchroom myself which caused a bit of a rumpus in the snooker world because I was joining the stable of my clear-cut rival.

I'd had a selection of different managers since leaving Henry West including a music mogul called Harvey Lisberg and then I'd briefly joined a company called Framework (set up in direct competition to Matchroom by a geezer called Howard Kruger) before finally joining Barry's boys. It was a bit strange being inside a camp that had for so long appeared to be The Opposition.

Being part of the 'Matchroom Mob' of me, Davis, Willie Thorne, Dennis Taylor, Tony Meo, Neal Foulds, and Terry Griffiths was a lot of fun at times, even if I did cause Steve and Barry some major headaches from time to time – usually while we were away in Hong Kong.

Barry loved nothing more than getting his Matchroom stable to Asia so he could get some wheeling and dealing done. We went quite often for about three or four years with Barry, performing in Matchroom exhibitions and tournaments that he organised. He used to impress clients while we were out there by hiring a boat to take everybody out into the harbour because Barry, being Barry, never missed a chance to do business.

Me and Tony Meo got to know this very rich, political family in Hong Kong called the Chans and they couldn't do enough for us. They were incredible and me and Tony Meo couldn't believe our luck when we visited the place. S-Class Mercedes' were put on for us, we had big suites wherever we went and we never paid for a meal or a drink so we used to have a great time. I used to love going to Hong Kong because it also meant we could smoke these little cannabis Thai sticks. I was always laughing and having a great time – and getting paid for it!

Soon after I'd joined, we were playing a tournament in the Queen Elizabeth Stadium and there were 3,000 in there all going mad.

All the Matchroom boys were there and me and Meo were fucking about as usual. We were in the back, in the dressing room, smoking these Thai sticks and Terry Griffiths knocked on the door and wondered what we were up to.

"What's that you're smoking boy? Why you laughing?" "You wouldn't like it Tel," I told him. "You don't want none of this."

SINK OR SWIM

"Why boy, why, what is it?" Terry said, before taking the Thai stick out of my hand and taking three massive lungfuls.

At first, he was fine and then he started giggling and messing around with us. That was the calm before the storm.

Next thing any of us knew, the intercom crackled and went "TERRY GRIFFITHS FIVE MINUTES TO MAIN STAGE, TERRY GRIFFITHS FIVE MINUTES TO MAIN STAGE."

As part of the entertainment, we'd play a couple of frames against each other and then do some trickshots. Each player would do one or two and the Hong Kong crowd loved it. I never really liked doing them so would always try and get out of it but Terry was great and was the last one on that night as Barry wanted the evening to end with a bang. Little does Baz know that his plans were going seriously wrong.

All of a sudden, this Thai stick comes on Griffiths in a big way and his eyes started going in opposite directions.

He picked up his cue, wobbled out of the dressing room and tried to walk down towards the arena where Barry, who was the MC that night, was giving Terry this big intro, trying to whip the crowd into a bit of a frenzy.

"LADIES AND GENTLEMEN, THE 1979 CHAMPION OF THE WORLD... TERRRRRRRY GRIFFITHHHHSSSSS..."

Nothing.

Terry is nowhere to be seen.

Barry tried again, getting a bit concerned by now about where his showstopper was. "LADIES AND GENTLEMEN, THE 1979 CHAMPION OF THE WORLD, TERRRRRRRY GRIFFITHHHHSSSSS..."

The next thing, Terry started staggering down to the stage – eyes gone, legs gone – he picked the microphone up from

Barry and spoke into it... "WHAT HAVE YOU DONE TO ME WHITE?"

Barry put his hand over the microphone, grinned to the bemused crowd and whispered, "Where the fuck have you been?"

"I've just had one of Jimmy's fags," Terry said, giggling like a madman. "They're fucking brilliant!" and with that he turned around and just walked off stage! Totally gone.

All of a sudden, me and Meo knew that Hearn was going to come after us. "Fuck, quick, go," I shouted at Meo, crying with laughter, and we were out of there in no time at all. It was like Zan's again as we legged it out of the fire exit door, trying to escape Barry – who was actually laughing as much as anyone about it.

About an hour later, it all settled down and then I started to get worried about Terry, who was my friend. I thought I'd ring him in his hotel room and apologise.

The phone rang, Terry picked up and that was it – the pair of us were worse than useless for laughing. I swear on my children's lives that Terry picked that phone up and didn't say a word for a full 20 minutes. Not a single word. He couldn't because he was hysterical. He finally got his voice – and sanity – back and we started chatting.

"Jimmy," he said. "I'm going to ring the wife in about four hours' time, will I be alright by then?"

On that trip, when we checked into the hotel, I was searching for my wallet and this bag of hash fell out onto the floor. Now back then, that was still a big deal. Nobody would bat an eyelid today but in the '80s it could've got me in some serious trouble. Barry clocked this weed and wasn't happy. "Jimmy, what the fuck are you doing?" I looked him straight in the face and went, "I wonder who's just dropped that? It's nothing to do with me Baz, definitely not" and I got away with it. Again.

●●●●●●●

As I say, me, Tony and the Chans became big mates. Me and David Chan got particularly close. His dad was very influential because he was a Hong Kong politician and we really started hanging around with some movers and shakers. On this one trip, Barry kept making us go on these junk boats in Hong Kong harbour with all these people that he wanted to impress.

I said to David, "Your uncle has a big yacht doesn't he? Why don't we pull up beside Barry's junk and give them all a bit of a surprise?" David jumped at the idea and the next thing you know, we're on this yacht, worth about £10 million with its own crew. We chased after Barry's boat which had the rest of the lads on board, including Davis. Barry was probably fuming that I wasn't there – he always wanted me to do 'client hospitality' because I was the only player in Matchroom who could drink all night and then play all day.

We got the captain of the yacht to pull up next to the junk boat and I thought it was time to surprise Barry. "COME ON BOARD, EVERYONE," I shouted over the side of the junk. "THERE'S PLENTY OF ROOM FOR YOU ALL."

Barry probably couldn't believe it because he'd been looking for us all morning anyway. Everyone got off the junk and on board the yacht and we went off towards this island off Hong Kong.

We had to anchor up about half-a-mile from the island because it had become too shallow and suddenly Eddie Charlton jumped off the boat and started swimming to the shore. 'Steady' had been a really good swimmer as a kid – probably because he was an Aussie – and he just took off. I wasn't in the mood for any of that but we all jumped into the sea wearing these big lifejackets you could sit up in. It was all very nice, a joint or two was getting passed around – away from Hearn because of the smell – and there are definitely worse ways to spend a Sunday morning. We had a lovely hour or two and a right laugh.

This yacht also had its own speedboat that was towed behind it. And this is where things started going wrong.

The crew of the yacht started ferrying people to the island where Eddie had swum to. I watched him do a few trips and thought 'fuck it, I can do that'.

"Eh mate, any chance I can drive that thing?" I asked and the crew said yes. The Chan family really liked me so the poor bloke couldn't really say no. Davis jumped in with me. He was a bit scared of the water – not to mention his half-stoned driver as well. I was really gunning this boat, doing doughnuts around the yacht and grinning like a madman. I was giving it maximum and spray was going everywhere before I finally dropped Steve off at the island. He was paler than me when he got off but I thought 'job done!'

The next thing you know, this fucking speedboat is sinking. What's happening here? Turns out I'd got too close to the island when I dropped Steve off and the boat was stuck to the bottom. I couldn't do a thing about it and sweat started pouring off me. 'Oh shit, what do I do know?' was all that was running through my head.

I thought it would be alright as this massive white speedboat, covered in cushions and with its own mini-bar, looked to be able to handle itself.

Some of the crew from the yacht swam across to where the speedboat was to assess the damage/how much I'd fucked it. I swam off to the island for the rest of the afternoon and left them to it. There was no point all of us standing around, scratching our heads, wondering how to get a dodgy boat back up and running. Plus, all that sweating had left me in need of a drink to rehydrate. I put it out of my head and we headed off for lunch and loads of wine in this fabulous seafood restaurant before we decided we should all head back to see what the fuss was about.

As we got back to the shore, I knew I'd done a proper job on this speedboat. They'd had to bring the yacht in as close as they could to the shore without that also getting stuck on the bottom as well. They'd attached a big rope and they'd started towing it but the next thing, it flipped upside down. Leather cushions were floating all over the place, the seats from the boat were drifting around and away and all you could see was about a foot of the boat sticking out of the water – the rest completely gone, submerged.

Now I'm no expert sailor but when a boat is flipped upside down, 90 per cent of it is under water and it starts looking like The Titanic, I'm pretty sure that means you've got a problem.

It was time to admit defeat. We somehow all climbed back onto the main yacht and it was time to cough up. I stood in front of my mate David, weatherbeaten, sunburnt, pissed from lunch and stoned from the joint and with the speedboat next to us, slowly sinking and looking worse than I did. "I'll have to pay you for this mate," I told him. "Just send me the bill and I'll sort it. How much is it?"

"Jimmy, Jimmy, don't worry about it," David insisted.

"No, I mean it – how much is it? What's the damage?" I said. They were my friends and I'd broken their boat so I definitely would've paid for it but the answer sobered me up in no time. "It cost £35,000," David said. I don't know what the equivalent would be today but that's still a lot of money now, never mind the best part of 25 years ago. As it turned out, they let me off in the end – the Chans were a very generous family – and I got away with it but the speedboat was properly wrecked and they had to get a new one.

Just another quiet Sunday afternoon with The Whirlwind…

•••••••

Hong Kong is my favourite place in the world – even if I did cause Barry headache after headache there. Another time I played Neal Foulds in the final of a tournament and I raced into a 5-0 lead. Nobody was more surprised than me – mainly because I'd prepared for the final by not going to bed.

I'd spent the night before racing around Wan Chai, getting pissed and having a great time. I ended up in a place called Joe Bananas, enjoying the Happy Hour Screwdrivers and the bad karaoke. Hong Kong is a fantastic place for a night out – plenty of dark and dingy bars, plenty of places to go looking for trouble.

I staggered back to the hotel as the sun was coming up, I got changed and went straight to the Queen Elizabeth Stadium to play Neal. It was the first to six and I was absolutely flying but then, as always, I tried to force it, tried to get over the line too quickly. Neal started to peg me back. He could see I was trying to rush and he got into it before I finally fell over the line, winning 6-5.

The crowd was going berserk and it was a fantastic win so I decided to celebrate by going out again. I started on the booze and necked a few vodkas but was so knackered by now that I didn't last long. I went back to the hotel and collapsed.

The next thing I knew, Barry was outside my hotel room, threatening me with all sorts unless I get out of bed sharpish. I'd overslept and was in trouble with Headmaster Hearn.

"Jimmy, you've got a golf exhibition and it starts in an hour, get up," he kept shouting, worried that the winner of the tournament wouldn't show up to schmooze with Barry's business mates on the golf course. "If you don't get out of bed, I ain't paying you," Barry said.

There was no way I was moving so Barry got a bit drastic. He went down to reception, got some spare room keys and let himself in. "Jimmy, move it, NOW," he kept shouting until he ended up tipping a bucket of water all over me and the bed. We ended up screaming at each other, nose-to-nose, and nearly came to blows. In the end I just accepted he'd won and started to do as he asked. But I could barely walk, never mind play golf. Barry had invited loads of bigwigs to play that morning and I just couldn't handle it. There was some big opera singer there as well as some actors and the head of Hong Kong television. Barry had put me down in a four-ball with them.

I got to the course and it was about 200 degrees. It was so hot, I felt shattered and it all just felt too much. I staggered over to my golf bag, got the three wood out and hoped I wouldn't make a prick of myself.

I closed my eyes, swung and I hit this ball straight down the middle of the fairway, the perfect opening shot. I'm a bad golfer so nobody was more surprised than me.

The opera singer teed off and so did the rest of the group as I started walking towards my ball, sweating pure alcohol. I was so hot that I can still remember vodka stinging my eyes as the sweat poured off me. That's how messed up I was. I eventually took a seven on that hole and was starting to wonder what to do. 'I can't play another 17 holes,' I thought. 'I've got to get out of here'.

As we walked to the second tee I hatched my plan. To my right was a wall, about six-foot high, and behind it was a row of taxis. "Hold these," I said to my caddie, passing him my clubs. I went over to the rest of the four-ball and threw myself at their mercy, playing the sympathy card big time. "Listen folks," I told them, "I'm really, really ill. It must be something I've eaten. I just cannot carry on." They were in complete shock and couldn't work out what was going on. They were probably even more shocked a few seconds later when this sweating, red, half-pissed Englishman took a running jump at this six-foot wall, heaved himself over it and was last seen legging it towards the cab rank.

I got back to the hotel, knowing Barry would go crazy. I got the concierge to pay the cab fare because I had no money and went straight back to bed.

About six hours later, the rest of the lads finished the game and came off the course, sweating, bright red, sunburnt and all knackered.

They staggered through the hotel reception and I was sat there, nursing a drink – showered and as fresh as a daisy with a big grin on my face. Hearn wanted to kill me! "Barry, you said

I had to play," I told him. "And I played. You never said it had to be the full round."

I've got a lot of respect for Barry Hearn. He always quips that most of his grey hairs are named after me. I can't blame him for that and I wouldn't be surprised if his great mate Davis doesn't also have one or two greys with my name on them.

On a different occasion, Barry sorted me out for an exhibition in Deauville in Normandy. Barry had agreed a fee of £25,000 to play just two hours of pool – an hour on the Saturday and an hour on the Sunday. I wasn't even a pool player but they wanted me, so fair enough.

We went off to Deauville, which was a beautiful place. We stayed in this big hotel, ate lobster and drank vodkas all night and were treated unbelievably.

After the first hour of pool – which was only a knockabout – I got paid and I had money in my pocket. That was never a good thing.

"Baz, there's a casino here isn't there?" I asked him and Hearn told me it was a top drawer place.

In 20 minutes I did £20,000.

"Jimmy," Barry said. "I worked quite hard to get that 20 grand for you. Any chance you can start looking after your money a bit better?"

"Baz," I told him. "I'm still five grand up on the weekend aren't I? I'm still doing okay!" That was my mindset back then.

"But you've still got to pay tax on it Jimmy," Barry said. What?

"Ah fuck that, Baz," I said. "If I'd known that I wouldn't have bothered coming and I wouldn't have gone anywhere near the fucking Blackjack."

Thanks to Barry, me and Steve once had the chance to go to

Hong Kong and make some serious money in no time at all. Barry was in his office one day when he got a phone call from a bloke who lives over there. A bloke who went by the name Bobby Moore – or 'Mad' Bob Moore.

Bob was a Kiwi and a real eccentric, a massive gambler who seemed to live at the Happy Valley racetrack and a man who had plenty of friends and enemies in Hong Kong.

"Barry," Bob said. "How much would it cost to fly Steve and Jimmy over for a private tournament? I want them to come over and play a game in my club in Kowloon." Barry thought he was taking the piss so quoted him £20,000 each plus first-class flights and a suite for both me and Steve.

"Okay Barry, no problems," Bob said. Barry thought that was the end of it until his accountant let him know the next day that £40,000 had just turned up in the Matchroom coffers from an account in Hong Kong.

So me and Steve flew over there for, literally, a 36-hour trip for just the odd game of pool. It was very strange. Bob had lots of cash and was not scared to let people know it. He always wanted the best tables in restaurants and he wanted to always try and sign up bands and mates and sports stars and whatever else.

On that trip, him and Barry had a big falling out about something but it didn't bother me. I was halfway through Hong Kong's supply of Dom Perignon so I let them get on with it.

Me and Steve would play a frame and Bob would shout out "I'm doubling the prize money" and he was always true to his word.

Soon after that trip, me and Steve got another invite to Hong Kong to play in another invitational pool tournament. The pair of us were in Bangkok after the Thai Open when we were meant to get to the airport for the flight.

'Fuck that,' I thought. I'd got to bed at 7am after a night in Bangkok – the world's maddest place – and there was no way I was fit for anything.

Davis, who's never been late for anything in his life, kept nagging me to get up but I wasn't having any of it.

I flew later that day instead and when I got to Hong Kong I was practically jumped on by these massive minders. They were seriously big lads. "Okay fellas, what can I do for you?" I asked as I was almost lifted off the ground and taken out to this big car. Bob Moore had done his homework and knew I was partial to getting up and running off whenever I felt like it. (He must've heard about the golf incident…)

These massive bouncers finally dropped me off at Bob's suite and there was Davis at the wrong end of a few glasses of champagne.

I'd never seen Davis pissed before – he must've been just about the only player in the world back then who didn't hit the bar straight after playing – and he mumbled "Alright Jimmy" before crashing through this drinks cabinet and onto the floor. I'd probably necked more than him on the plane but he was well gone.

Shortly after that trip, Bob Moore was gone as well. He committed suicide. I was so upset to hear that. He was a lavish fella and someone who lived a big life, enjoyed himself and as a result we'd got on very well. And, unlike Davis, I hadn't trashed his drinks cabinet.

●●●●●●●

The 1980s were undoubtedly Davis's era and the longer the decade went on, the more it felt like he had a hoodoo over me. I started to think that I just couldn't beat him when it mattered most, that I always gave him too many chances and that his nerve never failed. The more I tried to beat him, the more aggressive and spectacular my shots. I kept pushing the boat out on the table (and in my private life) and he made the most of it. Occasionally it came together for me but it wasn't that often, as my preparation was nowhere near as good as his.

He beat me in the 1986 and 1987 World Championship semi-finals as well as the 1987 UK Championship final and although I did enjoy some notable wins like at the Masters and The Classic in 1986, Davis has a far better head-to-head record. I should probably have played in a more cautious style against him but I couldn't do it any other way. That was just the way I played, it was why the crowd loved me, it was why the crowd had loved Higgins before me and it was why the crowd loves O'Sullivan today. We don't know how else to approach the game and we wouldn't change it even if we could. It takes all types to make a sport and I was lucky enough to be a flair player.

It felt like Davis's dominance would last forever, even when I finally beat him at the Crucible in 1990. I'd waited a long time for this, having been at the wrong end of matches against Davis there since 1981. He was the defending world champion (when wasn't he?) and the semi-final was one of the greatest matches the Crucible has ever seen.

Occasionally he would inch ahead and then I would get my nose in front. Davis had made every final for the past seven years so had to be the favourite but everything came together for me perfectly. My potting and temperament were great, I was relaxed and confident. He did open up an early 5-2 lead after one session and he was 8-6 up after the second but I never panicked and the match just flew by.

After the third session I was 13-9 up and when we reached the 30th frame of the match, I knew I had finally got the chance to put him to bed at the Crucible. It wasn't a classic frame, my top break was just 38 to leave him needing snookers but that proved to be enough as Davis conceded and applauded me with a big smile as he got out of his chair.

Davis never won the world title again and I was back in the World Championship final, this time against a bloke called Stephen Hendry...

That 1990 win aside, though, you can see what I mean when I say that Davis must've been rubbing his hands during this period. His most dangerous opponent wasn't practising for 10 hours a day, sipping tonic water and getting eight hours of sleep – he was crashing boats and legging it from golf clubs, he was drinking every minute of the day, he was smoking weed and, well, we'll get to what else he was up to in a bit...

If I'd have been like Steve and hadn't lived the way I did, I'd have won 10 World Championships without a doubt. I don't say that with big regrets or any bitterness – that is just a plain old fact as far as I can see.

Davis still plays in tournaments and exhibitions. He is a bit like me, he wouldn't know what to do with himself without playing snooker. This is all we've ever done and to just suddenly stop would leave us scratching our heads. Steve commentates as well but he won't get the golf clubs out yet; he still wants to play.

In 2010, I beat him in the final of the World Seniors Championship at the Cedar Court Hotel in Bradford and I was really delighted. I played very well in that tournament. I'd been completely off the booze for a couple of months, I'd been practising hard and it felt like my months of good preparation had paid off. I was soon 3-0 up in a first to four and I'd not put a foot wrong. In the next frame, I only needed the yellow and green but I missed the yellow and Steve cleared up to make it 3-1. 'Oh no,' I thought. I had visions of another Davis comeback and victory against me. However, I made an 80 in the next frame and that was enough to win it.

When we do face each other today, at an exhibition or on the Snooker Legends tour, we still do everything we can to beat each other. The punters deserve that and me and Steve have that much respect for each other that a win over him is still a satisfying feeling, but there are bigger smiles on our faces these days. Steve's a father now, we're both dads to teenage kids who drive us mad so he sees the bigger picture in life. He's learned how to relax and enjoy the game more, the same as me. It's always great to see him and to keep tussling with him.

My last words about Steve are these.

These days snooker is obsessed with stats, comparing today's century makers to players of the past and trying to work out who would be the greatest. It really pisses me off because I watched the TV recently and some statistician was asking the question: 'Would Steve Davis at his peak be in the top 16 today?'

That is a loads of bollocks. There is no chance at all that Steve would be in the top 16.

He'd be in the top four.

He'd be a regular winner, make no mistake.

I've every admiration for him.

5

Fame Game

'Go on Kirk, just keep going,' I say to myself, knowing that the frame is well gone. There's not much else to do but sit here quietly and watch my mate, in his terrible suit, rack up the points. Kirk Stevens looks comfortable and cool, the odd grin on his face from time to time. He pots his 15th red and 15th black and the balls are nicely placed. Wembley might be about to see something special. 'Don't let it go now, son. Take your time'...

Losing to Davis in the '84 final didn't feel like a huge setback because there was no doubt I was his major rival and also one of the best players in the world. That fact alone was a bit of a miracle when you consider my lifestyle.

I was 22, a father to Lauren, me and Maureen had now got

married – a 20-minute job at a register office in Wandsworth (something neither set of parents were too happy about) – and I was all over the papers and on the television every five minutes.

There's no doubt that the 1980s was the best time (up until that point) to be a snooker player. There were only four telly channels so we were all getting piped into the nation's front rooms during major tournaments. The press lapped it up – they loved my 'badboy' persona – and my style on the table seemed to get more attention than most.

And I'd really hit the big time when I won the Masters a few months before that defeat to Davis.

The Masters is the finest invitational event in the world. Everybody wants to win it and the crowds at Wembley are something else. It probably helps that I'm a London boy and I always had the noisiest and best support when we played there.

To be honest, I'd shown no real form at the Masters before I beat Terry Griffiths 9-5 in the final that year. My other two performances at the Wembley Conference Centre had seen me lose easily to Eddie Charlton and then Ray Reardon, so I wasn't expected to do much by the time the tournament came around in January, 1984.

It was a wonderful feeling to beat someone as fantastic as Terry – who remains a big mate – but, ironically enough, the final itself has been pretty much forgotten by most people in favour of my semi-final win over Kirk Stevens.

I'll discuss Kirk in more detail in the next chapter but some of the most memorable moments in Masters history happened in our match, a game we both played with a big smile on our face because we knew we were entertaining the massive crowd and because we were mates who were having lots of fun.

FAME GAME

Kirk is best known for his white suit but he was also a superb snooker player. Before a match in the 1982 World Championship, Kirk was running around trying to find some black trousers to fit him but he couldn't find any clean ones so he had no choice but to take a deep breath and walk out in the 'ice-cream suit'. You can imagine how that went down with the lads on the tour but Kirk brushed it off and it became his trademark.

I was 5-3 up in the Masters semi-final when he produced one of the most fantastic breaks I've ever seen. It seems weird to say that one of your career highlights happened when you never got out of your seat but watching Kirk hit that 147 against me was absolutely brilliant.

Not a lot of people know that when Kirk went and sat down afterwards, he looked up and saw a fellow Canadian in the crowd going crazy. Donald Sutherland, the Hollywood star, had snuck into the audience to watch. It was the first frame of snooker he'd ever seen live and Kirk went and produced a 147. Sorry Donald, it's only downhill from there son!

Kirk broke, I didn't really leave anything simple on but he potted a long red and he was away. He managed to break the pack quite early. 'He could win it at this visit,' I thought. 'And the 147 is on as well'.

He got to 120 with no problems and by then I was willing him on more than anyone. The frame was long gone. I had the best seat in the house and I love Kirk to bits so I was probably more nervous than he was.

After potting the last red, he then kissed the pink which left him a touch out of position on the yellow but he played a great rest shot to rescue it. However, that left him out of position on the green which meant he had to go all the way around the table to come back up for the brown. Fortunately he nailed it. The crowd were cheering every shot by now and I was sat in my seat praying he would get there. He then potted a fantastic pink which left him perfectly on the black and the rest is history.

I was out of my seat and over to Kirk as soon as I could once the black rolled in, genuinely delighted for him. You couldn't hear yourself think and Kirk deserved all the applause he got.

If anything, though, that 147 helped me more than him as, understandably, his head went a bit after that. He was almost getting dragged into the crowd by fans who wanted to celebrate and Cliff Thorburn, his fellow Canadian and the man who'd hit the Crucible's first 147 the year before, almost pulled Kirk's head off his shoulders, he was hugging him that hard! There was a bit of a circus then as Benson and Hedges, who were the tournament's sponsors, handed him a tenner as a deposit for the £10,000 he'd just won for a maximum break and all this, bit by bit, took his eyes off the fact that the match was not over yet...

When he eventually sat down again, he was so full of excitement and adrenaline that I knew if I just relaxed and stayed calm I could kill him off.

In the 10th frame, we traded safety shots before Kirk left me a very long red, right from the back of baulk. I knew that if the red went in, I could clean up from that point.

The red didn't even hit the sides of the pocket on the way down, the rest were beautifully placed and I was determined that Kirk wouldn't get out of his seat again.

Sure enough, red after red disappeared, my place in the final got even closer – especially when I fluked a red into the middle pocket – so I thought it was time for some fun. I couldn't let

FAME GAME

Kirk take all the glory could I? Turning the flair on and off came naturally to me. Some players have it, some don't and I could just size up the table, size up the shot that would get the crowd roaring and then, crucially, produce the goods when it mattered.

Kirk sat there throughout all this, his left leg folded over his right, looking like the most relaxed man in the room. As I say, he was happy with his 147 and the attention and thrill that gave him.

I got onto the colours, potted the brown for the century break, eased the blue down and then really turned it on. I smashed the pink in, the cue-ball flew off the bottom cushion and left me perfectly on the black. "Shot, Jimmy," Kirk said, patting his leg and laughing in appreciation, enjoying the moment almost as much as I was. I then hit the black even harder into the top pocket to seal the break and the match. Me and Kirk just hugged and laughed with the crowd going crazy.

Both of us hit the champagne together almost straightaway because that's what we were like, two young kids, excited by what we'd just produced, excited by our talent and excited by the future. It had been a fucking amazing match from both of us – the time of our lives.

The next day against Griffiths I continued where I left off, racing into a 5-0 lead and it looked like my hands would be on the Masters trophy in record time. However, Griffiths was a tough opponent, a former world champion and a man you had to drag off the table.

He pegged me back to 5-3 before I pulled away again to 8-3 and Griffiths couldn't see me from there as I ended up winning by four frames. I finished with a pink over the middle pocket that I couldn't miss. In it went and I heard the sweetest noise of my career up to that date – the crowd cheering me, the youngest ever Masters winner.

Off the table, I'd been through a whirlwind of a different kind over the previous 12 months as my manager Harvey Lisberg, a man who'd made his money in the music business, tried to change my image by cleaning me up and attempting to give me 'sex appeal'. Good luck with that. I was this buck-toothed kid who didn't really say much to anyone and Lisberg, along with his business partner, Geoff Lomas, felt that they could transform me into someone who the public would take to their hearts – completely missing the point of why I was popular in the first place.

I was just me – the bloke who played with his heart more than his head, the man on the street who just happened to be good with a snooker cue. I smoked, drank, stayed out too late and too often put my mates, good nights out and gambling first. But that is why I was growing in popularity. Nothing against Davis but I was the exact opposite of him and the public loved that; they loved someone who wasn't a machine, who could miss, who could drive them mad or make them cheer within the same frame.

However, Harvey and Geoff still tried to sort me out. They had my teeth done and I even had my bloody hair permed. Then they got Lord Lichfield, the Queen's cousin, to take loads of photos of the 'new' me!

I actually went to see Lord Lichfield 25 years later (to the actual week in fact) to do some photos for a testicular cancer charity and we got on really well. "Jimmy," he said. "I must have a bottle of wine with you. I've always loved watching you."

FAME GAME

We sat there drinking this nice expensive bottle of red and we had a good laugh. "Taking your photo now is 100 times easier than it was back then," he grinned. Apparently I'd been a bit of a nightmare. It just wasn't my scene, having to smile and grin like an idiot. I also did an advert for Softmints and the director said it would take four hours and it took four fucking days. I just couldn't be arsed with it all. It wasn't for me and everyone was taking the piss, Maureen included.

Geoff owned Potters snooker club in Salford, a very famous club where John Virgo played. He also tried to influence my style of play, telling me to practise in a certain way, think like a winner and so on. The problem with that approach was that it was too structured. I play on instinct and on adrenaline. Long-term planning on a snooker table is pointless until you see how the balls are lying.

However, I liked Geoff and his wife Helen a lot and I eventually moved up to Manchester for a bit during the week, staying with them most of the time before flying back to London at weekends to see Maureen and Lauren. It just made sense at the time. Manchester was the place where loads of players used to practise, the exhibitions available up there were decent and it suited me because it meant I could still have my space in the week – space to go out, play a few frames of snooker and see what trouble I could get myself into.

The great thing about Potters was that it opened at lunchtime until about midnight for people to play snooker and then it would re-open at about 3am so that all the croupiers and DJs who'd been working all night could go somewhere for a drink.

You used to get coppers, villains, footballers and birds in there. It was an amazing mix and I was in my element, away from home and away from anybody telling me to have an early night. In those days you could just walk on a flight in no time at all so I'd get the 10pm to London on the Friday and then the first flight back up on the Monday.

Half the time, Maureen couldn't work out why I didn't seem that bothered about a big night out when I was back in London, not knowing that I'd spent all week on the piss until 6am in Potters.

None of that affected my style of play and the 1983/84 season turned into one of the most fantastic of my career – apart from losing to Davis at Sheffield, of course – as I also won the New Zealand Masters, Thailand Open and Carlsberg Challenge beating Kirk Stevens, Terry Griffiths and Tony Knowles respectively.

The prize money convinced me and Maureen that it was time to move to a nice place in Wimbledon although, to be honest, it felt a long way from home for a Tooting boy. I was still spending a lot of time in Manchester and I know that Maureen also felt isolated for a time there because I was always out but she had to be around for Lauren.

The most surprising thing about the Wimbledon house was the fact I still had enough money to buy it. I'd earned more that year than any other in my career up until then and had somehow managed not to burn it all at the racetrack.

Gambling had started to really get a grip of me, even more so when me and Peewee and Victor used to back anything with four legs in the early days. I'd think nothing of putting five bets on at £500 a race, seeing what happened to them and then repeating it, chasing winners and chasing my money back. And despite doing my best to practise more – and stay out of mischief as demanded by Harvey and Geoff – I still found myself drawn to some old haunts and I still found myself getting into some stupid positions – usually when I was in Ireland.

Take the World Amateur Snooker Championship that year.

They were being held in Ireland and I'd agreed to go over there to hand out the trophies.

What I obviously didn't know at the time was that a crew from London had been over and flooded the town we were staying in with forged £20 notes. I landed in Dublin, went straight out on the piss and got back to my hotel, in Malahide, where the tournament was being played. Then I decided to head to the bar at 3.30 in the morning for one final drink.

After finishing my drink, I was about to go to bed when a geezer approached me. "Have one for the road with me Jimmy," this bloke said, practically insisting that I stay up for yet another nightcap. I wasn't that bothered but I did the courteous thing. This guy handed me a £20 note and I gave it to the bar staff and thought nothing else of it. I finally went to bed, got up at midday and there was bad news.

"There's a phone call for you downstairs Mr White," the receptionist said. I staggered down the stairs, barely dressed, and got nicked on the spot. Two massive Irish policemen cuffed me, tore up my bedroom – they did a proper job on it as well – and dragged me down to the nick.

I was bundled in to see the town's chief copper and he wasn't best pleased. "Listen here. You fucking cockneys have completely ruined my town," he said, seriously pissed off. "You're going to fucking prison."

In Ireland in those days if you had the evidence (which was the £20 note); the witness (who was the barman) and the culprit (who was supposedly me), then you were fucked. You were bang to rights. The lads who'd brought all the dodgy money with them had caught the 6.30am flight back to London, leaving me up to my neck in it.

I sat with this top policeman and started to talk him round. "Look," I said. "I'm a professional snooker player, my dad's a carpenter, I've never done anything illegal in my life" (which was kind of true, give or take a few fruit machines…)

My words weren't having much impact and I got ready to stay in Ireland a little longer than I'd first expected. There was £5000 worth of snide notes in the town and I was looking at some serious time in jail but then things took a turn for the better.

As I'm sat with this copper, his phone starts ringing off the hook. A butcher's and a pub here, a baker's and a hotel there, a bookies somewhere else; all ringing to complain about a till full of snide cash. The copper started getting more and more irate as the day was going on but in the end he believed me. "Off you go now then Jimmy," he said. "It's been a pleasure having you here." He knew I wasn't bent and we'd really warmed to each other by the time I was let out.

In fact, we got on so well that me and Higgins even ended up going back over to Ireland to do a charity exhibition for him one night in Dublin!

I knew who the people were who brought the money over and when they read this story, they will know that I know. I was very disappointed in them – it was a bad thing to do to that town and for snooker in general. A lucky escape…

•••••••

FAME GAME

I was living two, or even three lives during this time. There was the Jimmy White on the television, winning tournaments, cashing cheques, saying the right things to the camera; the Jimmy White of old, missing his old haunts, the dodgy and dangerous days with Tony Meo, Victor and Peewee and the flash Jimmy White, living it up at every opportunity in the West End.

Somewhere along the line, I was also a married man with a little girl although me and Maureen constantly fell out about where I was, who I was with and what I was up to. She thought I was becoming flash and big-headed (and she might have had a point...)

For example, whenever I played in a tournament or an exhibition, I always used to make sure I had a suit and a driver ready so I could get changed quickly and get straight out.

I was always living above my means. If I couldn't get to one of my suits, I'd just walk into a tailor's anywhere in the country and get a new one fitted, as simple as that. A tailor called Tommy Nutter would have suits made for me all the time. It was mad! I come from working man's cloth, a very proud family and I couldn't pull a bird to save my life and then all of a sudden, birds were throwing themselves at me. I was getting VIP treatment everywhere I went.

I was having a ball, a total fucking ball. Looking back now, I must've looked a bit stupid but I didn't care. I suppose it just goes to your head.

One night I'd be playing a tournament on the television then the next night I'd be back in a dodgy pub, smoking weed with my old mates, getting pissed, not going home. The night after, I'd be in The Grosvenor hanging out with the rich and (more) famous. That's how life was. I just wanted to be out and about.

Over the years, people have tried to work out what all the boozing and going out has really 'meant' – they've second-guessed me, tried to get inside my head and work out why I am like I am. Could I not deal with the limelight, the expectation, the pressure or whatever else?

The truth is a lot simpler than that and I'm not that 'deep' I'm afraid. There was nothing tortured about me, I just liked a nightclub, a joint, a Screwdriver and a gamble. It's as clear-cut as that.

Looking back, I was a nightmare for Maureen because she spent most of her time trying to make Wimbledon into a nice home, looking after Lauren and trying to keep our marriage going. We'd have some almighty rows about me going missing and Maureen could more than hold her own in an argument but I was only 22, too young to settle down – not while there was a big world out there, with plenty of people ready to buy me a drink or two.

Growing up, I'd spent a lot of time in a pub called The Invitation in Battersea Rise and I used to be drawn back to it with Peewee all the time. It was a right desperadoes' pub, it had loads of atmosphere and you could get up to all sorts. There were some good lads in there and it was rough but me and Peewee used to love it because you could smoke cannabis and the police never raided it.

There was that much smoke in there that if the alarms went off, the fire brigade never bothered coming because they just knew it was some of the boys smoking a joint or 10.

It was run by this massive bloke called Gerry who was scared of no-one, apart from his missus – this tiny five-foot bird who used to give him loads of grief. During a lock-in, she used to fly downstairs and give him a final warning. "Gerry, get everybody out, NOW!" she'd scream and he used to take his medicine and kick us out. He was terrified of her and always did as she said.

It was a right spit and sawdust joint and one night I was in there knocking a few pool balls around. This guy came over to the table and clearly wanted something. "You're Jimmy White," he said. "Let's play a game of pool for a fiver."

Now, this night I really couldn't be arsed playing for money. Nobody on earth had played more games for cash than me at that point but I just wanted a knockabout with the lads. "No thanks mate," I said, nice and politely, but he wasn't having it. "Come on, one game," he said, and I finally gave in. I broke and immediately kicked his arse, potting all the reds and the black. He hadn't had a shot. "Thanks for the game mate," I said and that was the end of it.

Or maybe not.

We then went to a nightclub called Nelson's which was at Wimbledon Football Club. It was nothing flash but it did the job. John Fashanu used to go in there and we'd have a drink and a laugh. I was at the bar when all of a sudden one of the bouncers came over. "Jimmy, there's a bloke outside who wants a chat," he said. "You better come and have a word."

I looked across and could see it was this bloke I'd done for that fiver. And I could see he wasn't there to give me a Christmas card. All of a sudden this bloke produces this axe from nowhere, like a fucking rabbit out of a hat, and he starts doing these wooden doors in. 'Best of luck lads,' I thought as these bouncers started wrestling him and trying to get him on the ground. Somebody rang the police (that was unheard of as well) and it turns out that this bloke was wanted for GBH or attempted murder or something like that... and he had me on his hit-list.

He went down for about six years and, well, I don't know what else to say – I hope he ain't around any more or reading this! I had some mates talk to him in prison and they said he was really out to get me. I was with Peewee, who was about as hard as me, so we'd have been in real bother if he'd got his hands on us.

•••••••

By the time the 1984/85 season came around, me, Harvey and Geoff had decided to go our separate ways and a mate called Noel Miller-Cheevers, who I'd known for years since our playing days together at the Pot Black Snooker Club, had offered to manage me. That seemed like the best thing to do at the time because he knew snooker inside out and he had some big plans for us both.

The Pot Black Snooker Centre had 26 immaculate tables. Davis used to travel all the way from Romford on a Tuesday night to practise there because the club had that many good players. He never spoke to anybody – that seemed a bit weird – but he kept himself to himself.

In there was me, Tony Meo, Wally West, Flash Bob, Noel, Patsy Houlihan, Eugene Hughes and loads of other fantastic players. There was a used car lot nearby and all the car salesmen used to come in there to play and gamble. We used to give them mad starts, like 100 or something, and we'd still clean up. We used to play in the Pot Black until everybody got thirsty and we'd then pour out of there into The Invitation.

FAME GAME

Soon after, Noel decided he couldn't dedicate as much time to me as he needed so I was on my way again and passed on to a a geezer called Howard Kruger.

Howard was a very flamboyant man, he loved the limelight and he soon set up Framework Management and recruited Higgins, Joe Johnson, Tony Knowles and a few others.

Howard immediately had to try and defend Tony, who, God bless him, had recently been stitched up in *The Sun* by an old flame who claimed that he loved to wear stockings and suspenders in bed. That caused plenty of giggles among the rest of the schoolboys on tour. Then he faced even more trouble when the WPBSA did him for £5000 for bringing the game into disrepute! He almost fell off his high heels when he heard that...

Again, unlike Davis, who only had one manager, I'd been jumping around (and would keep jumping around) for years, changing managers, but my game was coming together nicely and I couldn't put a foot wrong in the early non-ranking events, winning the Thailand Masters and Carlsberg Challenge as well as the Irish Masters at Goffs, one of the noisiest and most intimidating places in the world to have a game of snooker.

Goffs was a horse-trading ring for most of the year and had these really high, steep tiers as well as fans sat all around you. When you were at table level, it felt like you were surrounded by a million faces and the atmosphere was always exciting and electric, a mixture of adrenaline, booze and cigarette smoke. No wonder I felt comfortable there. Beating Higgins 9-5 may have upset some of the crowd – Ireland's never produced a more-loved sporting hero than Higgins – but I couldn't help but fall in love with the event, the crowd and some of the troublemakers who led me – little, innocent Jimmy White – astray...

A bloke called Con Dunne was the biggest culprit, and one of the biggest characters I've ever met.

Con was a chronic alcoholic, a fantastic snooker player in the 1970s and someone who'd turned to promoting snooker tournaments and exhibitions in Ireland. Whenever there was a frame of snooker played in Ireland, Con was either playing it, organising it or both. Whatever he did, it always involved alcohol. You can see why we got on. In fact, Con used to drink so much, his own brother Richard used to ban him from drinking in his own bar. Con would get round this by filling up water bottles with gin and then start toasting the health of all the punters. This went on for months until Richard finally worked out why his brother was asleep at lunchtime every day, head on the bar, following a long morning sipping 'water'.

Con is a great bloke and eventually moved to New York where he opened a nightclub, left the booze behind and hasn't touched a drop since.

Tony Knowles ended my World Championship hopes in the 1984/5 season with a 13-10 loss in the quarter-finals. Tony outplayed me and although my season ended on a low point, I felt that a ranking victory was getting closer.

Tony may have celebrated that win with a trip to Josephine's nightclub in Sheffield. That was where all the snooker players used to hang out (except Davis, of course). Tony was a regular there and wasn't called 'The Melter' for nothing. He'd been given that nickname by Geoff Lomas's wife, Helen, because he was a good looking boy and the girls used to flock to him. He literally used to have women hanging off him, one at the front and one at the back.

"What you do is this Jim," he'd start. "Stand in t'nightclub at t'highest point where all birds can see yer and then about ten-ter-two make yer way t'bar." He'd only have about three drinks all night and he was fighting them off.

Tony was great fun and a good bloke who had throat cancer about four years ago. As you get older you sometimes only get back in touch with people when they're ill and it's only then that you realise how close you were to them and what an amazing time you had with them. Seeing Tony again was great and, touch wood, he's fine now.

Anyway, the 1985/86 season opened with another win in the Carlsberg Challenge – I always liked events sponsored by booze – before we all jumped a plane to Australia for the Winfield Masters. Sydney is one of my favourite places in the world and I'd move there tomorrow but, fuck me, it's not exactly around the corner is it?

We had a nightmare journey Down Under but about 30 hours later we finally landed. The tournament was an invitational and that year there were a few of the usual faces involved; me, JV, Tony Knowles, Willie Thorne and Eddie Charlton.

There was also Big Bill Werbeniuk.

Big Bill has gone down as one of the legendary characters of the game because he used to suffer from the shakes and came up with the now famous idea that can after can of lager would stop them – even I hadn't thought that one up. He even managed to convince the taxman that the booze was tax deductible because it was a necessary function for his job – now that is a dodge that anyone in Zan's would be proud of.

After landing at Sydney, looking and feeling like shit, some of the boys wanted to go to the hotel to freshen up but fuck that, there was fun to be had.

"Take me to the City Tatts please mate," I told the cabbie.

I turned up at the City Tatts – an old social club close to Darling Harbour – walked to the bar and surprise, surprise, Big Bill was standing there, nursing a lager.

He'd got to Oz about three days before the rest of us so felt pretty good. The jet lag was gone and the beer was cold.

"Hi Jimmy, fancy a game?" he asked, knowing that I couldn't resist a challenge. "Let's play for a dollar a point."

I'd not even got my cue out of the case by this stage. I've been in the same clothes for two days and I'd had no sleep. Bill could see some easy money heading his way for sure.

"Okay Bill, you're on," I said, knowing that I'd have to be pretty good to avoid an expensive trip to the bank to get Bill some (more) beer money.

I was more than just good.

Five minutes later, Big Bill owed me exactly $147 dollars.

I'd done him for a maximum break, half an hour after leaving the airport. I hit another ton in the next frame and all of a sudden Bill didn't fancy playing any more. "See you back at the hotel Jimmy," he said, walking off.

Tony beat me in the semi-final of the Winfield Masters but my form was still good and when the Goya Classic arrived, the first ranking event of the season, it felt like my time had come to win one.

Yeah, I'd done great up until now in invitational events. I was one of the most famous snooker players in the world but the bottom line was I'd not yet won a ranking tournament and that had to change if people were going to stop whispering that I didn't have what it takes when it mattered most.

I flew through the early rounds, easily beating Warren King,

FAME GAME

Dean Reynolds, Davis and Neal Foulds to set up a final spot against Thorburn. I absolutely battered him early on, taking a 7-0 lead with no problems whatsoever.

But, not for the last time, having a lead as big as that worked against me. I found myself drifting off and losing focus. I just couldn't stay in the zone long enough to kill people off and Thorburn knew that. Plus, he was one hard bastard to beat – he wasn't called 'The Grinder' for nothing.

Thorburn just hung in there, fighting for his life, even in the eighth frame when he needed five snookers! When he got out of his chair to even play the balls – it was 74-4 – I thought he was wasting his time but Cliff was a fighter, he needed some time at the table to get himself going and slowly he chipped away – not helped by some poor shots from me that saw the fouls start to increase. Before I knew it, Thorburn was closing in on me and he eventually – somehow – won the frame 77-74 to pull one back. That really affected my already poor concentration and as I got worse, he got better and the day ended with me just 8-6 up.

It felt as though Cliff was in the lead because of his magnificent comeback and he carried on where he left off the next day. I just couldn't stop him in the end as he beat me 12-10.

I personally wasn't arsed in the slightest about losing because that's sport for you, it's what happens, but I was aware that commentators and the press were starting to question whether I could get over the line in a ranking event.

Fortunately, they didn't have to wait long as soon after I pulled off one of the most dramatic wins in the history of the sport, made all the sweeter because it was against Cliff again.

We faced each other in the final of the Mercantile Credit

Classic at the Spectrum Arena in Warrington. Me and Cliff had again battled hard, him giving me nothing, me trying to finish him off too quickly and when it came down to the final frame I needed a snooker to win, with only the pink and black left.

Snookering someone when you've got so few options – and when you know one false move sees you lose the match – is one of the hardest aspects of snooker but I stayed as calm as possible and I finally managed to get him tied up behind the black.

He missed and I can still remember the roar of the crowd and the feeling of excitement when I got back to the table, ready to end my wait for a ranking win.

The audience went crazy when the black went down and I was delighted to win, if only to quieten my enemies down a little. It was a classic tense, nervy victory and I don't think anybody has ever won a tournament before or since in that way.

I was aware, though, that even to win a ranking tournament I'd had to climb mountains to get there and Cliff was pretty devastated to lose like that.

I won on the Sunday, had a big party with my family on the Monday and I then went home to see Maureen and Lauren. On the Tuesday I felt like I still wanted to celebrate with my oldest pals so went to The Invitation and there was this dog tied up with some rope outside.

I went to stroke the dog and as I did so this old, straggly dog cowered and tried to get away. It had obviously spent its life being beaten and messed about with. I went inside and finally came out at about 4am, pissed and stoned, and this poor dog was still there. 'I'm not having that,' I thought and I took it to Mum and Dad's.

FAME GAME

"Jimmy," Mum said the next morning. "Do you honestly expect us to look after that?" I nodded that I did but I knew she would anyway. I could do no wrong at that moment in time, especially after beating Cliff. She let the dog run past her, it found Dad, started barking and they became best mates for about 10 years. They even called him 'Mercantile' after my win!

My first ranking win felt great, as did the prize money, but I was still missing most of the time. Maureen never held back when it came to letting me know how upset she was by my Lord Lucan impressions – that's if she could find me – although a tour round South London's worst, roughest and most dangerous pubs would probably have turned up something. When we did see each other, we fought like cat and dog over everything and anything. One minute it would be love at first sight, the next minute we'd be bawling each other out – usually over nothing. Well, she sometimes had a point.

On one occasion, I heard that Con was in London to play snooker for the Irish amateur team in a tournament at the Connaught Rooms and I was invited along to give out a few prizes and generally give the event some colour.

Con, being Con, somehow managed to get run over by a black cab after the first day's play and he was in absolute bits when I finally caught up with him the next day. His left leg was enormous, it was twice the size of his right one and it was crystal clear that he'd broken it. "I'll be okay Jimmy, just get me some aspirin," was all he kept saying but we carted him off to hospital where the doctor took one look at it and knew it was bust – there was barely any need for the X-ray. "Jimmy, it's fine, it's fine, let's go for a drink," Con kept saying, totally out of his head with pain.

I couldn't just leave my pal in that condition so I eventually took him home to Wimbledon where he could stay with us while his leg healed. It was great having him around, to play cards and have a glass or two with – just to help with the pain of course. At first, Maureen completely agreed and she loved Con so she was more than happy to have him hobbling up and down the stairs.

The peace lasted for about 10 days before Maureen had had enough of Con staggering around with crutches in one hand and a bottle in the other. "Jimmy," she whispered to me one day. "I've not been to bed properly for a week, Lauren is tired all the time and you and Con are playing up. Either he goes, or I go."

So we went!

I picked Con up, told Maureen not to wait up and we staggered out of the front door. The next month is a bit of a blur to be honest but it involved us moving from hotel to hotel around London, drinking all over the West End every night and going to as many nightclubs as would let me and an alcoholic on crutches in. What can I say? It worked wonders for Con's leg and he was soon on the plane back to Ireland, as fit as a fiddle. Or as fit as an Irish snooker player is ever going to be anyhow.

I finally summoned up the courage and went home and smoothed things over with Maureen and, to be honest, I'd missed Lauren to bits. Despite being off the radar for a month, I still wanted her to know that she was the most precious thing in the world.

Throughout all our rows over the years, the one thing I'm proud of is the fact we kept the kids out of it. We didn't raise our voices in front of Lauren – or any of our children – and we were good parents, just bad partners. I was too immature to settle down, I had the bright lights of London on my doorstep, a gang of mates who loved a night out, a raging thirst and that snooker-hall mindset of always looking for the next pub, the next dodge, the next party.

It was a hell of a lot of fun and at the time it didn't feel like it was affecting my snooker. I lost to Cliff in the Masters final – but only after I called a foul on myself towards the end of the match that let him back in. I was the only player who used to call their own fouls and although it cost me at Wembley, I've never regretted it. Throughout my career I've run the risk of fouling because I feather the cue-ball so closely. It's happened a few times and I've always told the referee straightaway, which is just how it should be. End of story. It does offer a bit of a strange contrast, though. There was the off-table Jimmy, running wild whenever he could and the on-table Jimmy, who I like to think has always displayed a very respectful attitude towards the sport. There has been only one occasion I can think of when I've really let myself down at the table, when I stupidly conceded a frame to Matthew Stevens in 2002 at the Crucible as my temper got the better of me and I lashed out at the black ball. I apologised immediately for my stupidity – it hurt nobody but me and that was the end of it.

After the loss to Cliff, I retained the Irish Masters title with a win over Willie Thorne before the season ended with another loss to Davis at Sheffield.

Overall, it had been a decent season, I'd gained my first ranking title and I'd won a lot of money, made a lot of new 'friends' and generally done exactly what I wanted to. There were even some 'friends' I made without knowing it.

When I was growing up, my mum got mugged once and her handbag was taken. These two massive coppers knocked on our front door and found Mum really shaken and they started going crazy on her behalf, determined to find out what had happened.

Anyhow, the bag got found because a South London gangster, who I'd better not name, heard about my mum being done over and wasn't going to let that liberty lie. The next thing, the doorbell at Mum and Dad's rang and her handbag was on the step, with everything back in it.

A few years later, the same gangster got in touch with me because he wanted a favour in return for what he'd done for mum.

I thought it would just be to go and visit a granny who liked me or a charity do or something – I've always tried to do as much as possible to help people out because it doesn't take much time and it can make someone's day. Anyhow, this favour was anything but as easy as that.

"I want you to visit someone in prison," this geezer said.

Oh God.

"Erm, okay then, who is it? One of your mates?"

"Yeah," he said. "It's a mate called Ronnie. Ronnie Kray."

Fucking hell.

Ronnie was in Parkhurst prison on the Isle of Wight but I agreed to do it. They booked me a visit in but I was away on the piss, with the fairies, partying, whatever, so missed the first trip.

The gangster, unimpressed with my no-show, went through the paperwork again and got me another visit sorted out and, again, I was at the bottom of a bottle of vodka somewhere and I missed that visiting slot as well.

FAME GAME

I'd really blown it this time.

Finally, by some minor miracle, I was at home in bed with Maureen when the front bell went early one morning. Maureen raced downstairs in her dressing gown and answered the door.

"There's two guys downstairs and they will only talk to you," she said.

"What are you on about?" I replied before going downstairs to talk to these lads. They were huge. Like two mountains with heads. And they weren't taking no for an answer. "Come with us Jimmy, you've got no choice today mate," they said.

I got in their car, a big Mercedes, and drove to the ferry at Southampton. I got on the ferry and tried to chat to these two fellas but they weren't having any of it. They were so big I thought I'd better not push my luck. They never said a word to me. I had a raging hangover and was in last night's clothes so the day was not going well.

Anyway, we got to the Isle of Wight and it was like nothing I'd ever seen before. By this point I've done the odd prison exhibition so I think I know how it works inside. I couldn't have been any more wrong.

I went through security and we were taken into this wide open public space and there was Ronnie. It was unbelievable. He had full silver service, he was dressed immaculately in a suit and tie and there was just one guard keeping an eye on him; one guard who Ronnie could easily have overpowered if he'd wanted to. It was insane.

You might be wondering what I was feeling at the time and let me put it like this: I was meeting Ronnie Kray, how would you feel?

Anyway, he gave me a big hug – there were no handcuffs

– he gave me a little doll for Lauren's birthday and he was a complete and utter gentleman. All he wanted to do was talk about snooker, he loved the game to bits. We chatted for about two hours, about snooker, Zan's and London in general, and the time absolutely flew by.

We sat there and discussed everything and anything, sipping tea out of china cups and picking at finger sandwiches. It wasn't quite the Ritz but it wasn't far off. The food was excellent and it was delivered by Ronnie's own waiter.

The meeting was obviously a big thing for him and he certainly knew his snooker. He talked about shots, how to play with spin, safety – the lot. We didn't talk about any of his crimes, he just wanted to know about my Masters win in 1984 and the flair shots against Kirk.

The next thing, the two hours were up and I was off, back to Oxshott, with the two massive blokes who still haven't said a word to me. I got back home and just shook my head to Maureen. As the guys pulled out of the drive, I just saw one make the slightest smirk at me as if to say 'It was a good job you were fucking in today Jimmy son, or else you'd be in serious trouble'.

How do you sum up a day like that? Like most other areas of my life at the time, you simply can't. Put it this way, I bet Davis wasn't doing that.

As well as secret admirers like Ronnie Kray, now that I'd started making my name in snooker, I had a list of friendly landlords the length of my arm. One night we were in a gaff called The Grecian Grill, all looking flash and legit, when the lights came up and it was time to go home. 'Fuck this,' I thought, 'the night's barely started.'

FAME GAME

I found a payphone, made a few calls and then piled everybody into the back of this big minibus. "Follow me," I told the driver and we drove around London until we arrived at a big housing estate with this moody pub in the middle of it. I knew exactly what I had to do because I'd spoken to the landlord about 30 minutes earlier. "The keys are under the mat," were his last words. I searched around, found the keys and lifted the shutters on the back door. We were good to go and the party carried on.

It was 4am in the morning and I'd packed this pub out, the drinks started flowing again, the music went on and we picked up where we'd left off.

This used to happen all the time, wherever I was in the country.

Publicans always let me get away with that because when they dared come downstairs in the morning they'd find the right money in the till and the place in perfect condition. I never wanted the lights to come up or the music to stop and that's why I boozed as long and as hard as I did.

In my eyes, a good drink meant a good laugh and who doesn't want a good laugh? I never had work the next morning, I had a bit of fame and a full wallet – what would most 20-somethings do if they were offered that kind of deal?

I've never, ever, ever woken up and had a drink as my first drink of the day, otherwise there's no doubt I'd be dead by now. But back then I could keep going without the hangovers.

Drink was never my downfall, never my achilles heel.

Oh no, that was something else altogether...

6

The Devil

Temptation/
You can take it or leave it/
Temptation/
But you'd better believe it...

I'm in Flickers nightclub in Tooting, I've had a dozen Screwdrivers with another dozen on the way.

Flickers isn't the classiest of gaffs but it's exactly what I'm after tonight. I'm 20, there are birds in here, I'm getting spotted by a few people who know who I am, I stand at the bar, loving life and all the attention.

What more could you want than this? The drinks and the good times are flowing.

THE DEVIL

A mate walks over, a mate who's just got back from Amster-dam. "Jimmy, you've got to go over there," he yells in my ear, above the music in this crammed bar, bodies pressed up against each other as we all fight for a drink. "It's a fucking amazing place. Here try this." I look him in the eye but I know exactly what it is. He opens a little packet, sticks some on the end of his thumb and shoves it under my nose.

I've just done my first line of coke.

It won't be my last.

Temptation/
You can take it or leave it/
Temptation/
But you'd better believe it...

Five minutes after taking that first line, I got on that dance floor and I thought I was God himself, banging into everybody, jumping up and down and going mad.

I'll never forget that 'Temptation' by Heaven 17 was playing and my mouth was so dry. The five minutes I'd planned to spend dancing turned into three hours. I felt incredible, amazing, unstoppable – I felt pretty much the same as anyone else does when they first take the stuff. I've had bucket loads of cocaine since but it never beats that first high. You're always chasing that same bang but it turns out you never get there.

I suppose it had been coming for a while.

In the 1980s, it was hard to move in London without someone offering you coke in a nightclub or in a bar. Scratch the surface of the West End or any other London nightclub and under-neath the glamour, the champagne, the VIP bars, the roped-off entrances, the bouncers who know your name, there's a world of shit just waiting to get you. Coke might look glamorous – especially to a young dickhead like I was – but if I could have my time again, I'd tell that guy to fuck off and never come back.

Cocaine is The Devil's Dandruff, make no mistake.

I'd first tried drugs when I had my first joint, aged about 16. All the pubs in South London used to have blokes in them who'd sell you dirt weed which wasn't too bad. It wasn't like this skunk stuff that is around now and blows your head off and is sprayed with something that makes you addicted. This modern skunk is bad news and too strong. We used to just smoke the mild weed that Jamaicans used to smoke. In every snooker hall we went in, there would be blokes getting all giggly and stupid and chatting shit. It appealed to me a lot. It was a bit of harmless fun that meant nothing and I really enjoyed a smoke as a way of relaxing.

I'd had no real urge to go onto harder stuff than cannabis until I tried it that night in Flickers. Even then, it wasn't until about 1985 or 1986 that it got a proper grip on me.

When you first take cocaine you become really friendly and chatty and your sexual appetite goes through the roof. There were what you called coke whores everywhere in the '80s. It wouldn't take you five minutes to pick up a girl in a club, especially if she knew you had money and a gram of coke on you as well. When me and Maureen were having trouble at home – usually once a month, at least – I'd be chasing these girls, playing around and basically being an idiot.

I'm not proud of it, but it happened and that's all there is to it. There's no point me hiding it now, is there?

As the years went past, cocaine went from being a Class A

drug that I didn't want to go anywhere near to knowing places all over London and the country where I could get it.

My story is no different to a million others really. A young man from nowhere gets fame, fortune, drugs, birds and money thrown at him and he can't say no to any of them.

The worst thing coke did to me, looking back, was sober me up. That might sound a bit strange but I could drink and drink and drink all night – be as pissed as 20 men – and then a couple of lines of coke would sort me out. I'd stop zigzagging and walk normally again. So what did I used to do with my new-found sobriety? What else but get smashed again. Coke allowed me to just keep going, turn an afternoon pint into an all-dayer, an all-dayer into an all-nighter and all-nighters into two, three or four days straight. No wonder Maureen used to go mad at me.

And, ultimately, it was behaving like that which cost me 10 World Championships. No disrespect to the other players around, but I genuinely believe my name would be on the trophy 10 times if I hadn't found coke.

Some people might read this and say "that's sour grapes" and accuse me of not having the bottle to go all the way but I'd tell them that it takes more bottle to score cocaine from the front-lines of Brixton at four in the morning than it does to win a snooker tournament.

It wasn't bottle I was lacking, it was brains.

●●●●●●●

On the table, the 1986/7 season got off to a decent start as I won another ranking tournament, the Grand Prix, beating Rex Williams in the final.

I was 5-3 down going into the night session after a shocking afternoon and I was something like 1/9 to win the match by then. Even I wouldn't have bet on that – and that's saying something... I just had a great night and managed to turn it around, finishing with a nice break of 72 to win 10-6. Another ranking victory so early in the season let Davis know that I was coming after him that season, even if it meant I had to beat a great player like Rex to show him.

Rex had a lot of class. He was an old-style snooker player who was a big believer in manners around the table and the proper etiquette of the game. I'd been taught by Ron Gross how important it was to act properly at the table. I suppose that was one reason why even I'd been embarrassed by playing pissed-up against Steve Newbury in that tournament at Pontin's. Kids play today and bang their cues and I can understand their frustration because they're trying to make a living but when I was growing up and learning the game, there was a bit of class about it and Rex certainly had that. At the end of the match he was genuinely pleased for me, he made some nice comments in the press and I always respected him for that (although I don't think he'd have been as complimentary if he knew what I was getting up to in my own time...)

I was living a life of constant upheaval. There was no calm in my life at all – not that I felt like I needed any at the time. I was young, I'd come from nowhere, people recognised me and I started to think I was somebody that I wasn't. Coke makes you feel that as well; it makes you feel as though you really are invincible and the most famous, powerful man in the world when, in fact, that is all just a load of bollocks. If you take a line and a couple of girls smile at you, then you think you're God's gift.

THE DEVIL

It also didn't help that I kept getting involved in some mad plans; like recording a bloody song!

When I was still with Howard Kruger and Framework, Higgins hatched an idea that we should release a record to try and beat Matchroom at their own game.

Barry Hearn had got Chas & Dave on board, alongside his Matchroom boys, and they'd reached the Top 10 with 'Snooker Loopy'. I won't remind you of it but I bet you can't get the tune out of your head now can you?

It was a terrible song but it gave snooker a bit of a publicity boost and Framework wanted to do the same, so before you knew it, we were singing 'The Wanderer'. Higgins, Tony Knowles and Kirk Stevens all went down to Bournemouth to sing this song and film the video. They were some of the best, funniest times of my life. We partied every night and went to every nightclub in Bournemouth (twice). Like I say, we felt invincible.

None of us could sing a bloody note, though! We sounded like cats being locked up. It was such a piss-take. We tried to keep a straight face while we were recording the song but we just couldn't do it; I just couldn't take it seriously. Do yourself a favour and don't go listening to it on YouTube – your ears will thank you for it.

Soon after, my move to Matchroom followed when life with Howard got a bit too much. I wanted to be managed by someone who knew snooker first and who had a sound head for business and Barry certainly had that. I also thought the Matchroom bollocks involving singing was over. What I didn't realise is that five minutes after I'd joined, we'd be back in the studio recording 'The Romford Rap'. For fuck's sake Baz!

In contrast to 'The Wanderer', I really hated 'The Romford Rap'. It was Baz's way of cashing in on 'Snooker Loopy' and you couldn't really blame him for that. Snooker was that massive back then that anything to do with the game was like printing money. Baz even brought Matchroom aftershave out!

The Matchroom lads all had to dress in different coloured suits and sing a different line and the video was filmed in The Hippodrome which totally freaked me out. I used to go to The Hippodrome all the time at night, when it was dark and mysterious and fun and suddenly there I was, in the same place in the middle of the afternoon, far too sober and far too clean.

"Have we really got to do this?" I asked Barry, but he wasn't having it. The song flopped and was quickly forgotten. And I never, ever went near The Hippodrome in daylight again. There were far too many memories in there – even if I couldn't remember them...

Once again, it reminded me of the two lives I was leading. In one, I was the bloke in the dickie-bow on the telly, potting snooker balls for fun and doing stupid music videos. In the other, I was getting up to all sorts, snorting coke constantly and drinking all night. I thought I was getting away with it but I suppose I wasn't as clever as I thought and the whispers about what I was getting up to started to grow.

I was in The Invitation one Friday afternoon and the phone rang. "What plane are you catching?" the voice at the other end said. It was Bernard Manning's son, also called Bernard. "What are you on about?" I asked. "You're playing in my club tonight, get yourself to Manchester. Now." There'd been a mix-up and I didn't know what had happened. "I'm stuffed," I told him. "Re-organise it for next week and I'll do it for nothing."

THE DEVIL

The next week we went up there with a mate who is black and we walked into the Embassy Club, where Bernard Senior was there to greet us. He wasn't working that night as he usually was and broke the ice by saying, "Not only is he a week late, he's brought a fucking n****r with him." That was it, my mate wanted to kill Bernard.

I wanted to leave that second but Bernard put the charm on and won us round. Everything calmed down and within the hour my mate couldn't stop laughing at some of his jokes – all of them just as offensive to somebody, somewhere.

We played the exhibition and as I was getting down for the shots, Bernard would walk around to the other side of the table and pretend to do a massive line of coke off the cushion. All you could hear, every time it was my turn to play, was Bernard sniffing and snorting. He'd obviously heard something on the grapevine. Fucking murder it was, even if he was funny.

●●●●●●●

When you've been on coke a while it becomes so easy to spot the person in a club or a bar who's dealing the stuff. I had that snooker hall knack of spotting a rogue from a mile off.

You could walk into any busy pub back then, take a quick look around and pick out the geezer you should approach. A quick nod of the head or a wink and you were outside, the deal was done, you'd pass the twenties over and you were away. As simple as that.

I hated it but I needed it. When I used to have about four or five drinks my nose used to run, as if my body knew that coke was on the way soon. I only rarely have a big drink these days but if I have four or five bottles of beer, my nose still runs like my brain is still telling me it's time to get some cocaine. If I had three bottles of wine tonight, within 10 minutes you'd think I had the flu because of the state of my nose.

One thing I didn't do was take coke during a tournament. Why take the risk when you knew you could play the system and be 'clean' when it mattered? You knew that if you stopped taking coke a week before a tournament began, you'd probably get away with it.

Saying that, it didn't stop me worrying. There were plenty of times that I'd give a urine sample and be thinking to myself 'Well Jimmy, you've done it this time' and I'd picture myself having to explain what I'd been up to.

If I'd have been caught out and the WPBSA had thrown the book at me and shoved me in front of a press conference then I couldn't have had any complaints. I'm not stupid, I knew it was wrong and I knew it was harming my game but I enjoyed doing it and it meant I could keep drinking all day and night.

But the stuff is fucking evil.

I call it 'The Devil's Dandruff' for a reason. Without a shadow of a doubt it ruins lives. Look how many famous people it has messed up. The list of celebrities that have died because of the stuff or have gone bankrupt or whatever is as long as my arm. When you're on it, people talk shit, they lie and cheat their families and friends. They do anything they can to get their hands on the stuff, they stop working and thinking and caring about anything other than cocaine, cocaine, cocaine. When you see people trying to be cool on cocaine I just feel sorry for them. After a while, blokes can't get the horn, they let themselves go and it makes you paranoid. It's the worst thing on the planet.

THE DEVIL

When the World Championship used to finish we had two months off and I'd be on it solid. Buckets of the stuff. I'd think nothing of doing a couple of grams a night, three or four nights a week.

I became very selfish and it came before everything else in life. Maureen tried to intervene at some point. My brothers and brother-in-law would try and have a word but I just told them that I had it under control and that I didn't need any help. I was a madman really.

After beating Neal Foulds to win the British Open, me, Maureen and Lauren soon moved from Wimbledon into a beautiful place in Oxshott. We'd really arrived now. This place was beautiful. It had the swimming pool, the double garage, the big swanky gates; the full Footballers' Wives treatment. My ranking tournament successes meant I was clearing £250,000 a year and we were determined to enjoy it.

We'd not been in Surrey long when Maureen fell pregnant again with Ashleigh but even that didn't straighten me out. I was living a bullshit life – the Tooting boy done good, living it up in Middle England in this big house with a loving wife and two beautiful kids when the reality was that I used to drive in the middle of the night to Brixton to score my gear. I'd be on the A3, snorting it off my thumb and having a great time in the car. I was a fucking rogue and I look back on some things I used to do and wonder if that was really the same person.

Whenever I went over to play in Ireland – and I seemed to be there every five minutes – I used to get on the phone, ring a few people in London, and then pay for them to come over to Dublin with bag after bag of cocaine on them.

Back then, security was pretty relaxed and loose. I'd be playing in exhibitions and I couldn't wait for those planes to land so I could get my hands on it.

I used to bankroll the entire trip and I'd think nothing of ringing certain numbers up and telling them where I was and how much I needed. "I'm in Dublin for a fortnight, come and see me as soon as you can," I'd say down the phone, trying to keep it vague in case anyone was listening in. I'd meet these lads at the airport, clammy and sweaty, needing a fix, before doing the deals there and then and escaping back to my hotel room to get stuck into these bags of coke.

If I was flying anywhere myself I would be up and out of my seat the minute the seatbelt signs pinged off. I'd be in the toilet, snorting away like crazy, laughing away to myself about just how smart I was.

Football matches, nightclubs, airports, hospitals – wherever. There wasn't a place I didn't snort it, outside of tournaments of course. You could've taken me for tea with the Queen and I'd have found a way to have a line.

The inevitable effects of being on coke and the problems this caused at home meant my snooker took a turn for the worse for a good 18 months.

I went from being a regular semi-finalist to slipping down to a quarter-finalist at best, losing more regularly to players I should've been blasting off the table. No disrespect intended to the likes of Mike Hallett, Barry West or Dave Martin but I wouldn't have lost to them if I'd have been living like Davis – or just living half-normally. I occasionally managed to regain some form but I couldn't twist the knife, losing to Davis in the 1987 UK Championship final and to Terry Griffiths in the semi-final of the 1988 World Championship.

THE DEVIL

The following season, I lost to Davis in another ranking final, the International Open, before finally beating him in the Canadian Masters final. John Parrott was too strong for me at the Crucible, sending me out in the quarter-final.

Again, I've got nothing against these geezers – I've known them a long, long time – but, looking back, I can't help but think that it was the coke that beat me more than they did.

None of this does me any favours and I know I come out of this sounding like a twat – which I undoubtedly was – but the reason I'm coming clean is to warn people off the stuff.

Just don't try it.

Don't even get started.

Cocaine is the worst drug in the world.

As if snorting it wasn't bad enough, for a short while in the mid-80s, life took an even darker turn...

•••••••

Kirk Stevens was a big cocaine taker on the snooker circuit.

I always got on really well with Kirk, he was a real pretty boy and all the ladies used to love him. He's gone public with his coke problem in the past and admitted he used to really be in the grip of the stuff.

Back then, he was always surrounded by dealers and people trying to push coke on him so when I spotted this, I knew we'd become good pals. We just had the same sort of outlook on life – about booze, girls and drugs. Kirk barely tried to disguise his problem and the blokes who used to sell it to him were unbelievable, turning up in the audience at tournaments and not really bothering to hide what they were doing.

Me and Kirk got close because of our love of the stuff and became really close mates. He's a lovely, lovely guy and I'm so pleased to see that he's healthy and happy these days. The way he's managed to turn his life around is an absolute credit to him and goes to show you how strong he is. He's now as anti-drugs as I am and he'd back me up when I say that all drugs are bad news.

Back in the mad days, though, we were as bad as each other. We used to love doing a line or three together and then going to nightclubs and dancing, enjoying the attention from all the girls and the feeling that anything was possible.

Our favourite spot was a place called Bootleggers in Piccadilly. Bootleggers was a really top club, very posh with some top looking birds in there. All the women loved him and he loved them back.

Someone who worked there used to sort us out for coke and me and Kirk couldn't get enough of the stuff, spending days snorting, boozing and partying like there was no tomorrow.

On other occasions, we'd go to the Kings Cross Snooker Centre, on Pentonville Road, and play our own little game on the tables as we tried to do the 'D' in cocaine. You go along the line, around the 'D' and then down the other line. We'd empty a bag out in the snooker club, which was always open late and nobody ever bothered you on the back tables, and off we'd go. Neither of us managed to do the entire lot. I could only ever get to the brown spot. *Must try harder Jimmy, must try harder...*

At the time it was a real laugh but we were bad news for each other. Coke puts you on a downward spiral that you don't notice because you're too busy enjoying it. It's like being mugged by someone who's making you laugh while they're at it.

THE DEVIL

And me and Kirk really fucked ourselves up when we went from snorting coke to smoking it...

I can't really explain how I made the jump from snorting to smoking crack cocaine. Jimmy White... Snooker Hero, People's Champion...Crack Addict. Sounds far fetched doesn't it but for about three crazy months, it was true.

Me and Kirk just got dragged into it, I suppose. I think he tried it first but I'm my own man and I don't blame anyone else for making me do something as stupid as smoking crack – the blame for that lies at my door and my door only.

I suppose it was the next step after snorting bags of the stuff and the temptation just got too strong. 'This is bad news Jimmy,' I thought, but then I smoked it once, then again and before you know it, I was hooked.

And if using cocaine is sniffing The Devil's Dandruff then smoking crack is sucking The Devil's Dick.

Over the years, the prize money and exhibition money had mainly been frittered away on drink and gambling but I still had ways to smuggle a bit to one side every now and then, away from Maureen and the bookmakers – whose kids I must've put through private school 10 times over.

I had one sneaky account with Natwest that had £30,000 in it – a massive amount of money back then but the kind of sum I could burn in five minutes flat at the racetrack – and I started dipping into this every now and then to fund my new crack habit.

And I did the lot in less than three months.

Every single penny, up in smoke.

We used to smoke crack at Kirk's flat in Putney. Snooker was very good to us both in the '80s. We earned a fortune and we both liked the finer things in life, including this apartment that he had. We knew that if we got in there we could close the curtains, lock the doors and get cooking up safely away from the public, the press and anyone else who could shop us and ruin our careers.

Kirk's flat could've been fantastic – I bet it is these days – but he was gripped with a bad addiction and he just couldn't be bothered doing anything with the place. I'll always remember, he only had one cassette tape for his stereo system – 'Dancing In The Dark' by Bruce Springsteen – and during that mad period we'd sit in his flat, scratching around waiting for the crack to be cooked up, listening to that over and over again.

Three months of our lives were lost doing that – lying there, glassy-eyed, spoons, tinfoil and rocks lying everywhere. We didn't give a shit about anything else – practice went out of the window and our families didn't know where we were half the time. We were two mad kids doing our best to kill ourselves. When you're that gripped by the drugs, even for a relatively short time, you don't have the brains to take a step out and look at what you're doing to yourself.

All you care about it cooking up and carrying on.

We were in his flat one night, sat around in a scruffy pair of jeans – snooker's two supposed glamour boys – and as Kirk was cooking up, he set his thumb on fire with some lighter fluid or something, fuck knows what.

The end of his thumb started crackling and smelling really bad and Kirk didn't move a muscle. We both just lay there, off our heads, watching his thumb slowly turn blacker and blacker. Kirk was too far gone to feel any pain and I was too far gone to tell him to run to the tap and put the flame out.

THE DEVIL

We just wanted to make sure the crack was cooked up properly; fuck Kirk's thumb, just make sure the drugs are okay.

Along with Kirk and I, my mate Peewee also sucked The Devil's Dick with us. Now Peewee is as honest, as straight and as genuine a bloke as there's ever been. He'd never, ever do you an injustice but when we were on the crack, I once saw a rock fall on the floor as we were trying to cook it up and Peewee clocked it straight away. He managed to sneak this rock into his hand while we all were desperately searching for it on our hands and knees, crawling around Kirk's flat, trying to find this tiny bit of evil. I saw Peewee smuggle it away and then deny he knew where it was – just so he could have it to himself later on.

That's what crack does to you. That's what crack had done to us. That's how bad it is. We were flirting with death and we didn't give a shit. Everything else went out of the window – our self-respect, our families, our money and our snooker.

Me and Kirk were always the same after we smoked it; as paranoid as it gets. We'd race down to the front door of this flat, unopened mail all over the floor, the windows grimy from where they'd never been cleaned, and he'd clamp his hand down on the top lock while I'd put all my weight on the bottom lock, sweat pouring off us, panicking that we were going to be busted by the police at any moment. Nobody had phoned them, we were just that far gone we thought we'd end up in jail. Meanwhile, all the time, all you could hear was 'Dancing In The Dark' blaring out of Kirk's speakers.

I ain't nothing but tired/
Man I'm tired and bored with myself/
Hey there baby, I could use just a little help

You're not wrong there, Bruce.

I still can't listen to that song without coming out in goose-bumps and the shivers. In fact, I don't feel too clever writing this, and we're talking almost 30 years ago now.

One time we were both due to play at the Irish Masters and we prepared for it by getting totally out of it on crack in the build-up. I couldn't hold my cue I was that messed up and Kirk was the same. Three days before we were due to leave for Ireland, we tried to sort ourselves out but you can't just flick a switch and get your form back and me and Kirk were hopeless. He lost in the first round to Willie Thorne and I lost to Willie a few days later in the quarter-final.

The pair of us were holed up in The Keadeen Hotel in County Kildare. We had all the time in the world on our hands. We were bored and we were drug addicts; plain and simple. Eventually it all got too much and we had to score some crack, otherwise we would've gone mad – we were sweating and shaking, pale, not able to sleep and generally ruined.

We got our hands on some from somewhere (I might even have had it flown in, I can't remember) and then we got down to it. "Jimmy," Kirk said. "Go down to the bar and get every-body's cigarette lighters would you?"

So I did as I was told and I went down to the bar. I had more front than Kirk so made my way around the room, shaking hands with everyone, having a bit of a laugh and a joke with these punters, all of whom wanted to buy me a drink and, cru-cially, lend me their lighter. "Thanks mate, I'll bring it back in a bit," I told everyone, making sure that nobody clocked that I now had about 15 lighters on me. Some people might've guessed I was an addict by then because I must've looked awful but at the time I thought I got away with it and I ran back to Kirk's room, emptied my pockets and spilled these lighters all over his bed.

He had a couple of rocks on him so he started trying to cook them. Unfortunately for us, though, we couldn't get these rocks to burn properly. "Give me a hand mate," I said to Kirk and I started trying to dismantle the door of the wardrobe so we could use it as firewood. I'm not joking. We started breaking down the furniture in the room, a table here, a wardrobe there, trying to get a fire started so we could cook this stuff up.

That's how sadistic the drug is – that's how crazy it had sent us. Two of the best snooker players in the world, holed away in an Irish hotel room, smashing up chairs and ripping up a duvet so we could make an indoor fire and smoke some crack. We would've paid all the money in the world for a bunsen burner about that time.

The next day we were at the bar when somebody told me Maureen had turned up. I'd been missing for weeks. She was fuming about what a twat I was being and she'd flown over to Ireland to find me and to kick my arse. I can't say it wasn't deserved but I couldn't handle seeing her. "Fuck off, she's not here," I said but then I spotted her near reception.

Fuck that. I ran upstairs to my room and tried to hide but Maureen wasn't having any of it. She walked into my room and was about to go off on one at me before I was ironically saved by what we'd been up to the night before.

"Jimmy, where the hell have you been?" she started screaming before she tried to sit down on this vanity stool. Unfortunately for her, me and Kirk had tried to burn the legs off the stool the night before and when Maureen sat on it, the legs gave way and she fell to the floor. We all burst into laughter. That broke the ice and I got away with it.

We came back from Goffs and me and Kirk went our separate ways for a few days. I went to my bank and tried to get some money out only to be told I'd done the lot; the account was empty, finished.

I was getting desperate for a score by now so I raced to Kirk's to try and get a rock. I knocked on the door and I will never forget it for as long as I live. I frantically banged on the door then realised Kirk wouldn't open it unless I let him know who it was. "Open up mate, it's Jimmy," I shouted, and finally I heard the locks open and Kirk stuck half his head through the gap in the door.

I had an apple in my hand and when Kirk spotted it, he lunged for this apple and ate it whole – the entire lot; not just the fruit but the pips and the core and the entire works.

He'd been so paranoid on the crack that he'd not left the flat for three days straight and was ravenous. I stood there and watched my mate, one of the best snooker players in the world and a man I loved, throwing this apple down his neck, a stick-thin, pasty mess.

It was the turning point for me.

In that instant I knew I had to get off the rocks and try and straighten myself out.

"I'm never going near that shit again," I said to Kirk. And I meant it. My three months of madness was up.

However, saying you're binning crack and then actually doing it are two very different things and the next fortnight was a nightmare. Your body and mind are constantly screaming at you to give in, to just have one more pipe, to just let your hair down and enjoy yourself and you have to ignore all that and get through it.

For a fortnight I barely moved, lying in bed, crying, shivering, paranoid, angry and covered in cold sweats. I felt like I was dying but I knew I had to stick with it. I was a father, I was a husband, I had this snooker gift that I was smoking away.

For fuck's sake Jimmy, sort yourself out.

In the end, the cravings and the cold turkey passed and I recovered but it was a horrendous time for everybody. Looking back, I don't think any of the other players knew we were crackheads and we were never caught but, saying that, none of the players were stupid either. They knew the life I was leading and the places I was hanging out. They also saw me barely able to string a sentence together and looking like shit most of the time, so I'm sure plenty of them put two and two together. Even if they had guessed, I wouldn't have given a shit, to be honest.

As the '80s went on, Kirk finally returned home to Canada to try and sort himself out and that was the best thing for him, while I continued to snort my way around London.

I suppose that getting off the crack should have given me the strength to push on and ditch the powder as well but I didn't really get there. Not then anyhow. That would come a few years later. As I say, I don't blame anyone else for what I was up to and plenty of close friends and family used to try and make me grow up but I was deaf to their pleas and I was seriously addicted to the stuff.

At home, soon after Ashleigh arrived, we discovered Maureen was pregnant again. Georgia was born in March, 1989. Becoming a father again was, obviously, a fantastic feeling and having three little girls meant the world to me.

Me and Maureen would still be fighting and bickering a lot and I packed my bags more times than Michael Palin but that never stopped us from doing the right things by the kids. I was no angel but the girls never witnessed the madness and that is something I look back on with some pride. The girls were wonderful and the same as daughters everywhere; funny, loving, excitable and they had their old man wrapped around their little fingers even if he went missing for God knows how long to God knows where.

Throughout the mad days like that, and the mad days on the coke, I still had to try and produce. A big house in Oxshott and three kids doesn't come cheap and that's before I even start on the gambling and the boozing – both of which were running out of control as well.

•••••••

1989/90 didn't have much going for it really until I won £100,000 at the World Matchplay, beating John Parrott 18-9 in the final but by the time the Crucible came around in April, 1990, I was actually feeling surprisingly good. I'd prepared well – despite everything else going on in my life – and I wanted to put my bad season behind me.

I'd even been over to Hong Kong to star in a film.

Having done loads of exhibitions over there with Matchroom, I was really popular and got approached by a bloke called Steven Chow to appear in 'Legend Of The Dragon'. You should watch it, it's a classic in Hong Kong; it's their Shawshank Redemption! Chow is a big star over there, he's like Bruce Forsyth, and he wanted me to add a bit of snooker skill into the plot. He had to try and beat me at snooker in order to win his family land back. It was filmed in Hong Kong and it's still on YouTube so go and have a look. I was sat there, surrounded by all these mad extras as they fought and kicked the shit out of each other.

At one point, Steven Chow's character jumps about 30 feet in the air and then slams down on the table and plays this masse shot that sends the cue-ball around corners. Well, it was actually me who played the shot for Steven because he didn't have a clue what he was doing. (Mind you, looking at the tape again, my acting was as bad as his cue action so we're quits).

Being sat there, in my dinner suit, watching all this action around me was crazy. It was a lot of fun and I loved it. Steven was so friendly and I was pleased to help out.

It was hardly 'The Color of Money' but it was a really great experience. Here's me, a kid from South London, getting paid to act in a film in Hong Kong. That doesn't happen every day does it? It was only a cameo but I enjoyed it and it meant that whenever I went back over there I was treated like royalty.

Back at Sheffield, I'd managed to get off the drink and the coke in the build-up and it worked like clockwork, as I beat John Virgo and Terry Griffiths before squeezing past Davis, 16-14 in the semi-final, a real bruising match that Davis reckoned was the best he'd played in a losing cause. I had to agree with that – he'd been in fantastic form but everything clicked for me and I held him off.

Going into the final against Stephen Hendry I felt great. Finally, I was back in the World Championship final. I was really up for it, my confidence was back and I felt that it was time to prove to everyone, and myself, that I could be the world champion.

Hendry was only 20 but had previously gone public about his belief he could win it before he turned 21. That confidence and cockiness was great for the game and he had the skills to back it up. But not this year, this year was going to be my turn. You don't beat a competitor like Davis in the semi-final and not think you can win it. If you can beat Davis at the Crucible, you can beat anyone.

That was the theory anyway – the reality was a lot different.

Maureen was pregnant for a fourth time during that Crucible effort and I so wanted to win it to celebrate that news, but it wasn't to be.

I don't have any regrets about that final; Hendry just beat me fair and square. My safety game wasn't tight enough and he punished me, plain and simple. There was nothing in the early frames. The first session was tight and I was still in it at 9-7 down after two sessions but he then won the first four frames of the third session and I couldn't catch him.

Every time I got near him, he eased into a higher gear. I threw as many punches as I could but just couldn't get close enough to him and he won 18-12 in the end. A six-frame margin tells you all you need to know and when he finally put me out of my misery, I walked across and applauded him, just as he deserved.

Hendry had clearly been nervous – he admitted as much afterwards – but he played superbly and there wasn't much I could do about it. I knew I'd be back. Unfortunately, so would he...

Maureen gave birth to Breeze soon after but I'd by lying if I said I saw the light or anything like that. I stayed on the coke, the booze and in the bookies and kept enjoying the limelight when it suited me and the dark, dingy pubs of South London when it didn't.

THE DEVIL

Coke even cost me my nightclub, 'Whirlwind's' – the only club in history that had its opening and closing night all on the same evening!

I was approached by a geezer in Surrey who wanted me to put some money up for this gaff in Earl's Court. It was a really swanky place. He spent about £200,000 doing it up and it looked great. A big plush bar, VIP seats all over the place, a big dancefloor; the works.

On the opening night, me and Maureen turned up – me in a sharp suit, her in a big dress and we spoke to all the TV news crews who were there. We got loads of coverage and the night was going great.

At first.

The place was full of people I knew and it also had gangsters from all over London in there. They all came to meet me because I knew them from being out and about but it all started getting a bit moody. The gangsters from X started giving the guys from Y the eyes, and vice versa and it felt like it would go off at any second. I put two waitresses on each group of lads, desperate to make sure that no one group was getting served quicker than anyone else. I wanted to keep everyone happy and I managed to keep them all apart but I was terrified they'd meet in the toilet and World War Three would start there and then.

It all went great until I left at 3am – and then the police arrived. I was on my way home and the joint was raided, the police found a load of cocaine on some punters in there and they closed us down! We'd only been in business eight hours! But that was it, goodbye to Whirlwind's.

We'd spent some serious money in there as well. It cost £20,000 alone for this massive sign we'd made. There it was

JIMMY WHITE

– Whirlwind's – written in massive letters, 10-foot wide with all these lights around it. Eventually, when we were getting it moved it fell off a lorry and broke apart which somehow sums everything up.

Another occasion when coke messed things up was when Ronnie Wood had a birthday party one night at his place in Wimbledon. It was a lovely night, all very respectable until I did a couple of lines. The food at this dinner party was sushi – really top end, expensive stuff – but the coke had started playing tricks with my mind. I'm sat there in my best suit and Maureen is asking me over and over again what was wrong. Nothing was wrong, I just didn't fancy raw fish.

I started using my cigarette lighter to cook it at the table. I had a piece of tuna in one hand and this old lighter in the other, watching the tuna crackle and spit (a bit like Kirk's thumb!) and you can imagine the looks I was getting from everybody. Ronnie just laughed and didn't mind. He's one of the coolest men I've ever known, so nothing bothers him but Maureen wasn't happy.

But that's what coke does to you – it turns you into a dickhead.

I don't know how much I burnt on cocaine but I did at least a couple of hundred grand.

I was the only one out of my group who could afford it so I always had people around me who wanted to get a line as well. I was known for having a lot of hangers-on, especially at the Crucible and I'd say that the reason for that was that most people wanted the drugs rather than my company.

By the time the 1991 final came around against John Parrott, I was still properly gripped by the stuff but I can't blame that when world title chance number three went begging.

John is a really nice guy and a credit to the game. I love doing

148

exhibitions with him these days and he loves his horse racing. He's a classic Scouser – full of life and chat and he's a great ambassador for the sport.

I'd beaten Steve James 16-9 in the semi-final and I got a phone call from Stephen Hendry that night. "Jimmy, I just want to stay well played and good luck in the final," he said. "Go and win it." That was a nice touch because I know how much Hendry was hurting after losing to James in the quarters.

John had been buried by Davis in the 1989 final. And I mean seriously buried, losing 18-3 with a session to spare. It had been a brutal display by Davis but John had done brilliantly to dispel any demons from that and he was once again one of the world's top players by the time we faced each other in the final.

Third time lucky Jimmy? No chance.

I never got near him because he played like a god. The first seven frames he played were out of this world. I've never seen snooker like it I don't think and even John himself will tell you that he played in a way that he'd never done before (and certainly since!)

He was just unbelievable. Every pot went in, every snooker was perfect, every safety shot had me tied in knots – it was the dream opening session and I was always chasing it after that. He went into the match on the back of a revenge 16-10 semi-final win against Davis and that meant he was flying, mentally.

It just wasn't my night. I'd got to the Crucible in one of Barry's limousines, the Matchroom boys always liked to be a bit flash when we could, so I turned up in a car with POT 147 as the numberplate and the fucking thing got a parking ticket! I should've known then that John had it in the bag.

John not only won a few quid and the World Championship

final, he also got a holiday to Australia out of the final. There used to be this big character nicknamed 'Harry The Dog' who was a massive gambler. And, unlike me, he was actually pretty good at it. He used to bet on Parrott and really fancied him in 1991. It paid off. He had massive cash on him in every round and then backed him again in the final and was quids in. To thank John for his efforts in filling his wallet, Harry sent Parrott to Oz for about a month, which isn't too bad is it?

Parrott often says in his after-dinner speeches about that final that his first plan was to quieten the crowd down but I don't think that was it. I just think he had the sporting day of his life against me and good luck to him for that.

Afterwards, David Vine (at "wages time" as he always called the cheques being handed out) asked him about his win and John had enough class to demand an extra round of applause from the crowd for me, which was a nice touch and sums the guy up perfectly.

I never really recovered from that first session and he played extremely well. It happens in life, in sport, in loads of different areas. When I spoke to Vine myself I told him I couldn't be too upset. "You only have to watch the misery on the news," I said, "to realise how lucky we all are to be here."

I meant those words then and I mean them now.

I'd have to stick to that attitude for the next few years.

Especially at the Crucible.

Especially against one player in particular.

7

No Regrets

It's September, 1987, and I'm in a hotel in Hong Kong with Stephen Hendry, Willie Thorne and Ian Doyle, Hendry's manager.

Me and Willie have just done Doyle for £4,000 after he gambled on Hendry when we were all playing a pound a point. Doyle, renowned as being a tough manager and a geezer who gets on Hendry's case a lot, wants me to have a word with the young spiky-haired kid to try and keep him on the straight and narrow. Doyle tells me that Hendry doesn't really like practising and isn't yet fulfilling his potential.

I don't know much about that, he's just beaten me in the Hong Kong Masters semi-final and seems to be a fantastic prospect. But I take Doyle's words on board and decide to help. I'd been *a kid on the tour myself and I could've done with a few wise words of advice from time to time too.*

"Stephen, you've got to practise mate," I told him.

"One day you could be the world champion."

I've always been very kind to Stephen Hendry.

He was one of those, like O'Sullivan, who idolised me as a kid. I first met him when he was about 14 at the World Amateur Championship in Dublin in 1984. He was shy and he didn't smile much but there was no doubting his skill on the table.

The whole snooker world was talking about this kid and what an incredible potter he was. There aren't that many professional players and we all travel and work together, so when rumours start going around about there being a new talent in the game, you soon get to hear about him.

Hendry had started playing when he was 12 and never looked back. He just looked so composed and calm. He soon started winning amateur championships left, right and centre and he was one of the youngest ever professional players.

I remember the first time I watched him play and I knew right there and then that he had all the tools to become an absolutely fantastic player.

At the 1986 World Championship, I stood at the back of the Crucible arena and peered through the gap in the seats as Hendry faced Willie Thorne. Now, Willie had been around a long time by this point, he was a superb break builder and he had a very good game. Hendry on the other hand was only a kid but he pushed Willie all the way. There was nothing between them for the entire match until Willie just got going towards the end and held on to win 10-8.

NO REGRETS

Hendry hit a 44 break in the last frame but it wasn't enough and when he went to shake hands with Willie, I remember saying to myself that I'd just seen a future champion. He was only 16 at the time.

I first played him later that year in the Scottish Masters and I hammered him 5-1. It was the quarter-final and you could tell he was nervous. His arm was tight and he never looked relaxed. I felt great during that match, scoring a big century in one of the frames to leave Hendry looking glum in his chair.

I knew how it felt to be the new wonderkid in town and I also knew exactly how it felt to have older players trying to dominate you. It never bothered me when the older guys used their experience to frustrate me or slow me down and one thing is for sure – it didn't bother Hendry either, not one little bit.

If I had to sum him up in one phrase I would use: 'Hard as nails'. That's exactly what he was. He still is.

He had massive self-belief and was always comfortable at the table. Hendry would leave a four-foot pot and back himself every time to hit it perfectly. In golf, you see some professionals leave themselves awkward 12-foot putts and they go to pieces and then you see some players who love them. Hendry was the same at snooker – he was never put off or bothered by difficult long pots. He backed himself massively and he usually delivered when it mattered most.

We faced each other in the 1988 World Championship in the last 16 and the shy kid from Scotland had been transformed into this self-confident player who knew he had all the tools.

That match was a Crucible classic, it was like a Spaghetti Western shoot-out. The pair of us went for each other from the absolute start. I barely had a safety game and Hendry was as attacking as I was (on his day) and we just went for it. We both missed easy shots in the last frame as the tension gripped us a bit but I then played one of the best shots of my career under pressure. I was at the top of my game and so was he. It was tit for tat. He left me a long red and I had no other option but to take it on.

I got down to it and thought, 'This is the match, this has to go in' and I smashed it in. I made it a bit harder for myself than I would've liked as I then had to pot another long red from baulk but when that went down, there was no way I was going to look back. The blue followed and then the frame wasn't far behind.

"Well played," I said to Hendry at the end and you could see his winner's mentality then, disappointment written all over his face. He always had a lot of class, though, and thanked me for the game, wishing me luck in the quarter-final.

A lot of young kids would've been delighted to take me, one of the world's best players, all the way but he was showing then how tough he was. I was obviously delighted to win and I suppose it was Hendry's way of showing how much he'd improved and really 'arrived'. He truly belonged among the world's best and pushed me so hard.

We next faced each other in a really big match in 1990 at the Masters where he beat me 6-4 in the semi-final on his way to the title. He won five Masters in a row – from 1989 to 1993 – and by now he was looking unstoppable.

The thing about Stephen was that he used to prepare for tournaments so well and he used to love the pressure, the tension and the excitement of competing.

When I walked out to play him in the Masters or at the Crucible, the crowd used to be massively on my side. They'd cheer and scream when I won a frame or when my name was announced and while that was a lovely thing for me, it actually worked against me in a way because it just spurred Hendry on. The louder the crowd got, the deeper he used to go into his own little world, concentrating even harder and wanting to win even more.

That is the one thing I'll always remember about Hendry; I don't think there's ever been a player who wanted to win as desperately as he did.

He didn't want century breaks (although he hit an incredible 700 of them) and he didn't want the affection of the fans – he just wanted silverware and world titles and he was fantastic at making that happen.

During a tournament, while I'd be out with my mates until all hours, enjoying my freedom and far too many Screwdrivers, Stephen would keep himself to himself.

I had a mate called Geoff who had a Chinese restaurant in Swiss Cottage and during the Masters every year, Hendry would take himself off there every night for his dinner. While I was running around, trying to keep everybody happy, seeing all my mates and sponsors and whoever else, Hendry would be sat in this Chinese restaurant with his Dim Sum, nice and relaxed and ready for the next day's play. He was the master of keeping himself to himself whereas everybody wanted a piece of me, and I usually gave it to them.

Of course, Stephen coming to prominence in the game also happened to coincide with when I was enjoying some of my finest years. Hendry v White World Championship clashes would go down in snooker folklore... not necessarily for all the right reasons as far as I was concerned.

JIMMY WHITE

1992 World Championship Final, The Crucible, Sheffield,
Stephen Hendry (SCO) 18 – Jimmy White (ENG) 14

By the time I came to play him for the second time in the World Championship final, I really fancied my chances. I was in the form of my life in 1992, winning the British and European Opens and generally playing fantastically, hitting 25 centuries in competitions, my highest ever in a season.

In the British Open I'd beaten James Wattana in the final 10-7 after an amazing show of bravery from him.

During his last 16 match against Tony Drago, Wattana was taken to one side and told that his dad had been shot during an incident in Bangkok. Somehow he still managed to go out and play and he hit a 147 against Drago under those circumstances, an amazing feat that should be recognised more often than it is. By the time he'd come off the table having won 5-1, his dad had died but he stayed in the tournament and I eventually ended up getting the better of him.

After I won, I was still in awe of his courage for managing to continue to play and I remember thinking that his 147 against Drago was something else. Of course, I had no idea then that I'd also be hitting a 147 against the same player just two months later.

I've known Tony forever and we were practice partners for years so we knew each other's game really well. Tony is a fantastic player although his Mediterranean mentality means he can sometimes lose his temper over nothing and that, in turn, can affect his game at times. He is an underachiever really because he is still one of the most talented players ever to have picked up a cue. He is also one of the nicest and most decent players around – something that he proved when I hit my maximum against him.

In our first round match, I was winning 8-4 and felt great – nice and loose – when Tony took on a long red and missed. I got out of my seat, sized the table up and knew the balls were in a lovely frame-winning position. I wasn't thinking any more than that at the time.

I certainly wasn't thinking about a 147. Not yet, anyway.

I've made over 250 of them – one in the World Championship, 50-odd in exhibitions and about another 200 in practice and they're always special, even in practice, even with nobody else watching.

When you're playing on your own, making a 147 is like throwing a nine-darter; the best players can do them all the time but when the pressure is on, that's something different.

And if a darts player tells you he's not nervous as he lets that last one go – even in practice – then he's lying and snooker is the same. As you get down for that last black, I don't care what anyone says, your heart is racing and your palms are sweaty – you desperately want it to go in.

You can imagine then how it felt to be trying to get one in at the Crucible with the world watching.

As the break continued, the reds just kept getting better and better. I was quick around the table, I was playing by sheer instinct, knowing what shot I had to play before I'd barely seen the previous ball disappear.

After the fifth black, I went into the pack and the reds split perfectly for me. 'It's on,' I kept saying to myself. 'Just stay steady, let it build slowly, don't rush your shots'.

The tension kept creeping up because the Crucible audience

is the most knowledgeable crowd in the world. They knew the maximum break was a possibility and by this point there was no way I wasn't going to go for it.

If you take a cold look at a snooker frame, you should never really attempt a 147 because the risks involved are too great. What you should do is worry about getting to 74 as safely as possible, potting reds with care and then coming back up the table to pick off plenty of blues. The longer you play in and around the black, the higher your chances of making a mistake, losing position and handing your opponent the chance to get out of their chair.

But fuck all that.

This was the Crucible, this was the World Championship, this was me.

If I'd not gone for the 147 and won the frame I'd still feel guilty about it to this day. Better to lose the frame going for glory than win the frame and bottle out of snooker's hardest achievement.

The reds kept disappearing until I got slightly out of position so I had to take on a long red followed by a black with the rest. The audience applauded me but it felt like I couldn't miss. I was in the zone – I just had to stay calm and deliver.

As I kept going and got past the century, I knew that nobody wanted me to do it more than Tony.

After the 15th black and with 120 on the board, the crowd began to get really restless and nervous for me. The odd shout came from the crowd but I didn't mind that – I was so focused I could've been playing anywhere. 'Nice and relaxed Jim,' I kept saying to myself. 'One ball at a time'.

I potted the green and if you watch YouTube you can see

NO REGRETS

Drago's nerves in the background. His right hand was shaking and he was hitting his own leg because he was so tense for me. He didn't watch the match back for about three months but when he did, he came out in cold sweats over that green because he was sat there, shaking in my eye-line, and he thought he might have put me off. Fair enough, the green did rattle in but that wasn't Tony's fault.

The brown was straightforward but I pushed the cue ball a bit out of position meaning I had to stun the blue which left me a long pink. The tension was starting to get to me now – I was on the verge of achieving a lifetime ambition, raising the Crucible roof and also earning £100,000 – and I knew I had to keep it together for just two more shots.

The pink was a bit of a stretch but it disappeared and I was down and in position for the black before I knew it. This was it. Don't miss this Jimmy. Do. Not. Miss. This.

I pulled back the cue and the black rolled into the middle of the pocket as the entire Crucible went crazy. I barely had time for a little clench of my fist before Drago was out of his seat, on the verge of tears, hugging me. "Well done mate, well done mate," he kept saying as he threw his arms around me. That hug seemed to last forever and I knew he meant every word of what he said. It was one of the classiest and most touching moments of sportsmanship you will ever see and it was Tony in a nutshell; passionate, snooker crazy and a great bloke. I'd been the same when Kirk Stevens did me for a 147 in the Masters in 1984 and I hope it is a tradition that continues forever. At the end of the day, as well as being players we are all snooker fans and the moment you can't win a frame yourself, all you want to do is watch your opponent go all the way.

After beating Drago I progressed to the final against Hendry after wins against Alain Robidoux, Jim Wych and Alan McManus and I thought it was my year.

Fourth time lucky Jimmy, this is it.

And for a long time in that final, it really did look like this was it. When I was 14-8 up against Hendry I was absolutely cruising it. I was just flying in that final. My potting, safety play and positional skill in the first three sessions was just something else and I was good value for my six-frame lead.

There was no doubt whatsoever in my mind that the World Championship was finally mine.

Hendry was a great player, I knew that even by 1992, but then so was I and there was no way I was going to let that lead slip, not in a race to 18 anyway.

But I suppose the signs were there.

Because I was winning so easily, I sat in my seat during the 23rd frame and snooker was now the last thing on my mind.

My head was racing, not with what I needed to do to beat Hendry, but with what I'd say afterwards in my speech. In my mind's eye I'd already lifted the trophy, I'd already shaken David Vine's hand, I'd read the back page of the next day's papers, I'd given my dad a hug, I'd thrown the biggest fucking party of all time.

'I'll start by thanking my mum and dad and Maureen,' I was saying to myself. 'Then I'll thank my mates, and my family. I'll mention Mr Beatty and the lads from Zan's and then I'll say a few words about a few others who've ripped me off and tried to fuck me over'.

I just couldn't wait to get the night started. As for the rest of the final? No worries, give me half an hour and I'll be the world champion. I was so far ahead, so ridiculously far ahead, that when I did get out of my seat to play, I was too concerned about showing some flair, rather than killing the match off.

At 38-33 down in that 23rd frame I played an amazing long pot for the yellow. The ball went down but what are the percentages of that shot? I ended up snookering myself and although that wasn't a fatal error, it was a sign that my head was not where it should be.

Soon after, I went for a very long red that rattled the pockets for about 20 minutes before it missed and that let Hendry back in to win that frame. Again, other shots were available but nobody loses a World Championship final from six frames down, so I took it on.

It's just the way I'm put together. If I see a shot that I fancy, no matter how difficult it looks or how the balls are spread then the temptation to take it on gets too strong to resist. Higgins knew what that feeling was like and so does O'Sullivan.

When Hendry got it back to 14-9 after my error on the long red, it still barely registered. He might've been the World No.1 but I was flying and in the form of my life.

At 14-9, Hendry potted a wonderful brown that helped him clinch the frame so the session ended with me 14-10 ahead. In the evening session, I then missed a simple red that would have made it 15-10 but, instead, it was 14-11, then 14-12 and before I knew it Hendry was smelling blood and he was all over me.

Looking back now, I can barely recall what happened. It just seemed to go past in a blur. Like all sports, snooker is about momentum and confidence and Hendry seemed to improve by the second while I got worse. He knew that I didn't like being too far in front so just told himself to chip away, play solid snooker and wait for his chances. That's exactly what he did and credit to him for that.

He had nothing to lose as well, don't forget, and that made a big difference. The gap had been so big and his chances so small that he could just go for it whereas I got tighter and more distracted the longer it went on. I just couldn't stay focused.

It's hard to explain but when you get out of the zone and lose focus then it's so hard to get back into it. Trying to regain your focus is impossible and the more you become aware of it, the more you know you're gone and it does your head in. You stop being in control of what's going on and that's fatal.

Fair play as well to Hendry, he played some incredible snooker in that last session, including three century breaks. He was unstoppable and I would've needed to be at my absolute best anyway before you even mention how gone my head was.

I was exhausted as well.

I'd had such a great tournament and a great couple of weeks. I was winning, I was having loads of parties, going out to Josephine's nightclub all the time and living like there was no tomorrow. Every day of the World Championship was a holiday, a party, a day of freedom for me.

I was absolutely knackered. When you're surrounded by mates and card games and more booze than you can drink then it catches up with you. I was so tired going into that final.

When he came back at me, the pressure got to me, I was completely gone and I just couldn't handle it. Hendry made a 112 break in the last frame but by then I barely knew who I was or what I was doing there.

A few moments later, David Vine shoved that microphone under my nose – the one I'd been daydreaming about earlier –

and rather than delivering my victory speech I had to pay my respects and congratulations to Stephen instead.

"I wasn't at the races in the end," I told David. I was barely on planet Earth, never mind the races and I was just pleased to get out of the arena. Watching Hendry lift the trophy made me feel so sick, again, even though I didn't really have anyone to blame but myself.

Seventeen days of playing snooker is tough for anybody, especially if you were living the life I was. If you played your game, went for dinner and then went to bed, you'd find 17 days of competition to be tiring on its own. I was playing all day then on the piss all night and at the very highest level, it comes down to margins like that.

I don't blame anybody else for that other than myself and, to be honest, I don't really blame myself that much either because at the time I didn't think I was doing anything wrong.

You can only live your life as you see it in that moment and in 1992, aged just 30 (the final was always around my birthday), there was no way I was going to live a life other than the way I wanted to.

Other people might've seen it and been aware of the damage I was doing but I didn't and I wouldn't be told. My family would beg me to have an early night and a soft drink but fuck that. Why should I go to bed when I had a suite full of mates, a pack of cards and booze on tap? It was madness – but it was a madness that, at the time, I thoroughly enjoyed and that is why I can't feel too down about it. I'm my own man and it was my own decision. End of story.

That's not to say that I'd do it the same way if I had my time again...

One of my biggest problems, looking back, was the amount of people I had as an entourage. You could call them hangers-on I suppose, but I just looked on them all as mates. I don't want to mention names but there were far too many people having far too good a time around me – paid for by me as well.

They would turn up in Sheffield pissed after the train journey with nowhere to stay and they wouldn't have a suit to wear to go into the players' lounge or anything like that.

They really shouldn't have been anywhere near me but I used to try and help them all out, put them up in my suite, sort them passes and suits out and do whatever else they needed to have a good time. Meanwhile, I wasn't getting the rest I needed. I was always on stage, always performing to my mates and seeing everyone right.

And that was wrong.

Listen to this as an example. During the interval against Hendry, the World Championship tournament director, Mike Ganley, came over to me for a quick word. Mike is the son of Len Ganley, a great referee who passed away a few years back, and he needed to speak to me urgently.

"Jimmy," he said. "We've got a potential problem with some of your mates. I've picked up that if you beat Stephen, they're going to come flying out of the crowd and onto the playing area. We can't let this happen."

"Okay Mike," I told him. "Leave it with me, I'll sort it."

The boys involved were two brothers and although they meant no harm by what they were planning – they just wanted their five minutes of fame – it would obviously look very bad for the game and for me, especially with the final being live on the telly.

So rather than spending the interval relaxing, I had to run

around the Crucible until I found the lads and warned them off their little stunt.

That didn't cost me the World Championship because Hendry played well and I lost concentration – but it's not hard to see why I was struggling at the table when I had so much on my plate.

Unlike Hendry (and Davis), I didn't have a long and solid relationship with a manager either and little things like that add up in the end. If one of Hendry's mates had planned that stunt, Ian Doyle would've sorted it with a few choice words. I didn't have that and so I had to sort all this shit out – the suites and the suits – myself. Not ideal.

Hendry was as good as gold off the table after that final and we genuinely still get on really well. I'd always tried to give him good advice, ever since he was a kid, and I'd still be all ears today if he wanted to chat about something.

He used to ask me all about a career in snooker and my advice was always the same – do the opposite of what I'm doing.

"Save your money and get an early night," was my usual advice and he stuck to it well. I'd been in the game a long time before he came along so I knew how the world worked.

1993 World Championship Final, The Crucible, Sheffield, Stephen Hendry (SCO) 18 – Jimmy White (ENG) 5

I was lucky to get five.

As I potted the last ball against James Wattana in the semi-final that year, I knew that would be the highlight of the World Championship for me. There was no way I could beat Hendry in the final and I knew it before I'd even put my dickie-bow on.

Why did I know?

Well, because I'd not picked a cue up for a month before I made the trip up to Sheffield that year. My private life was a shambles again at this point because me and Maureen had finally split up for good (or so we both said, anyway). I'd spent months on the piss and coke, running around like a madman, and generally just forgetting about snooker.

Over the years I must've furnished 20 flats in and around London. I should own half of Dixons, the money I've spent in the place. Mine and Maureen's turbulent lifestyle and the amount of time I was spending going out with my mates had finally become too much. I was gone.

I'd moved out of our place in Oxshott and into a new flat and for the first and only time, I fell out of love with snooker.

I just couldn't find the motivation to practise, I dropped out of the Sky Sports International in Plymouth and I had no interest in playing, whatsoever. Day after day was spent sitting around or going to the pub or the bookies. Sheffield kept getting bigger and bigger on the horizon but I wanted nothing to do with snooker or anyone. I wouldn't say it was depression, more just a general feeling of disappointment that my marriage was curtains and that my love for the game had dribbled away.

On form and preparation, I didn't deserve to play at Sheffield and I knew I had absolutely no chance whatsoever. You know your own game far better than any coach or fan does. Nobody can tell you how you feel at the table and that year I knew I was well out of sorts.

On the way to the final I beat Joe Swail, Doug Mountjoy, Dennis Taylor and Wattana but I fell over the line in every match. I never felt like I could really get going and score heavily and I knew that, at some point, that would cost me. I'd only won those matches on reputation and because I knew how to win but there was no doubt I was going to get kicked sooner or later and it just so happened that it was Hendry doing the kicking again.

And what a kicking it was as well.

Hendry showed his class from the very first frame, firing off a 136 break. I never stood a chance.

If you watch the replay, when I shake his hand at the end, you see me smiling. That was because he'd just put me out of my misery.

Every sportsman will tell you the same thing; some days it just ain't your day and that final was one of them. I'd been out-played and outclassed by the best player in the world. Again, he'd probably spent months preparing with a calm manage-ment team and a settled life. I'd been moping around, moving flats, and getting lost in coke, horses, birds and drink.

These are not excuses at all – Hendry was fantastic on that occasion and deserves all the praise in the world – but I was living a hectic life and you can only bluff in snooker for so long before it catches up with you.

The £105,000 runners-up cheque helped ease the blow a bit, especially after I'd only won five frames – not bad for half-a-day's work!

I knew I was beaten before I even went out there so I wasn't worried about it at all. In fact, the night before the final I'd gone out in Sheffield. I got in at 7.30 in the morning. I'd ended up in a place called Pinky's – I don't even know if it's still there – before staggering back to the Grosvenor House Hotel to try and get some kip.

I had a mate with me – I don't want to say who it was – and by about 7am he was crying. "Jimmy, what are you doing?" he kept saying, but I just carried on partying and drinking Screw-drivers. "Please Jimmy, just go and get some sleep." I wouldn't listen though – I knew that I could've slept for a month and still got nowhere near beating Hendry.

He simply proved me right the next day.

1994 World Championship Final, The Crucible, Sheffield, Stephen Hendry (SCO) 18 – Jimmy White (ENG) 17

He's beginning to annoy me.

If I'm going to be remembered for anything I suppose it's going to be that black in the 1994 final.

Everybody thinks back to the black I missed off the spot in that last frame and I can't really blame them but I think something has been overlooked before that.

In the 32nd frame I had to clear up to win when Hendry was 16-15 up and then 30 minutes later when he'd gone just one frame from winning the World Championship at 17-16, I hit a 75 break to make it 17-17.

People forget those frames.

People call me a 'bottler' for missing that black and losing the last frame but that break of 75 was more pressure than you can ever imagine and I managed to pull that off and make the final go the distance.

If your bottle's gone, it's gone long before it's 17-all.

Before the final frame – only the second ever Crucible final to go all the way following Taylor and Davis in 1985 – I nipped off to the toilets to compose myself and get myself together.

NO REGRETS

I felt confident, I'd played some fantastic snooker, especially early on when I went from 5-1 down to lead 9-7. Stephen had then gone into a 15-13 lead but couldn't get away from me. I just kept pegging him back.

When I walked back down to the table, the reception from the crowd was unbelievable. You could almost taste the desperation and desire of the audience for me to win it and at one point, it looked like I was about to make their dreams, and my own, come true.

I broke and the nerves and tension just continued to grow. The Crucible was as electric as I've ever known it, including my epic matches against Higgins and Davis.

Hendry got off to the better start until he potted a blue and then lost position. It would've been a hard shot in the pub, never mind the World Championship final and at 24-8 down I was suddenly out of my chair and a step closer to the trophy.

I potted two reds and two blacks before going into the pack, hoping something would break for me. It didn't. The cue-ball sat surrounded by reds and none of them would go, apart from a near-impossible one into the corner.

I needed my cue extension to even reach it and it was certainly a gamble – but I knew by then that I had to play my natural game if I was going to feel like I'd done myself justice.

The shot paid off, the red disappeared and I came out for the blue and everything was looking fine. Two more reds soon followed, with a blue in between, until I got down to pot a simple black.

That black.

Of course I was nervous, of course I was tense, of course I wanted the world title more than anything else on earth at that moment in time. I had made a break of 29, I was 13 in front and I was another four or five minutes away from achieving my dream.

'Keep your cool,' I kept thinking, fully aware that the Crucible sounded empty. It was so quiet in there that I could've been playing a practice game. Nobody dared move, nobody made a sound. After 15 years of being the fans' favourite, the one title that me – and the public – wanted me to win more than any other was around the corner.

The BBC commentator Clive Everton has said in the past that having to attach my cue extension for the long red might have burst my focus but I don't really think it did, I just think I got down too quick and I twitched and threw my cue at the shot.

I used to take about 14 seconds per shot but I got down well before then. It cost me. Golfers can get the yips before a big putt and that was what happened. I just rushed and the ball didn't even come out of the jaws. It missed by a mile.

I thought I'd lined it up right but I obviously hadn't done and the black stayed up. I knew then that it was all over. The groan of the crowd is not something you forget in a hurry either.

Hendry got out of his chair in no time and as he did I had a little scan of where the remaining reds were. I knew that I'd lost. Hendry was too good, too cool and too talented to miss this golden opportunity I'd just given him. Not a lot of players would have cleared up from there but, as I say, he was as hard as nails.

Walking back to my chair was the longest walk of my life. 'You've fucked it again,' I told myself, and I knew I wasn't lying.

There are few more exposed places to be in the world of sport than your seat in the corner of the Crucible as your opponent wins the World Championship while you're sat on your arse. If you lose the Wimbledon final you do it by running and stretching for a ball, if you lose the World Cup final you do it while running about or trying to block a shot or save a penalty. But in snooker there is none of that. You're stuck there, in the middle of a theatre as your opponent inches his way to the trophy and there's not a single thing in the world you can do about it.

When I sat back in my chair I just felt empty. I just wanted to get out of there. Hendry is an amazing competitor and a true champion but, for fuck's sake, I was going to have to stand up and say a few nice words about him again. I was going to have to shake David Vine's hand again and pretend I couldn't hear the sadness in his voice. On the telly, Dennis Taylor said he could've wept for me. That's a bit strong – it's only a game – but at that moment in time, my stomach was in my shoes and I just wanted to get out of there.

I'm not an emotional man so I was never going to burst into tears or anything like that but I was obviously devastated to have got so close once again. But that's sport isn't it? If I'd have made that black, what's to say there wasn't another one I would've missed at some point?

I always put it like this. When I got my MBE in 1999 I got it for services to sport and a bit of charity work. That day, I met nurses who worked 100 hours a week, injured servicemen, firemen who pull kids out of burning houses and loads of other people who actually do something that really matters. Proper heroes.

So to cry over a bit of sport is never going to be, and it never has been, me. After I'd lost I returned to the players' lounge where all my family were and I was easily the most relaxed of the lot. Mates were in there, pale with shock and my dad didn't look too much better either. "Don't worry," I said. "It's only a game." Of course part of me was eaten up when that black missed but I'd always played the game with that attitude and I wasn't going to change now. Nobody had died, had they?

•••••••

Those three famous defeats weren't the last I had seen of Hendry, of course.

I lost to him in the 1995 World Championship semi-final – he was fantastic in that match, including a 147 – and it was as if I'd simply forgotten how to beat him.

By the time the 1998 World Championship came around, my head was in pieces when it came to playing him. Sure, I'd put to bed those final losses but I just couldn't seem to get hold of him at all.

I lost to Hendry in 14 straight matches ranging from Thailand Open defeats to losses at the Irish Masters, the Masters and even the Premier League. It just felt like my game had gone and wouldn't be coming back and I needed to do something about it.

As the 1998 World Championship approached, I did an interview with a newspaper about my troubles and I eventually got contacted by this company called Advanced and they said they could help me. "Jimmy, we can give you some tips and hints on how to beat Hendry," they said. "Let's set up a meeting and talk about what we can do."

This company was run by two geezers called Andrew and Michael who were really determined to help me out. We met up in Surrey and they were just so, so positive and convinced me that Hendry was just another player and that I had the tools to beat him.

I got to that meeting and thought they might be a pair of nutters like you see on the telly shopping channels, just feeding you shit to con you into getting involved. But they soon had me believing what they were saying. They worked with loads of golfers, millionaire businessmen and big companies and they tried to instil confidence and self-belief into people who'd taken a knock.

I was comfortable with not having won the World Championship and it genuinely wasn't keeping me awake at night but, still, you're not going to come runner-up six times at anything and pretend you're totally 100 per cent okay with it are you?

The guys spent loads of time with me, trying to get to the bottom of what makes me tick and although they thought I wasn't taking it seriously, I was on board and picking up everything they were on about.

Someone like me, who didn't bother going to school much and learned most of their skills on the streets and in rough pubs and bars, can pick up more information verbally that most people can when they write it down.

Andrew and Michael kept telling me they were worried that I wasn't making notes or really showing much interest but what they didn't take on board was the fact I'd always lived like this and that I was listening and understanding and – most importantly – believing every word.

To make matters worse, by 1998 I wasn't a guaranteed pick for Sheffield. My game had dipped so much that I'd dropped out of the top 16 and I had to qualify in Telford first.

This was the last thing I needed but it had to be done. I faced Bradley Jones, a lad from Croydon, in the qualifiers and managed to beat him 10-5. At one stage there was nothing in it but in the end my experience paid off and I got through.

I was so thrilled to be back at the World Championship – Sheffield felt like home for those 17 days and even though the Crucible obviously carried some bad memories, I loved the thrill of the crowd and the limelight and I wanted to prove I was still among the world's best.

Beating Bradley did wonders for my confidence and the guys from Advance were also working hard with me.

"Jimmy, you need to improve your body language and your manner," they'd say. "We want you to sit like a champion and behave like a champion because you can win this, you can do this." They were just full of good vibes and it definitely had a positive effect.

On the day the draw for the first round was made, Andrew and Michael travelled to my house in Surrey to watch it with me. The draw came out just the week before the tournament and we were all sat in my front room, watching Grandstand, waiting to see who I'd play.

"And Stephen Hendry will play... Jimmy White."

Fuck me. Not him again.

Life was different now, though, thanks to the boys from Advanced. Straight after the draw, the BBC interviewed Hendry and he said something like "I've got a good record against Jimmy in Sheffield and I look forward to the match."

As soon as he said that, Andrew and Michael put their cups of tea down, both looked at me and said, "He's scared of you. Why else would he try and remind everyone that he's a winner at Sheffield when he's the champion. Honestly Jimmy, he doesn't fancy this."

I don't know if that was a tactic or bullshit but they continued to tell me that I had the beating of Hendry.

Turns out they were right.

The media had a field day about the draw and many papers predicted that Hendry would 'PILE MORE CRUCIBLE HEARTBREAK ONTO THE WHIRLWIND'.

This was the new Whirlwind he was dealing with – but even I couldn't believe what happened.

I was nervous going into the match because I wanted to do myself justice and give my fans something to sing about. I'd been supported so well and so vocally for so long and I didn't think my supporters could cope with another Crucible loss to Hendry.

I'd have loved to have been playing him at a later stage of the tournament but I had to accept my ranking had slipped, and yet the minute I walked into the Crucible I knew instantly that it still felt special and that my fans were probably louder and more supportive than ever.

And just as Parrott couldn't put a foot wrong against me in 1991, I couldn't against Hendry in that first session. I opened with a century break which really put down a marker and it just kept getting better. 1-0. 2-0. 3-0. 4-0. 5-0. 6-0. 7-0. It was fucking crazy. I ended the session 7-1 up, it was sensational stuff and I couldn't have been happier.

Still though, old habits die hard and all that.

You would've thought by now, considering I had 17 years of experience at the Crucible, that I'd have gone for a cocoa and a hot water bottle that night, but no.

I ended up in Josephine's nightclub with John Virgo instead. The place had quite a few in. People were coming up to me and congratulating me for doing so well that day and I was buzzing. Me and JV just kept looking at each other and were laughing our heads off at the way things were going. I was 7-1 up against the world champion for fuck's sake! Happy days. We had a few more drinks to unwind until JV suddenly turned to me and said, "Jimmy, mate, please go to bed, don't mess this one up."

"John I'm miles ahead, God couldn't beat me," I said. "Have another drink."

But the message got through and I behaved myself, sneaking into bed closer to midnight than dawn, which was a massive improvement for me.

In the morning, it went 8-2... then 8-3... then 8-4 and I was thinking 'Here we go again', but I turned it around and finally won 10-4. The crowd went absolutely crazy and Hendry, because he is class, was the first one over to me to shake my hand. "Well played mate," he said. "You deserved that."

It's moments like that which stand snooker apart from most sports and also why I've got 100 per cent respect for Hendry. He probably went on holiday for a fortnight and then came back and got back into it – that was just him, a born winner.

I was completely thrilled because it hadn't been a fluke. I played good aggressive snooker but I didn't take any stupid chances. I remained focused and it was such a relief in a way to realise that I could still play the way I wanted to and win. I didn't force it, I just got the job done.

That night, somebody mentioned that my victory had come exactly a decade after my first Crucible match, and only other win, against Hendry.

Time of my life: There were some talented players and real characters in the '80s and '90s. Here I am in another airport departure lounge with Cliff Thorburn, Steve Davis, Willie Thorne, Higgins and Tony Knowles. Inset right: Kirk Stevens in that famous cream suit

It takes two: Unstoppable on the table, unpredictable off it. Me and Higgins in 1990

Lonely sport: There's no hiding place in snooker when you're losing. You just have to sit there and take it. Here I am watching Hendry clear up in the 1993 World Championship final

He's beginning to annoy me... This is 1994 and the World Championship trophy is so near yet so far away

Getting my own back: Stephen was the ultimate gentleman when I knocked him out in the first round of the World Championship in 1998. Dad was so delighted he even gave me a hug!

Games room: Pictured with my family in the snooker room in my house in Oxshott, Surrey. I don't know if Splinter is under the table!

Courting attention: Enjoying a laugh during a visit to Wimbledon with Ronnie Wood in '92. Ronnie once brought John McEnroe round for a night

Feeling the heat: Stuck in my chair watching Stephen Hendry complete a 147 at the World Championships in 1995. It was a miracle I made it to the semi-final considering what I had to deal with that year

A star is bo
I knew as s
as I first sa
him that Ro
O'Sullivan w
special tale

At Her Majesty's service: Me and Tony Adams picking up our MBEs. It was a proud day – even if I didn't do as I was told

New generation: I made it to the quarter-finals of the World Championship in 2000 where I came up against Matthew Stevens

In the shadows: Backstage, waiting to play at the 2002 World Championships. The Crucible is such a special place, it holds so many memories

Long shot: At the table against Stephen Lee in the 2003 World Championship. I can't get my head around what happened to his career

On the brown ball: When I was first asked to change my name to Jimmy Brown I refused – then I thought why not – snooker needs a bit of fun!

Too young, too soon: Paul Hunter was a great friend, a fantastic snooker player and one of the game's real characters. I've no doubt he'd have won the World Championship. Unfortunately cancer took him, aged just 27

Heartbreak: The snooker world was shattered by Paul's death and we all still miss him. I just couldn't hold back the tears at his funeral

Good times: With the late, great Peter Cook and Rod Stewart on our big day out at the football. My old manager Alan Stockton and Ronnie Wood also joined in the fun.
Below (from left): Dad, Peewee, brother Tony and me at The Albert Arms pub in Esher

Man in the spotlight: Preparing for a television interview during the 2007 tournament in Sheffield. It should always be the home of the World Championship

Irish hero: With former world champion Ken Doherty in Dublin in 2006. Above: Ken on one of our hilarious nights out in China

Prize guy: Presenting the Unsung Hero award with Dame Rebecca Adlington at the BBC Sports Personality Awards and (above, right) waving to fans at the Masters

Jail break: Being welcomed inside Mountjoy Prison...but only for an exhibition match I was invited to play in 2007!

NO REGRETS

Sure, it would've been lovely to have won some of the matches that fell in between those two but that is sport, and life.

People ask does it bother me that I'm known as a six-times runner up or *'The Greatest Player Never To Win The World Championship'* and I can look them in the eye and say that it doesn't bother me in the slightest. Getting to any final is a feat and to do it six times is an incredible effort.

I also feel that I can't really answer that question because I'm not finished either. I'm 52 years of age and although a realist – which I am as well – would say that my best days are gone and that I'll never win it, now and again I play some nights and it still feels like the easiest and most natural game in the world. I know it's still there.

So, no I don't regret the nights out or the losses to Hendry. It was a hell of a ride and a hell of a lot of fun at the same time.

Hendry remained an incredible competitor and eventually ended up with seven World Championship titles, winning his last one by defeating Mark Williams 18-11 in 1999. That was his last really major win. He lost one more World Championship final plus a couple of Masters finals.

The loss of form, stature and silverware started to affect him and Hendry was never going to be one of those players who was happy to keep playing for the love of the game.

Unlike me or Davis, who'll still be pushing a cue around until we're 80, Hendry was interested in winning and winning only. I play because I absolutely adore everything about it and that has kept me going over some pretty bleak years, but as soon as Hendry's high standards dropped, he was out of there.

He lost to Stephen Maguire a couple of years ago at Sheffield and he decided that he'd had enough. I think the public were shocked by his decision because he is still a young bloke and on his day he can still beat anyone and could still play to a very high level.

But Hendry is Hendry – only the very best will do and I respect him for that. He earned his money, he got all the glory and silverware he deserved and when he recognised that he was past his best, he decided to walk away and do some commentary gigs and lots of work in China.

He's a good lad and I'm thrilled for him. I see him at the Snooker Legends tours and he seems to be really happy, especially about not playing on the professional tour any more.

Why should he be any other way? He's won seven World Championships, he's remembered as one of the greatest players of all time and he's got nothing to prove to anyone.

8

Dark Days

"Come here boy, come here," I shout after Splinter as he races around Streatham Common. *It's Christmas Day and I'm at my lowest ebb. Me and Maureen have split up again and I'm spending the day in a flat in Streatham – one of the 20 I must've furnished over the last 15 years. The Queen's Speech is on, families up and down the country are enjoying themselves, opening presents, sharing the day with each other – just as it should be – and the highlight of my day is taking the dog for a walk, on my own. My life feels like a fucking joke.*

I have four kids, a big house and I'm one of the world's most popular snooker players and yet here I am with a two-day hangover following a three-day coke and vodka binge.

I miss my kids and I've got to sort myself out.

It was spending Christmas, 1994, on my own in that flat that convinced me to finally try and kick my coke habit. The crack problem had disappeared a long time ago but coke was still a big part of my life – apart from when we played at tournaments.

Like I say, I'd evaded the testers for years, mainly by being a step ahead, well prepared and absolutely terrified of getting caught out. It wasn't really the game's fault and snooker did its best to catch rogues but you just had to time it right. Weed used to take longer to get out of the system and there was this old wives' tale that used to go around about orange juice cleaning it out of your system nice and quickly. I didn't know if it was true or not but I used to down litre after litre of the stuff coming up to a tournament.

Put it like this, if Lance Armstrong can get away with everything he did without a positive test, simply by making sure he timed his drugs at the right time, then a snooker player tested every now and then had no trouble. Half the time back then, just walking into the test room should've set alarm bells ringing but I suppose I just got really lucky.

I didn't miss coke or weed at major tournaments because I could get as much fun from just getting pissed and playing poker until the early hours and, up to now, they've not designed a test for that. Maybe they should've done – they'd certainly have found me bang to rights on that score.

I was very lucky to get away with it for so long and I knew that wouldn't last forever but my main motivation to get clean was simply the fact I fucking despised cocaine with a passion I can't begin to describe.

I've said elsewhere that it ruined my game and I mean it but now was the time to forget that and get my game back to where it should be. Unlike the crack, which I gave up in one horrendous fortnight of cold turkey, I weaned myself off cocaine gradually, over a period of quite a few years. It went from being every day to once a week then once a fortnight until you finally realise how much you hate The Devil's Dandruff.

It's a life destroyer.

I'd go six months without any then go on three-day benders, going mad, before trying to get back on the straight and narrow. I'm not mentioning names but I've met plenty of sportsmen and rock'n'rollers who've struggled with it and they're all the same. They hate it like I do. You never know, when I'm retired I might have the odd spliff if I'm on the beach somewhere but I'd never, ever do cocaine again.

And that Christmas of 1994 had been the turning point. I knew that I needed to get my self-respect and some self-control back, and I looked at 1995 as a fresh beginning and a new start, for me and, hopefully, the family as well.

If I was making a new start, I decided that I needed a new look. For a couple of seasons by now, I'd noticed the bald spot on top of my head getting a little bigger, month by month, year by year. I'd see myself on the telly and it started bothering me – a classic case of stupidity and vanity if ever there was one.

Back then, people were having transplants left, right and centre and it seemed to make sense.

I discussed it with Maureen – when we were back together – and she wasn't very happy. "Jimmy, if you were having a brain tumour removed then that's something different," she told me. "But having your head cut open because of a bald spot is crazy."

Little did I know how right she was.

I decided to go ahead with it anyway so I went to this place in the West Midlands for the operation, which was described as being like a 'facelift for your scalp'. They cut out a bit of my scalp, pulled everything up as tight as they could around that gap, let it heal and then did it again.

It was an absolute nightmare.

The surgeons who did it were butchers and shouldn't have been anywhere near an operating theatre. When I came out of hospital I looked like I'd been in a car crash. I had two enormous black eyes and my chin was drooping that much it was touching my chest.

The operation gave me the worst headaches I've ever had as well. They would last for days at a time and I couldn't get out of bed, never mind practise, so my snooker really took a turn for the worse. I was useless, I couldn't sleep because of the pain, my face looked dreadful and it sent me into a bit of a depression. Nothing seemed to be going for me and I was really upset and disappointed.

I wear a weave now and that's because I have a really bad scar on top of my head. It's that deep and wide that you can roll a penny down it easily. I eventually settled with the company involved out of court, which was something I suppose. However, the pain the operation caused – and the fact my snooker was so badly affected – pissed me off then and it pisses me off now. I had to pull out of the European Open in Belgium because of the agony I was in and that cost me valuable ranking points and potential prize money. Instead of a fresh start, this was a sign of things to come.

Yet for all my anger about that, the troubles with my scalp were soon put in perspective as I was about to enter the blackest, darkest, most painful period of my entire life – a time I wouldn't wish on anybody.

And I was about to get the harshest possible reminder that what happens on a snooker table doesn't really matter, that it was only a sport, it was only a game, it wasn't life or death...

•••••••

Everyone has their heroes in life.

People like Muhammad Ali, John McEnroe and Alex Higgins have been among my biggest role models because of their style, their presence and the way they played their sports. And, closer to home, my eldest brother Martin was my hero as well.

I was the baby of the family and Martin was a good 20 years older than me and, as a result, he'd always looked out for me. You couldn't have dreamt of a better brother. As a kid, mum used to send him into Zan's to kick me out and drag me home but, don't forget, it was Martin who first let me play with him on a table and he played a big part in my early snooker career, even if he did try and actually stop it at one point.

For my 12th birthday he came up to me with a simple offer. "Jimmy, what do you want, a bike or a snooker cue?"

Mum and dad thought I should be outside a bit more, rather than clogging my lungs up in a smoky snooker hall with Tony Meo. I opted for the bike because then I got the best of both worlds; I had my own set of wheels plus I could always nip into Zan's and use anyone's cue when they weren't in there. Most of the time I borrowed the cue of a bloke called John Nielsen who had no idea I'd been using it until I told him about 20 years later.

Anyway, I got my brand new racing bike from Martin and I was as proud as anything. I could now race around Tooting as one of the bike boys but before I could do that, I fancied a quick frame in Zan's. I padlocked the bike up outside the front door, went inside and before you know it, one quick frame had become about 15. I finally left in the early hours and walked outside to see my bike's padlock on the floor, broken, with my bike nowhere to be seen.

That was the end of my riding days there and then! I stuck to Zan's after that and isn't it strange how you get to crossroads in your life without even knowing it?

In early 1995, we were dealt some devastating news. Martin had got lung cancer. I just couldn't get my head around it. I simply couldn't process the idea that my big, tough, fantastic brother could have a shitty thing like cancer. To be honest, I'm still in shock now and it's been almost 20 years.

I'll never forget where I was when the thought of him actually dying first took hold; when it went from being a 'no' to a 'maybe'. We were all in The White Lion in Wimbledon at my Uncle Winky's funeral. All the family were sat about, suited up and sharing stories about what a character Uncle Winky had been. He was one of my dad's four brothers, he took no shit off anybody and was a fantastic man.

As we were having a few drinks and toasting his life, my brother Tommy turned to me and my other brother, Tony, and told us what he thought about Martin's health.

"Look at him," he said. "I don't think he's going to make it. I think he's going to die." Martin had been having a lot of treatment and was very thin and frail. He was being helped to the toilet when Tommy gave us his opinion and as we looked across at him, his suit just hung from his frame. Before that moment, I'd never for a second thought he wouldn't pull through. Cancer doesn't care though does it? It doesn't look into a person's character before deciding whether they will live or die. It just does what it wants and takes who it wants.

I suppose Tommy's words cut through the denial I was in and finally hit home.

He was right as well. Martin died a month later.

We were more devastated than I will ever be able to tell you. He was a very smart guy, very dashing and he lived his life exactly as he wanted to. Martin's favourite working method was to get his head down for three or four weeks and then he'd take a week off to go to the races, he loved the track at Wimbledon and he loved life, full stop.

The grief of him passing away was like nothing I've ever experienced before. Those of you reading this who've lost loved ones know what I mean. It's this blackness and this anger, especially because he was so young.

There was nothing we could do for him but we at least wanted to give him a send-off that he deserved. The night before the funeral we all crammed into The Jolly Gardeners on Garratt Lane for a drink, a game of cards and a farewell to our brother. All the family were there and we managed to put away £4,600 worth of booze.

We had a massive drink until about three in the morning but as we were leaving this pub, I didn't want the night to end so, properly pissed, I got my driver, Mick, and sister, Jackie, to walk to the funeral home where Martin was lying. Mick was a good bloke, he's dead now, and he used to run me around everywhere.

The funeral home was across the road from the pub and I couldn't stand it any longer.

"Mick, wait here a second," I said, and I was off to the funeral home's gate.

These massive gates were locked up with this big padlock and I kung-fu kicked it out of temper and it just opened, as easy as that. I was full of drink, full of anger and I was just gone in the head as it started to hit me that Martin was dead.

The chains around the padlock were obviously not actually locked up, they were just meant to look that way. I took that as a sign and walked through. Jackie came in after me, and I started looking for my brother in this funeral home. We walked around for a bit until I finally found him, our Martin.

Well, I looked at him and decided there and then that he looked like he could do with a drink so I got him out of his coffin and started to walk him back to the car.

He'd been dressed for the funeral but he didn't have his hat on. I found his hat, stuck it on his head, lifted him onto my shoulder and walked out with him.

"Jimmy, what are you doing?" Mick asked in shock.

He knew me well enough not to push it. I was beyond devastated and beyond furious that Martin was dead. Mick took one look at me and guessed there was no point trying to get me to put Martin back. Mick eventually helped me out and stuck Martin on the front seat of the car.

"Mick, take us to Tommy's house," I said, and off we set for my brother's house. Tommy had left the wake a few hours before. Him and Martin were very close. Tommy lived in Cheam which was a 10-mile drive and we knocked on the front door, with Martin propped up underneath my shoulder.

"Jim!" Tommy said when he saw us.

"What are you doing? What the fuck are you doing?"

"We're going to have a drink with Martin," I said. "We need a last drink with him."

And so that's what we did.

We plonked him down in the corner, talking to him, crying, laughing, sometimes hysterical with laughter, sometimes hysterical with anger, chatting shit, playing cards and saying our goodbyes. "The last Martin would want is us to be upset," I kept saying. "He'll be pissing himself laughing watching all this."

It was one of the strangest nights of my life.

I was completely gone emotionally and I thought I was losing it. I suppose I must've done a little bit because getting a body out of a funeral home is not exactly normal is it? But you do mad things in grief, I suppose.

We sat around with Martin for a couple of hours until it freaked Mick out. "I'm off Jimmy," he said. "I'm sorry mate but I can't cope with all this."

Mick upped and left and that meant we had a problem getting Martin back to the funeral parlour. Eventually Tommy's wife called a cab and me and Jackie prepared to take my older brother back. We propped Martin up between us, flagged down the cab outside and tried to get Martin in the back.

"Are you sure your friend is okay?" this cabbie asked me. "He doesn't look very well."

What do you say to that?

Me and Jackie just started laughing. "Don't you worry mate, he's just having a little sleep," I said. "He'll be fine in a bit."

We headed back to the funeral home with Martin 'sleeping' on my shoulder and when we got back, it was exactly as we left it. The gates were still wide open, the door was wide open – nothing had changed. We put him back where he should be, chained it all up and prepared to say goodbye the next day.

The funeral went as well as these things can, it was a lovely service and we said goodbye to Martin again, although in a church this time, not in the back of a London cab.

I thought nothing else of it until two weeks later when I got a knock on the front door and two coppers were stood there.

"Mr James White," they said. "We're here to arrest you for breaking and entering and removing a dead body without permission." I thought I was fucked but these two coppers then got around to digging me out of a hole.

"You didn't do it did you Mr White?" this one geezer said, shaking his head, making sure I understood where he was coming from. "There's no way you did it, is there Mr White? It's just a rumour isn't it?"

"I don't know what you're talking about," I told them, playing the game. "I didn't do anything."

That was all I heard of it because someone in the police must've realised it was an emotional time. I've had plenty of run-ins with the police but I've always respected them and tried to do benefit evenings for them and whatever else because I understand how hard their job is and after that little incident, my respect for them grew even stronger.

Martin was a beautiful, beautiful human being and it was a privilege to have had him as an older brother.

If you look on the left side of my chest, I don't have the name MARTIN tattooed on it, I have the name NITRAM, so that when I'm having a shave in the mirror in the morning, I can read his name, say hello and tell him I love him.

DARK DAYS

As if losing Martin wasn't bad enough, there was more heartache to come for our family soon after. Just a few months after
Martin had gone in October, 1995, Mum passed away.

Make no mistake, she died of a broken heart.

Mum brought up five kids – my dad was always working or he
liked to be out and about – and she did everything. She bathed
us, fed us and got us to school. That's how life was in those days.
Her passing, so close after Martin's totally, totally crushed us all.
You don't realise what your family means to you until you lose
people so close to you.

My mum was my best friend, she was like my sister. When I
was a kid, I used to go home and I'd think nothing of seeing
half-a-dozen women sat in the front room, rollers in their hair
and a fag on the go. These weren't coffee mornings either; these
women would be sat there slagging their husbands!

I adored my mum. She was the most beautiful person. If you
met her, then you always remembered her. She had problems
with her lungs in the end and lived with Jackie as it became
clear she wouldn't pull through. She went from looking like a
frail 70-year-old to a really old woman very quickly. Jackie was
the woman of the firm, so Mum went to her house for her
final days. In the end it was a blessing that she could go and
join Martin. To see mum and dad suffer and watch them going
through the pain they did when they lost their eldest son was
awful. Who wants to live longer than their own kids? It was too
dreadful for words.

We scattered Mum and Martin's ashes together at Sandown
racecourse. Martin used to love a gamble (it runs in the family
then...) and we sponsored a race, all got together and remembered the two of them in the best possible way.

The story of my nightmare year doesn't end there. In March, 1995, just as Martin was starting to go downhill, I'd been booked for an exhibition in Hong Kong. It went really well and it was a way of taking my mind off everything that was going on at home with my brother and Maureen.

That was until I jumped in the shower in the hotel afterwards and my blood ran cold. As I was washing myself, I found this little hard lump and thought 'This is a bit fucking strange'.

I knew something wasn't right.

I flew back home, went round to see Maureen and the girls and I still felt really uncomfortable. "I need to get this sorted out," I said. "I don't like this." I went to see my doctor, a fantastic bloke called Richard Draper and he agreed with me that something serious could be wrong with me.

Unless you've been in those shoes, the fear you feel when your doctor tells you something might be up, is just awful. My bottle totally went. You spend your time thinking about everything that can go wrong and that will go wrong. You can be told all the survival statistics in the world but when it's you, sat in that chair, all you can think about is dying.

Dr Draper instantly referred me to Ashtead Hospital to get it checked out properly. They didn't like the feel of it either so I was whisked off to the Royal Marsden Hospital where I had my left testicle cut out.

As it turns out, it was a good job I'd spotted the problem and gone straight to my doctors and I was lucky that he was male as well because I might not have said anything to a female doctor, which is just crazy but that's the way blokes can be. The surgeons found a form of cancer called Leydig which is a really unusual, vicious type, so I was very lucky. Another couple of months and I wouldn't have survived. I suppose they're the margins we all live by.

When I went down to surgery, I'd not told Maureen because I didn't want her worrying too much but it got to the point where I could hardly hide it from her any longer. She was my wife and the mother to my kids and although we were having trouble in our relationship, she deserved to know. She understandably went mad at me and I couldn't blame her for that.

About a week after my operation, I played in the British Open qualifiers and managed to beat Mark Flowerdew. It was a great win under the circumstances, including a break of 141, and I was still full of painkillers and stitches. I then beat Steve James in the second round and lasted until the last 16 before I was beaten by Mick Price, simply unable to carry on playing in so much pain.

Finally though, the physical pain passed and I tried to get my life back on track. I was no angel but I knew that snooker was the one thing I was still capable of doing, the one thing that would take my mind off Martin, Mum and my own brush with cancer. A lot of the things I've done in my life I can only blame the guy who stares back at me in the mirror for, but at least with the cancer I knew that it wasn't my fault; there was nothing I could've done to prevent it – I was just a lucky bastard to have spotted that lump when I did.

Trying to get back into the groove again was tough. It just felt as if everything had come down on top of me at once. Plus, although the cancer scare should have been a wake-up call for me to change my entire lifestyle, I still wanted to be out all the time and if you look at my results from around those years, you can see that my game was on the wane.

The regular finals became semi-finals, the semis had become only quarters and so on.

At the Crucible in 1995, I managed to get to the semi-finals, as I've said, and that alone was a bit of a miracle considering all the other shit I was trying to deal with.

I was up against Hendry again and he beat me, just for a change, although the match is best remembered for his 147 in the 12th frame.

I'd not done enough to get the cue-ball onto the baulk cushion with a safety shot, he potted a great long red and didn't really look back, splitting the pack beautifully and looking calm and controlled as the points totted up.

It was Kirk Stevens all over again as far as I was concerned. Until he got to 74 I was thinking, 'the frame is still open' and then when he got there, nobody was backing him more than I was, just as it should be. Tony Drago had been desperate for me to do it in 1992 and I was desperate for Hendry.

As he got closer, the pink and blue ended up virtually touching and he also lost position on the green. Hendry was a fantastic long-potter and he managed to pot the blue and regain position on the pink, but he was then left in real trouble on the black. It was no trouble to Mr Calm himself and he rolled it in to join me and Cliff Thorburn as only the third man to hit a Crucible maximum.

"Fantastic mate," I said to Hendry as I left my chair to congratulate him. Welcome to the club.

The 1995/96 season was no better and the furthest I got was the quarter-final of the Masters, where Hendry – him again – thrashed me in the quarter-finals.

I faced Peter Ebdon in the last 16 in Sheffield that season and

DARK DAYS

we had a right tussle, the match never looking like it belonged to anyone and he finally crawled over the line, 13-12, after a really strong battle.

Again, the hopes of winning at the Crucible were dashed by a player in the form of his life (he eventually lost in the final).

The statistics didn't lie though.

Had The Whirlwind blown itself out?

9

Changes

I'm playing Anthony Hamilton in the World Championship. I'm winning at the mid-session interval and although I've taken a 3-1 lead I just feel like I can't get going. I go to use the gents at the Crucible, which is only a tiny little place with a urinal and a cubicle. A mate comes in to see me and I let him know my thoughts. "I'm not feeling good here mate," I tell him. "My action doesn't feel right and Hamilton is giving me all sorts of grief."

I end up losing the match 10-9 after Hamilton fights back from 5-2 down and then 8-4 down to squeeze past me.

A few years later, Hamilton walks up to me and can't stop grinning. "Jimmy, I've got to get something off my chest," he starts.

CHANGES

"Remember when we played in 1997? Well I thought you were potting like a dream and I didn't think I stood a chance."

"Go on," I tell him. *"Finish the story."*

"Well," he says. *"I thought I was gone and couldn't wait for the interval so I could sort my head out. Then all of a sudden I got this massive confidence boost from nowhere."*

"Oh yeah, who helped you out then?" I ask him.

"You did," he grins. *"While you were at the urinal moaning about being shit, I was in the cubicle!"*

Turns out we'd both been caught short. And I'd been caught out.

The day I faced Hamilton was May 2, 1997.

Happy birthday Jimmy.

By the time I was giving away all my secrets in that toilet, my inconsistency seemed endless, I couldn't do much to stop it and things got so bad with Maureen that we'd finally decided to split up, for good.

Well, almost.

We had argument after argument – never in front of the girls though – and in the end we used to leave our marriage certificate at the solicitors so we both knew where it was when we went through yet another round of divorce talks.

We fought like cat and dog, always had done, always would do, because we were too alike. The entire 20 years of our relationship was just a rollercoaster – big highs, massive lows and nothing in between. I was a rogue, always out with my mates and she rightly resented that and got frustrated at my behaviour. When I knew I'd been gone for 12 hours, I thought nothing of making it a day or three because I knew there was an argument waiting for me when I got back to the house and who needs that?

Talking of cats and dogs, no matter how bad it got between me and Maureen, nothing was as bad as what happened to another member of our family around this time.

Splinter was a beautiful dog. The kids loved him. But after they'd been out with him one morning, he disappeared and wasn't to be found anywhere. Before long, Ashleigh, Georgia and Breeze were crying all day, every day, asking why I couldn't find their beloved pet.

For one reason or another – I'll get to that – I already had some posters of Splinter made up, so I started plastering them on every lamppost in the south of England. I also went to the police station in Cobham and reported Splinter missing – that's how The Times found out and put the story on the front page. The police said there wasn't much they could do but as I prepared to walk out of the station – and as I'm wondering how to break it to the girls that Splinter was no more – this little boy walked past me and I overheard him saying that he'd lost his jacket at the fair and could the police get in touch with the owners for him.

"There's been a fair around here has there?" I asked this copper, knowing straightaway what had probably happened to Splinter.

I made a few enquries around Cobham and Oxshott and, sure enough, quite a few dogs had gone missing in the area. I rang some gypsy friends of mine and put a £300 reward out for the dog and that seemed to do the trick.

The next day I got a phone call with the voice at the other end telling me he knew where Splinter was.

CHANGES

"I've got your dog, meet me at Epsom clock tower at midnight. Come on your own."

I wasn't that worried about it, so I pocketed the £300 and made my way to Epsom to get Splinter back. At a minute to midnight, a white van came screeching around the bend and came to a stop on the other side of the road. All of a sudden, this figure came from out of the shadows and I knew it was time to do business. "Jimmy White," this voice said, and as I walked out in front of him, I realised I knew him. "Johnny Francome," I said. He was a bare-knuckle boxer and we had some mutual friends.

"Jimmy, I didn't know it was your dog," he said. He was as hard as fucking nails so I can hardly claim he was quivering in his boots. "I'm getting £150 for bringing the dog back," he said.

I wasn't bothered by any of that and just wanted Splinter.

"I don't care Johnny," I said. "Take the £300, just give me the dog." With that, he gave a sign to his mates to open the door of the van, Splinter was bundled out and as they drove off, the dog – as divvy as he was – tried to jump back in the thing while it was moving!

"Splinter, come here," I was shouting, laughing my head off at this stupid dog and wondering what I was doing in Epsom at midnight.

The kids woke up for school the next morning and it was like 10 Christmases all at once, even if the dog had tried to mess up their nice surprise.

Anyway, the reason I'd had the 'dogknapped' posters all ready to go was because in our home in Oxshott, there was a separate building which I used as my own snooker room.

It was the perfect place to practise because it got me away from the house. There was a well stocked bar, so you could have a drink as you played, or enjoy a couple when some mates came round.

One day, Splinter was nowhere to be seen. I didn't know where he'd gone and I started searching high and low for him. He wasn't in the garage or the main house or the garden; he wasn't in Oxshott or the woods nearby or anywhere. This dog had gone properly AWOL.

Three days went past and I had these posters made to try and get some leads (excuse the pun...). By now I'm frantic, the girls are crying their eyes out, Maureen's giving me grief for not being able to find him and it's not looking good.

My mind was all over the place but while all this was going on, I thought I better get some practice, so I let myself into the snooker building where I got the shock of my life.

Put it like this, I could smell Splinter before I could see him.

It turns out that one of my mates had left half an ounce of weed on the bar by mistake. He'd had a few drinks one day and forgot to take it with him.

Splinter has obviously jumped up, thought it was chocolate and wolfed this hash down in no time at all.

Fast forward three days and there was Splinter spreadeagled under the snooker table still stoned out of his tiny little mind.

There were piles of dog shit everywhere. It was a festival of dog shit. Up the walls. Under the table. Behind the bar. It was shit galore, as far as the eye could see.

Even though he was covered in it, I was so relieved to see him that I got down on my hands and knees and starting cuddling him. He looked up at me and pinned his ears back as if to

CHANGES

say 'What the fuck's happened to me?' I took him upstairs, showered him and made sure we never left him with a block of weed again! Poor Splinter, dazed and confused by life. I knew the feeling.

●●●●●●●

When it comes to me and Maureen, what I don't want to do is portray her as some weakling woman, too scared and shy to stand up for herself.

Believe me, she was from my part of London and she would think nothing of pulling back and giving me a right-hander when we got into an argument.

From day one of us going out, there had been strife, including the time when she smashed my cue up.

A player's cue is the most precious thing he owns and when something goes wrong with it, you're left devastated. I've had mine forever and I'd be gutted if it got damaged. When I used to play like lightning, I'd spin the cue in my hand to feel for the grain and that helped me slow down – one of my biggest problems – because it gave me an extra five seconds of thinking time.

When we were just kids, me and Lenny Cain had been out for about three days on the trot and Maureen wasn't happy. She knew exactly how to get her own back. At the time, I was playing at a snooker club in Wandsworth all the time so she went down there and sweet-talked the barman into giving her my cue.

And then she stamped up and down on it.

By the time I got to the club, the owner was white-faced and couldn't believe what had happened. "Jimmy, I thought she was serious," he said. "Maureen said you needed your cue and I gave it to her and she smashed it to bits." What could I do but laugh? Maureen had strength then and she had strength now, telling me to fuck off when I deserved to be told.

The worst bust-up we ever had ended with her getting a black eye, something I'm ashamed to say happened and something I need to apologise for.

I'd been out all week drinking with Peewee and Maureen had had enough (again) and changed the locks. I managed to break a window in the back of the house, still drunk, and crawled upstairs to bed where I passed out. About an hour later, Maureen and a friend of hers came back, spotted the broken window and called the police, thinking we'd been burgled.

Two coppers came and inspected the property and couldn't find any thieves. What they did find was a pissed-up professional snooker player, lying fully clothed in bed, fast asleep.

Maureen was red-faced and couldn't see the funny side of it at all – the coppers were pissing themselves – and when they left we got into a terrible scrape. She used to go for me and then when I defended myself we both got hurt – not that that's an excuse. Anyone who knows me knows that I'm not like that. In all the years of going into moody pubs and snooker clubs, I've never been an aggressive person – it's just not in my nature.

The next day, it kicked off again. It all started when the phone went.

"Hi, is that Jimmy White, it's GMTV here. We've heard there's been an altercation between you and your wife."

Shit. What now?

"Erm, no, she is fine," I told them.

CHANGES

"Okay Jimmy," this reporter said. "If she's fine, do you mind us coming to your house to interview you both about these hurtful and false allegations?"

"Yes, pop round any time you want," I bluffed. "The kettle will be on."

I thought I'd done a good enough job of shutting the story up but the next day, GMTV came good on their side of the bargain.

The door went and a reporter was stood on the step.

"Hi Jimmy, is Maureen in?" Thankfully, Maureen had heard what was going on upstairs, covered the black eye up with some make up and we put on an Oscar-winning performance for the cameras.

As you can imagine, none of this is what you can class as expert preparation for snooker tournaments and the more shit I had to deal with – and the more shit I got in – equalled less practice time, which then had a bad effect on how I was performing.

It wasn't always my fault though as the blame for some distractions – as annoying as they were – lay at the feet of others.

Like going bankrupt for a start.

As every bookie in the known universe will tell you, I've always been terrible with money because I've had it from such an early age and I've had it so easily that it's never really meant that much to me.

That is a great attitude to have in a lot of ways because it means you can enjoy life and share your happiness and good times with your loved ones.

However, when it leads you to bankruptcy then that is a different matter altogether.

I ain't going to get trapped into a court case now, all these years on, about who was to blame or what happened but I'll just say I'd not been advised well over the years and I also lost a fortune when Lloyd's crashed.

To cut a long story short, I'd been left with debts of £170,000, I'd been threatened with all sorts of court summons' – which went in the bin most of the time – and I was left with few other options but to go bankrupt and start again.

I knew the press would have a field day and would try and paint me as 'ruined' and 'finished' but it didn't bother me what they thought. I genuinely didn't give a shit what people were whispering about me behind my back – life's too short to worry about any of that. The only slight concern I'd had was that it might give opponents the edge if they thought I was feeling upset about it all.

I was fortunate in that I had a mate who stood all my living costs for me for a while. I had three girls all going to private schools, so he picked up the tab for that and he also gave me a credit card I could use to keep myself afloat. I was – and will always be – massively grateful for that because it dug me out of a hole. It didn't take me too long to pay him back. I was still a huge draw for exhibitions so I quickly earned the cash I owed him.

The bankruptcy never once kept me awake. A lifetime of gambling had taught me that you're either up or down and that neither will last that long. I just had to dust myself down and get on with trying to focus on playing.

And besides, I soon had something else to worry about as yet another shitstorm appeared on the horizon.

I was sat in my house one day when the phone went.

CHANGES

"Mr White, it's The News of the World here. We have pictures of you doing coke with a girl and we want a comment from you. This will be featured in the newspaper on Sunday."

By now I was only taking cocaine very occasionally, about once a month, but I had a woman on the go as well and my driver at the time obviously knew all my secrets. He was a biggish bloke who worked in a furniture shop and even though I paid him well, what happens is that some people see your lifestyle and decide they want some of it.

Lo and behold, I'm sat in my house and the phone goes. Oh fuck. I put two and two together and realised that this driver was the only bloke who knew my movements and who knew the bird involved. This was a Friday afternoon – reporters always leave it as late as possible to ask you for a quote so that you can't get your lawyers involved – so I was now running around London trying to find this bloke who'd stitched me up.

I called every mate I knew and I called in every favour I could to try and find him and ask him what the fuck had been going on.

I couldn't get hold of him on the phone, he wasn't at his mum's or his usual pubs and I knew I was in real trouble.

I barely slept that night as The News of the World had given me until 2pm on the Saturday to respond when, all of a sudden, I got a phone call from my friend Kevin Kelly in Jersey.

"Jimmy," he said. "Your mate is in my club."

The News of the World had given him £500 to hide for a bit and of all the places in all the world, where does he go? Kevin's club in Jersey. What are the chances of that? Fuck knows what odds a bookie would give you, and even then it wouldn't be worth a punt. Even Higgins would avoid that bet...

Kevin didn't have a clue who he was but my driver couldn't resist shooting his mouth off at the bar and he told all the punters in there that he was a big mate of mine.

In the meantime, I'd found out some information about him that might just save my arse and keep my name off the front pages.

When I'd been looking for him, a few mates told me that he was wanted by the police because he'd sold a pub in Croydon called The Two Brewers to some old woman. The problem was that he didn't even own the pub so the police were looking for him and wanted to nick him for that. This was my one chance to sort this shit out.

"Kev, you've got to keep him in your club and phone the police," I told him.

Kevin called the police, without letting my driver know that he knew me and he finally got nicked for stitching this old woman up over the boozer.

I couldn't get on the phone to The News of the World quick enough. "You can't run a story based on the rumours of a fugitive and a thief," I told them. "He's hardly a credible witness is he? And, anyway, it's all bullshit."

The paper had no choice but to pull the story and I got away with it. But talk about fucking pressure. At about midnight I told Maureen I was going out for a drive, I jumped in my car and raced to the nearest petrol station, waiting for the papers to be delivered.

I was shitting myself when I got my hands on a copy but I flicked through the pages as fast as I could, desperately praying my mug wouldn't be staring back up at me and, thank fuck, The News of the World had got the message and there was no coke story, no girl story, nothing. It does go to show you, though, that this was the kind of off-table crap and stress I was under – almost all of it my own doing.

•••••••

If I'd thought that going bankrupt, almost appearing on the front of The News of the World and having my stupid dog nicked wasn't enough to handle, there was no surprise bigger than when I went away to play an exhibition in Bahrain.

My professional game was struggling but I could still name my price when it came to putting on small exhibitions anywhere in the world. Bahrain wouldn't have been the first place on my wish-list but I needed to raise some cash after the bankruptcy so off I went along with the four girls and also Maureen.

Even though we'd split up, we still wanted family holidays with the girls so they felt comfortable with what had happened between the two of us. The exhibition went fine, the girls enjoyed the adventure and before you know it, four kids was about to become five!

That sums me and Maureen up really.

We were at each other's throats but then madly in love the next minute. One night, after putting the girls to bed, we had a bottle of wine too many and she was pregnant again. We were both totally stunned – and totally delighted.

If nothing else, it proves to any blokes reading this that testicular cancer doesn't mean you can't go on to have kids.

I'd always loved the girls to bits – and I always will do – but when me and Maureen found out that we were having a boy this time, I was completely ecstatic. My own son. It was almost too much to believe and the news was just what I needed to hear after a couple of really tough years. It also brought me and Maureen back together, at least for a while, and we really tried to make a big go of it. First, though, we had to knock back a bit of press activity – especially when they heard what we wanted to call our boy.

I was born in 1962 and through the years, every time I'd been to Hong Kong I'd been told that I was born in the Year of the Tiger. Because 1998 also happened to be the Year of the Tiger, I wanted Tiger to be his name.

That would've been fine, apart from a certain American golfer who was kicking everyone's arse back then. The press rang me up one day and asked me why I was naming my son after Tiger Woods! In the end, we decided to call him Tommy Tiger – Tommy after my dad.

Just as I'd marked the end of Martin's life with a tattoo, I marked the start of Tommy's with one as well. I went over to Jersey for an exhibition and asked for a Tiger to be inked onto my chest. When I'd had Martin's name tattooed, it didn't hurt at all because I was emotionally gone at the time but when I got the tiger tattoo, you've never heard screaming like it. I begged the bloke to stop so I could catch my breath. I cried like a little girl, it hurt that much. I was in fucking shreds. Only the champagne we had afterwards numbed the pain a bit.

Tommy's birth changed me because I wanted to be around a bit more while he grew up. When me and Maureen had Lauren, all those years ago, we were just kids ourselves and almost 20 years of travelling on the snooker circuit, plus all the other chaos, meant that I'd not been around enough to see the girls growing up. Sure, I was a good dad – where I'm from, you don't leave your kids, no matter what – but with Tommy I got a later chance to really be there for him, show him how much I loved him and how I wanted him to be proud of his old man.

I ended the 1997/98 season with that superb Crucible win over Hendry before losing to Ronnie O'Sullivan in the quarter-finals and although Tommy arrived safe and sound in September, 1998, a happier time at home didn't really lead to much success on the table during the following season, apart from winning an invitational tournament at Pontins where I beat Matthew Stevens in the final.

No matter what my form on the table, it was around this time that I opened a piece of mail that certainly lifted my spirits.

I remember reading this letter in complete and utter shock because it said I was to receive the MBE "for services to snooker."

Nobody was more surprised than me, this South London dickhead, getting an award from the Establishment. Fuck me. Who'd nominated me? How does any of this work? It was all a massive honour but felt very surreal – a bit like the day we had to go to Buckingham Palace for the ceremony. I wonder what my old headmaster Mr Beatty thought?

On the day, we got to the palace quite early and I bumped into Tony Adams, the Arsenal and England footballer. We chatted a bit, had a laugh and then it was time to get down to business. We were all lined up to meet the Queen, looking sharp with me and Tony right at the end of the queue. We had to pass through these little curtains towards where the Queen was standing.

In front of us in this queue were firemen who'd saved people, policemen and soldiers who'd risked their lives and loads of unknown people who'd done some amazing stuff.

JIMMY WHITE

I had plenty of time to watch these people as this queue didn't seem to go anywhere and we had about a three-hour wait to meet the Queen. Now, before you go in, a bloke dressed up in all that royal clobber comes out to teach you how to bow when you're meeting someone from the Royal family.

"Mr White," he said, before giving me my instructions on what to do. I wasn't listening to a word he was coming out with, I was too busy admiring all these coppers and squaddies and wondering what they'd done.

All of a sudden, it was my turn to go through the curtains and my head just went completely blank.

'What the fuck did that bloke say?' is all I could think to myself as I poked my head through this curtain, with all the families watching.

My head was gone by now. Totally gone. 'Quick Jimmy, what did he say?' I was screaming to myself, before remembering something or other about bowing when you stand in front of Her Majesty.

So what did I do? As I started walking towards the Queen, I didn't wait to bow while I was in front of her, I walked up this aisle bowing all the way, like a little nodding dog! Like a waiter in a shit Indian restaurant. I must've given a good four or five bows by the time I got down the other end to meet her and she must've been wondering what was going on!

The Queen is a true professional, though, and calmly pinned my MBE on. Then she got down to some serious business.

"Jimmy," she started. (*Hang on, the Queen knows my name? She knows who I am?*)

"Jimmy, Jimmy, please tell me this," she continued. "Do tell me why they put the snooker highlights on so late?"

CHANGES

"I know Ma'am," I blurted out. "My dad misses most of it as well. It's far too late for him too." And with that, I was shuffled along, knees like jelly, head still bowing. She must've thought, 'Who's this fucking nutter?'

•••••••

Despite Tommy being born, it didn't solve much between me and Maureen and we finally decided to end it for good. And we meant it this time. We just looked at each other one day, in the middle of an argument and started laughing. Why the fuck were we even bothering any more? It was crazy to try and pretend we could get on. So I moved out, permanently, and started the task of getting all parts of my life back on track.

As far as I could see, I had to try and stop the boozing and the gambling as well as the coke so, almost overnight, I did exactly that.

For me, the worst problem I'd probably had was the gambling because you can do your money in the bookies a lot quicker than you can do it in in the pub.

One time, I gambled £20,000 on a horse at Sandown races – and it won. It was about 1990 and I found this bookie on the course who'd take the bet. That's the problem, there's always a bookie somewhere who'll take the bet.

"Alright mate, 20 grand on the nose please," I said.

"Sure thing Jimmy, although I won't wish you good luck for obvious reasons," the bookie said, grinning to himself.

The horse came from nowhere to win but the scary thing is, I'd got to the stage where I was neither up or down emotionally. I didn't really care either way. That's the level it got to. I never panicked or chased my cash back or worried about my losses and I never lost a second's sleep over it, not even when I thought about the amount of money I'd done.

Finally, I just woke up and decided I didn't want to live like that any more.

I think I've burnt around £2m gambling – disgusting isn't it when you think about it? – and I'd just had enough. The hassle, the ups and the downs (mainly the downs) and the amount of my life I'd wasted in bookmakers all just caught up with me, all at once. Plus I could see what gambling was doing to my pal Alex Higgins, and I didn't want to go down that road.

Most gamblers do it for ego. It's not about winning or losing, it's about challenging your ego and showing your mates and family that you're fearless and will bet on anything.

That's alright to start with – and I'd survived on my wits for 20 years living like that – but I just got to the stage where I was sick and tired of having to travel all over the country to do exhibitions, just to pay off my gambling debts.

I was always up north in the week, playing the clubs, trying to make enough money to clear my problems. I was a fucking idiot because I'd earned enough in the professional game to mean I didn't – or shouldn't – have had to play night after night on the road but I did. That was when I woke up and thought I needed to do something about it.

I looked at booze the same way and, just the same, decided it was time to really try and sort myself out. I even went to see Paul McKenna, the hypnotist from the telly, in a bid to get off the drink.

I always knew, deep down, that I could give it up whenever I wanted to (and I rarely touch booze these days) but a few

CHANGES

friends recommended seeing somebody so I had no problems booking in with Paul.

I went to his place in Kensington, a really beautiful gaff, plush carpets, big front door, the works and he invited me in.

We sat down and got chatting about the gambling and the boozing and we went into my background a bit. I told him that I didn't think I had a problem with being physically addicted to booze, I'd just always drank, always known that world and the fun that came with it.

Paul sat in his seat, listened hard to everything I said and he asked me a ton of questions. He's a seriously clever bloke and he's helped millions of people so he knows what he's on about.

"Jimmy," he started. "From what you've said, you know and I know that you've got all the tools you need to deal with any issues with alcohol you might have. You don't need hypnotherapy, you just need to make the decision to stop bingeing on alcohol and once you've made that decision, you'll be fine."

That was what I thought anyway but it was nice to hear it from a professional.

"Thanks for that Paul," I said. "Just one more quick question."

"Go on," he said.

"Well, if I'm not an alcoholic and I can control this at any time – do you fancy a quick pint?"

Ten minutes later we were walking into his local boozer around the corner.

Only I could go and see an alcohol counsellor and end up going for a beer with him! He was a fantastic bloke and his words certainly helped me. I cut down pretty much straightaway and have stuck to it ever since.

Sure, there are days when I still go out and have a bottle of wine with a meal or a bottle or two of lager but the days of popping out for a beer and then coming back a week later are long gone. They were great, great times but they couldn't last forever; even I could see that.

•••••••

A more settled life, a baby boy and a conscious effort to quit the booze and gambling seemed to help my game but I wasn't being consistent enough to guarantee a high ranking position any more and that meant I had to run the gauntlet of qualifying for the World Championship.

Dropping out of the top 16 didn't bother me from a practical point of view – it only got you an invite to a handful of tournaments anyway – but I suppose it was a sign that snooker was no longer as easy as it had once been.

Some of the talent starting to emerge by the start of the Millennium was frightening. There'd always been skilful players on the snooker circuit during my time – just look at Davis, Higgins, Hendry and Kirk for example – but a new breed of player was making his mark and making life tougher for me.

The likes of Ken Doherty, Matthew Stevens, Peter Ebdon, Paul Hunter, John Higgins, Mark Williams, Stephen Lee and Ronnie O'Sullivan were all now fully established, lethal around the table, young and desperate to prove to the likes of me, Davis and John Parrott that our time was up.

In the end, the inevitable happened and I failed to qualify for the World Championship in 2001, although, ironically, I'd not had a bad ranking season, finishing runner-up to Ebdon in the British Open.

CHANGES

Regardless of that, I was beaten by Michael Judge in the qualifiers and it was a sickening, sickening feeling and one of the worst of my entire career.

Sheffield had always been so good to me; I'd had the biggest moments of my career inside the Crucible. Yes, some of those moments were painful, looking back, but I'd been at the top of my talents in that arena and to be missing out made me feel ill.

My mood wasn't helped by the fact I could've been enjoying the party in Yorkshire if I hadn't have been stupid the day before I played Judge in the final qualifier.

This is what happened. At the time I was practising at a mate's house in Surrey and as I was on the way to his the day before the qualifier, a stone hit the window of the Hyundai I was driving and cracked it. I rang for somebody to come out to fix it and they took the window out but then realised they couldn't get another one for me quickly enough.

The qualifiers were held in Newport in Wales and because I was playing Michael the next day I just thought I'd drive without a windscreen.

It was only an hour up the road so what harm could it do?

Wrong move Jimmy.

I didn't realise just how freezing it was, especially when the wind is coming straight for you as you're doing 70 on the motorway. By the time I got to the hotel I had my jacket wrapped around my hands because I was so, so cold.

I staggered out of the car and couldn't sign the register in the hotel, that's how gone I was.

I somehow made it to my room and just lay in a stinking hot bath for two hours but by then the damage was done. I finally rang the hospital in a panic – I can't have been far off full-blown hypothermia – but there wasn't much they could do, apart from telling me to drink loads of hot drinks and hide under plenty of blankets.

That's not exactly textbook preparation for playing professional snooker, is it?

The next day I couldn't stop my hands from shaking. I couldn't pot a ball and, no disrespect to Michael Judge, but I should've beaten him and I think I would've done if I was fully fit.

Once again, I'd been my own worst enemy at the World Championship. Not getting to Sheffield felt terrible. Nothing could cheer me up, not even when Davis failed to qualify that year either.

I did loads of press and television at the time, expressing how upset I was about missing out and I meant every word of it. The Crucible is where the action was, where I felt I belonged and I felt like I'd let my fans down. It was the end of a 20-year run for me at the tournament I loved the most and knowing I had no influence on it was tough. I was in no mood to watch what was going on because it was just too painful so I decided to go on holiday, away from the noise, the media and the entire thing.

However, saying all that, if I couldn't win it myself, there was one player there who I was desperate to see lift the trophy.

A player I'd come to know as a big mate, a wonderkid snooker player and someone who had his own destiny to fulfil.

If the Whirlwind couldn't make it, at least the Rocket still stood a chance...

10

The Two Ronnies

"Right then," Ronnie slurs. "It's your turn." Keith Richards looks at his fellow Rolling Stone and starts grinning wildly, cackling. The sun is coming up in Ronnie's house and I can't believe what I've just seen or heard.

The two greatest living guitarists have had a duel for the last hour, trying to outjam and outplay each other. The two of them nod at each other in mutual appreciation and then sit down, drinking Screwdrivers from jugs, happy that their little contest is over. Now it's me and Ronnie O'Sullivan's turn to show them that although there are four legends in the room, only two of them can play snooker.

And while we might have been amazed at what two Rolling Stones can produce, the night ain't seen nothing yet.

Being a snooker player has given me an incredible life and the chance to meet people I otherwise wouldn't have got to know.

And two of those people just happen to be geniuses.

Ronnie Wood and Ronnie O'Sullivan are two of my best mates and two blokes I've shared some incredible times with, up and down, good and bad.

I first met Ronnie Wood through our daughters. In 1988, I went to Lauren's Christmas school play. Being useless with technology meant that I didn't have a clue how to use this video recorder, so I stood at the back of this assembly hall and tried to work out what was going on.

I turned around and there was Ronnie, also struggling to sort his camera out. He was trying to take photos of his daughter, Leah. We gave each other a nod and a grin and we had a bit of a chat and that was about it.

I was a massive Rolling Stones fan, so knew all about who he was but I was stunned when I found out that Ronnie loved his snooker and was a big fan of mine. One thing led to another and we decided to meet up soon after to go for a couple of pints in Wimbledon.

It was nearly Christmas and we were meant to be getting Maureen and Ronnie's then wife Jo, a present or two. That idea soon went out of the window when we realised we were pretty much identical in terms of loving a laugh, a frame of snooker and long, slow afternoons boozing. We worked well together from the start because I can't play the guitar and he can't play snooker and we both wanted what the other one had! That first bender, which lasted about three days, was the sign of things to come. We both copped it off our wives when we found our way back home but by then the deal was done; I'd found myself a new mate who thought like me, drank like me, lived liked me and lived near me. It was the start of an amazing friendship that gets stronger and stronger to this day.

I've had some incredible times with Ronnie and we're openly in awe of each other. I love nothing more than watching him on the guitar and he loves nothing more than a frame or two of snooker against me.

The stories about me and Ronnie go way back and the sad thing is, neither of us can probably remember the best ones. Ronnie used to love a proper bender – he's a member of the Rolling Stones after all – and him and Keith Richards used to get on it and stay on it. That drove Jo mad for years and Maureen wasn't too much happier when I hooked up with Ronnie either. He used to have this beautiful house in Kingston and I'd nip round there for a quick drink and end up staying out with him all week. It had a wonderful snooker table in there – I should know, I got it for him! – and days used to pass by in a blur of booze and laughs.

Ronnie also has a place in Kildare in Ireland that is beyond belief. It's set in the middle of nowhere with loads of horses running around. It's got its own music studio, guest house and even its own pub where you could just help yourself to whatever you fancied.

I used to stay in the guest house all the time and come downstairs at whatever time and find local farmers and policemen helping themselves to a Guinness or two, all with Ronnie's permission because that's what he's like.

I remember one New Year's Eve in Kildare and someone had given us these magic mushrooms. They helped turn a New Year's Eve session into New Year's Day. We just kept drinking and going for it, playing in his wonderful snooker room. The bar at Ronnie's was called 'Yer Father's Yacht' because his dad had been a water gypsy and we just had the most fabulous time. All of a sudden, Ronnie goes, "Wait here" and disappears out of the room and he came back in about 15 minutes later with this massive, beautiful horse.

Ronnie had a wonderful relationship with horses. He could train them and whistle at them and keep them under control. I, on the other hand, couldn't do any of that stuff and I was convinced at any second that this horse was going to bolt around this snooker room and we'd all be trampled everywhere. They'd be making glue out of us, not him.

"Don't worry Jimmy, I've got it under control," Ronnie said, which was a bit brave coming from a bloke who'd been on magic mushrooms all night, but I took his word for it and this horse was as good as gold, standing in this snooker room while we played and drank. You don't see that every day do you?

Those days were a lot of fun. On some occasions, we'd wake up, have some breakfast and then start on the Guinness all day. These horses would be running around outside, the fire would be blazing and we'd play frame after frame of snooker. Ronnie has to be one of the most loving, generous men alive – nothing was too much trouble. I've stayed with Ronnie a million times at his house in England or Ireland, I get on really well with all his family and his kids and if I see his ex-wife, Jo, we always say hello and catch up properly.

Saying that, I once nearly caused a murder between the two of them during one of my Crucible tournaments. I'm pleased to say that I wasn't even in the same part of the country as Ronnie when he put his foot in it, but it was my fault anyway.

THE TWO RONNIES

The story goes that I was due to be playing an evening session and Ronnie wasn't around that night so he wanted to video it and watch it when he came in. Back then, of course, there wasn't any internet, so you couldn't really find out what happened unless you recorded it on VHS and watched it back.

Ronnie set the tape recorder, went out, came back in and poured himself a drink. Then he pressed play.

I can't remember who I was playing but I won and Ronnie was delighted. That is until he gets to the end of the recording and realises that he's only gone and taped over his fucking wedding day! You can imagine how that went down with his missus...

Ronnie is always full of energy, laughing and enjoying himself. He's the same sober as he is drunk. He has a bundle of stories and wisecracks and is one of the busiest men I know. He showed me his diary the other week and he's booked up doing radio shows in America and loads of other things until 2017. You don't get into a situation like that unless you're seriously talented.

He's also one of those people who is amazing at more than one art form. Sickening isn't it? Over the last 15 years or so, Ronnie has really focused on his paintings and artwork. There is absolutely no doubt now that he is one of Britain's greatest living artists. It isn't his name or his background that has got his work into loads of major galleries – it is how beautiful he paints and draws. I've got a few of his works in my front room and they are incredible. He's just a really creative, brilliant bloke. It's a miracle really when you think about how much he's drank over the years!

I remember one night when he threw a party at his place and

we really went for it. The Screwdrivers were barely touching the sides, neither was the Guinness. We were having a fucking great time. At times like this, nothing else mattered other than where the next drink, fag or joint was coming from and the craic was flowing nicely until Maureen, at her wit's end after trying to track me down, decided that the party had to stop.

"Where's Jimmy?" she screamed.

"I don't know," Ronnie replied, trying to keep a straight face. Maureen was no idiot so ran out into the garden to find me passed out at the back of his garden. I was woken by the shout "JIMMY!" before Maureen started dragging me into the house by my legs, calling me all sorts.

"Morning darling," I said. "What's for breakfast?"

That was too much for Ronnie and me as we collapsed laughing. Maureen eventually saw the funny side of it too.

The laughing with Ronnie never stopped, apart from one tragic occasion that I'll never forget.

We'd had a big night, playing cards and snooker and messing around when Jo's dad, Michael, came downstairs and saw that we were still up in the front room. "Morning lads, want some breakfast?" he asked. Neither of us fancied any but we moved into the kitchen with him, the kettle was put on and we all continued chatting and just enjoying each other's company.

Suddenly, out of nowhere, Michael laughed out loud at some joke or other then collapsed in front of us. He died just there, a metre away from me. Jo was obviously devastated and Ronnie was no better as he loved his father-in-law to bits. It was a very sobering moment and something I'd never want to repeat. I suppose it does show you just how fragile life can be.

Hanging around with Ronnie also taught me what real fame

is. Sure, I was well known in snooker circles but the man is one of the most famous guitarists in the world and famous people attract famous mates like nothing else.

Me and Ronnie were just two lads but the people he knew and introduced me to were incredible. One time in the late '80s, we went with Rod Stewart to watch a football match at Highbury.

I can't remember who was playing but believe it or not, I was organising the transport. I told Victor Yo, "Go and hire a 10-seater Merc van or something for all the lads." I was only about 25, very flush and happy to spend it.

Me, Tyrone and Jesse Woods, Ronnie's boys, Ronnie, Peewee and Victor got into this van and we set off to pick Rod Stewart up. As you do.

Now, my road trips with Ronnie could last for hours. A 25-minute trip could take seven hours because we'd stop in every pub along the way. Eventually, we picked Rod up and then Ronnie, who'd already had enough to drink by now, piped up, "We're in Swiss Cottage. Peter Cook lives around here, let's pick him up."

Peter Cook? You've got to be kidding me. *The* Peter Cook? But the amount of people Ronnie knows is frightening so he got on the phone and told Peter to come out.

"We've got Rod Stewart and Jimmy White here," Ronnie said. Peter probably didn't have a clue who I was but Ronnie would always mention me. He was always proud to be out with me, which was always nice, if a bit embarrassing.

Ronnie gave Peter the big sell on this day out and Peter said, "Okay Ronnie, I shall be the strange looking gentleman standing outside the red pillarbox with the pink suit on."

Yeah alright...

Then we drove around the corner and there he is in this pink suit! "Afternoon gentlemen," he said. "Let's be gone to the football."

We went to Highbury and watched the game when all of a sudden, Peter Cook turned his back on the match and started chatting to the crowd. Before you know it, there were about 100 fans all craning to hear what Peter Cook was saying. They'd totally forgotten a game was going on – it was just like Peter's own private audience. They were all pissing themselves and then we all started pissing ourselves. The players must've thought 'What the fuck is going on there?'

It was unbelievable, watching the impact he had on the crowd and how they loved him. Later on, back in some pub, he did the same. We all crammed into this boozer, drinks were ordered and Peter was off again. "Let me tell you another story," he kept shouting to this audience and we lapped it up.

It's nights like that that I lived for. Priceless nights of fun and chat; loud music and overflowing glasses. It was never the next drink that I needed – it was the next buzz, the next feeling that I was alive and doing something extraordinary with myself.

As I say, Ronnie knows everyone and he introduced me to John McEnroe at Wimbledon one year. I loved the way McEnroe played tennis and I was in awe of him, even if he didn't have a clue who I was.

I was a bit flash that day at Wimbledon, wearing a red suit, and McEnroe soon let me know about it. "Hey Jimmy," he said. "Look on the bright side, you won't get run over in that suit."

A few years later, Ronnie had a tennis court installed in his garden and McEnroe was partnering Steffi Graf in the mixed doubles at Wimbledon but she pulled out because she'd made the final of the Ladies singles event against Lindsay Davenport the next day.

McEnroe wasn't best pleased that his chance of winning another title at Wimbledon had just gone up in smoke so Ronnie invited him around for the night. Next thing, McEnroe turned up at Ronnie's and you could tell he was not happy at all so he decided to take it out on the court. Ronnie's boys were on one side of the court and on the other was McEnroe – the real life John McEnroe – running around in a temper, smashing these balls all over the place.

I was stood there, yet again, wondering how the fuck I'd managed to get courtside seats to one of tennis's all-time stars and one of my all-time heroes.

Ronnie even sorted it once for me to meet The Greatest himself, Muhammad Ali.

I got an invite to his 59th birthday party at the London Hilton but we were originally on table 78, about three miles from the action, when Ronnie went, "Don't worry Jim, I know him".

I told him to fuck off but he was adamant. Turns out that Ronnie wasn't lying and they'd met in New York when Ronnie had been there for an art exhibition. The pair had spent some time together in Ronnie's hotel room, laughing and joking, and Ronnie had also donated some pictures to Ali's charity.

During this meeting in New York, Ali turned to Ronnie and told him he wanted to go downstairs with him and outside onto the Manhattan streets. "Why?" Ronnie asked. "Muhammad Ali on one side of the street and a Rolling Stone on the other – let's go and stop 5th Avenue," he said.

"Let's see who they'll try and arrest first, the black boy or the white boy!"

I rang back the organisers to let them know this and all of a sudden, me and Ronnie go from table 78 to table 2. The Greatest was about two metres from me and I couldn't believe it. Ronnie introduced us and he was very poorly with Parkinson's but we had our photo together and you could see that he and Ronnie really liked each other.

It was one of the proudest moments of my life. I was so in awe of him, the greatest boxer of all time, and so proud of my best mate for knowing so many extraordinary people.

●●●●●●●

I never feel better than when me and Ronnie are out and about, even if we have both now tidied up our act.

Ronnie had quite a bad drink problem for a few years but there was never a bad word between me and Jo because I was never encouraging him to go on benders. Fair enough, I wasn't stopping him either and I wouldn't try and hide it from Jo or Maureen because if Ronnie wanted to escape and get away for a bit then I was the mate he'd turn to.

He's a grown man and can do what he wants, so if a drink was what he fancied then as far as I could see, it wasn't my place to tell him to stop. Saying that though, I'm very proud of the way he's conquered his booze troubles. He's been clean for about five years now – there's been the odd mishap but nothing stupid – and he's done so well.

Looking back, we were a terrible influence on each other but that's only age and hindsight telling me that. At the time we had so much fun while we were out drinking. Nothing seemed to be impossible. No VIP club we couldn't get in, no drink we couldn't get – we felt invincible; two London kids who couldn't believe their luck – until my luck ran out one night...

After losing to Hendry in 1994, I royally messed up when I got caught and (rightly) done for drink-driving.

At the time I had a 535 BMW that I'd bought from Terry Griffiths. I had the steering wheel decorated in rasta colours and changed the 'Park, Drive, Neutral' and whatever else on the automatic gearstick to 'yellow, green, brown, blue, pink and black.' I thought I was the absolute bollocks. I was Mr Weed for about two years in this motor until this night.

Me and Peewee were on our way to Ronnie Wood's house at about four in the morning – as you do. There's no way I should've been anywhere other than bed, never mind behind the wheel of a car. Next thing I knew, a police car came behind me and flashed its lights. Great.

I wasn't thinking straight and stupidly decided to try and burn them off. I managed to lose them and we made our way to Ronnie's. I thought I was safe. All I had to do was get this car onto private land, hand the keys to somebody sober in the house and say they were driving.

I got out of the car at Ronnie's and tried to put my plan into action but little did I know that his house had been burgled the night before and his normal gates had been replaced with electronic ones. 'Oh fuck,' I thought, knowing this was a very bad sign. It wouldn't take long for the coppers to find us. Sure enough, they turned up and threw the book at me.

I'd legged it up the drive and was met with Ronnie who was even more pissed than me and Peewee. I turned to Peewee and decided that my mate would happily take the rap for me.

"You were driving weren't you Peewee?" I said to him in front of these coppers. "Driving?" he said. "Driving what?" Thanks for that, mate.

I got 120 hours community service and a three-year ban, all of which I totally and utterly deserved, and I then had to go to a meeting with this arsehole probation officer – a real tosser on a power trip.

I walked into this office and you could tell he was loving it straight away. He had this sneer on his face and asked me what I could do.

Could I paint, fix fences, do any plumbing?

"I can play snooker," I told him. "I can't do nothing else."

Unfortunately the Probation Service didn't have any need for professional snooker players at the time, so I was fucked.

I wanted to do anything to raise cash for charity or do exhibitions but they weren't having any of it so I was sent down to this old people's home to clean bathrooms and do whatever else they needed a hand with.

As you can imagine, this was not my idea of a good time. It was too much like a normal job for my liking. Getting up in the morning and going to work somewhere was something I'd never done and I didn't fancy starting now. But, as always, there's some fun to be found somewhere...

While I was cleaning an old boy's bedroom one day, we got chatting properly and this fella, called Harold, turned out to be a right character.

He'd been a journalist in Bristol but his family had forgotten him and he was now meant to just stare out of his window for the rest of his days.

He introduced me to his mate George – another old bloke left on the scrapheap – and we started having a right old laugh every day, taking the piss and watching the racing on the telly whenever we could.

Watching these funny, clever blokes just sitting around all day got too much for me – maybe I thought about my dad and didn't like seeing decent fellas left to rot – so I told my new mates, "Fuck the consequences, we're off out for the day."

I got my dad, Harold and George and we went to Kempton Park races. You should've seen them having the time of their lives.

Dad bought them a few (too many) drinks, we pushed our luck and returned the pair of them back to the home as pissed as you can be, both telling us how much fun they'd had. Old boys being old boys, we had to stop the car every 10 minutes on the way back from Kempton Park so they could get out and relieve themselves and one of them forgot to take his medication because he was so drunk. This caper went on for a few weeks until the matron/dragon who ran this old people's home busted me bringing them back in.

"Jimmy, have these two been drinking?" she said. She must've been watching Columbo to work that out – or maybe it was the sight of two 80-somethings completely pissed and practically crawling that gave it away.

"They're just having the odd drink to help them sleep," I tried to tell her. "It's good for them."

I started getting an almighty bollocking before the boys came to my rescue.

"I'm stuck in here all day, every day," Harold said. "I'm 85, what harm is a drink going to do me now?"

I could see his point, the dragon couldn't. It had been nice while it lasted.

I went back to the day 'job' of cutting the grass and mopping floors and this probation officer got back on my case. He thought he was a proper fella this bloke. I had 10 hours to go and I'd done about four hours when he came back, laughing that I still had to fit six more hours in that week. He just didn't like me at all. He probably thought he was the big fucking 'I am' in his local pub on a Friday night, telling all his mates how he was bossing Jimmy White about every day. I had no problem with the community service and I deserved to be punished but this bloke was taking the piss.

I'd had enough of all this so one day, as he escorted me from this nursing home, he was greeted by loads of paparazzi outside, taking my photo. "What's happening, what's happening?" he kept asking, in a panic.

"Don't know mate, the papers must've heard about this," I told him. What he didn't know was that the 'paparazzi' were my mates and it was part of a stitch-up.

The next day I smuggled a camera into the home with me, got someone to take photos of me mopping up and dusting and we then sold the story to The Sun for £10,000 which worked out at £5,000 each for me and my mates. Lovely!

I bet the probation officer never knew about that one but if Ronnie had had his fucking gates fixed I'd never have been in that position in the first place!

Still, I forgive him and I love him – he's a great friend.

•••••••

If Ronnie Wood is a genius with a paintbrush or a guitar, there is no doubt that Ronnie O'Sullivan is a genius with a snooker cue. In fact, he's the greatest player the game has ever seen, without a shadow of a doubt.

Higgins was unpredictable and exciting and a wonderful shot-maker, Davis was a machine and Hendry was as hard as nails, but in terms of all-round skill then O'Sullivan laughs everyone off the table, even me.

Back in 1992, I kept hearing about this wonderkid coming through the ranks. Apparently this Londoner played like he didn't give a fuck, was quick, could pot them in off the lampshades and was looking like a complete one-off. It rang a few bells.

Back then, most of the major qualifiers for tournaments took place in this gaff in Blackpool called the Norbreck Castle Hotel. There were about 20 tables in there and the place was full of blokes who were all trying to make their way in the game. Nowadays most qualifiers take place in Barnsley but Blackpool was the place to be then, even if it could be cold and fucking depressing.

Like I say, I kept being told about this young lad who was just doing everybody over.

He'd won his first 38 matches and only lost two out of his first 72 qualifiers.

The kid's name was Ronnie O'Sullivan.

His record already looked freakishly good and I knew the game had someone special on the way through, even if I did do my best to accidentally ruin it for him at the UK Championship that year.

In the first round in Preston, O'Sullivan was playing Cliff Wilson and I fancied O'Sullivan to win, so I included him on my betting slip.

The UK Championship that year was one of my mad tournaments where I was good enough to be able to drink and still pot people off the table. Back then I could stay up for three days, no problems at all – nowadays I'd be shredded.

I had a suite in a hotel and even though I was playing in the first round at 1pm, I didn't go to bed the night before, staying up all night playing poker instead. There was me, Danny Fowler, Alex Higgins, Barry West, William Allenby and a bloke called 'Maltese George' all sitting around, talking shit and enjoying ourselves. My suite was like an open house in those days, picking up all sorts of waifs and strays. I used to walk in to my suites at big tournaments and not have a fucking clue who half the people were. "Who are you?" "Oh, nice to meet you," some bloke still pissed in a suit would say from the couch, "I'm with Maltese George."

The cards and chatter were flying and I didn't really want to leave. "Won't be long," I told the lads. "Just got to go and play." I went and had a shower, got changed, came back to the table and finished the card game. Then I went and won my match. I got back to my room a few hours later and it was as if I'd not even gone. "Nobody's nicked my chips have they?" I asked, settling back into the game as if nothing had happened. I'd say that happened at about one in four tournaments. When I should've been practising, I'd be up all night, looking for mischief, shagging around, boozing or playing cards. Usually all of them.

Anyway, during that tournament I had an accumulator and I'd put £4,000 on. All my other boys had come in and O'Sullivan was my last bet. If he beat Cliff I'd stand to win about £20,000 which isn't a bad afternoon's work is it?

THE TWO RONNIES

As I was walking past him during the interval, I had a quick word with him, which turned out to be a bit of a disaster. "Any chance you could beat him?" I asked O'Sullivan. "You're far better than he is, you should be walking this. I've got you on my accumulator." It was a bad idea telling him. It shook him up and he ended up losing 9-8. Apparently Cliff Wilson also swore at him halfway through the match, calling him "a little cunt." Although that didn't help, it was probably my little motivational speech that did the damage.

Despite that personal setback, Ronnie had had a break of 145 in that match against Wilson, so it was clear that the kid had something special.

His cue-ball control was great and he wanted to clear the table every time he got in, which I loved. Ronnie is an instinctive player, he doesn't just see the game, he feels it – like I do – and like Higgins did before me. I remember giving a quote to the press at the time that he was "a breath of fresh air for the game of snooker" and I meant every word of it.

Ronnie has a lot of personal demons that have been well documented. I'm not revealing something unknown or taking a liberty by saying that. He's a man who loves his kids, Lily and Ronnie, but for whatever reason he doesn't get to see them as much as he wants and he's been involved in a tough custody battle with his ex-partner Jo. That has undoubtedly distracted him in the past and caused him a lot of heartbreak and grief that he could've done without.

There's no secret either that Ronnie has also struggled over the years because his own dad, Ronnie Snr, was jailed when Ronnie was just 17 for murdering a man after a disagreement in a Chelsea nightclub. Ronnie Snr got 18 years for that and it knocked Ronnie sideways because he had idolised his dad growing up and loved spending time with him. He's not had it easy by any means and not having a regular relationship with his kids tortures him, so that makes his achievements at snooker even more amazing.

I've met his all family and I regard Ronnie as a close friend of mine and we have had some great nights out.

The most famous one is when the pair of us, along with Ronnie Wood and Keith Richards ended up going back to Ronnie Wood's place at about six in the morning.

The table I'd got for Ronnie was the most beautiful snooker table you've ever seen. It belonged to Joe Davis before me and when Ronnie moved into his hunting lodge in Kingston, he bought it for £10,000. It was always a pleasure to play a game on it. The table was hand carved and had wooden chalk holders. It was about 150 years old and the slates were about three-and-a-half inches thick. It would take eight men to move the table – it was that old fashioned.

There was not a soul about at Ronnie's. Jo was away some-where, so we thought we'd have some fun. Ronnie and Keith Richards decided to have a bit of a competition on the guitar. None of us were sober, put it that way. Keith and Ronnie sat down with a drink and starting strumming, sometimes playing together on a favourite old blues track or improvising off the top of their heads.

The two of them are big friends and like all mates, they started getting competitive and wanted to get the upper hand on each other. "Come on," said Keith, "Who's the best, is it me or Ronnie?"

How do you answer that? Me and O'Sullivan just looked at

each other and were too in awe to even speak. We were there with two of the greatest guitarists the world has ever seen, drinking stupid amounts of vodka and orange and Guinness, and were getting treated to the best jam ever. People would've paid millions to have been in that room with us. It was a very special moment, even if we were all smashed.

The next thing, Ronnie turned to me and O'Sullivan and decided to up the stakes a bit. "Right lads," he said. "Me and Keith have had our turn. It's time for you two to do your thing."

I don't know what time is was by then but Ronnie started setting up a frame of snooker and it was time for us to return the favour. 'Right then O'Sullivan,' I thought to myself. 'Let's show these two what we've got'.

We were incredible that night.

We had 10 games of snooker, I had four century breaks and an 80 and he had five centuries. It was unbelievable. We couldn't miss, we couldn't put a foot wrong.

It was the 10 maddest frames of snooker you'll ever see.

We were nice and loose, it was a great atmosphere with Ronnie and Keith cackling away at what they were seeing and me and O'Sullivan enjoying putting on a show. We reckoned that was the least we could do after the jam session.

The longer the night (or morning) went on, the more we laughed and tried to play outrageous shots. I never played a safety shot (a bit like the whole of the 1980s, really) and Ronnie and Keith's faces were something else as they tried to get their heads around what me and O'Sullivan were doing on the table.

"Amazing," was all Ronnie kept saying and Keith wasn't far behind. Me and O'Sullivan knew then that we were on a par with those two and that they'd been as impressed by us as we'd been with them. What they did with their guitars, we'd done with our cues. It was just a priceless night.

Long before that night, in the early days, O'Sullivan was a bit of a lunatic and reminded me a lot of myself. He was running around having fun, surrounded by probably the wrong sort of people. He loved a night out and the buzz that alcohol gives you. 'I've seen this all before,' I thought. I liked him straight-away so decided that I needed to have a word with him about his life, just to try and straighten him out a bit.

I gave him the best advice I could.

We were at a tournament and I took him to one side and told him some home truths. It wasn't a lecture; it was just one older mate passing on a few words. "Don't do what I do," I told him. "I make it hard work to win these tournaments, don't do the same. Get your head down and keep your game improving." I think he listened to me because he seemed to focus himself a bit more and you only have to look at his results to see how he's improved. Ronnie's won the World Championship five times and he's the best player I've ever seen.

Besides myself...

He is better than Higgins because he's got such beautiful finesse and can create chances from nowhere. When he gets out of his seat, he gets to the table and immediately sees the balls in a way that is different to other players.

He looks at how the balls are set and instantly sizes up what he has to do to clear up. He doesn't see obstacles or problems, his brain goes into overdrive and immediately calculates how to win the frame. His brain is six or seven shots in front of him all the time. Most players are two or three (if they're lucky) and when O'Sullivan pots a ball he then goes a further shot in front.

THE TWO RONNIES

He's like a chess player in that he looks into the future and tries to work out every potential angle and shot needed to clear up. You have to be on a different planet to be able to do that and there is no doubt that is where O'Sullivan is.

•••••••

Another thing O'Sullivan is wonderful at is driving. He's a man who is perfectly at home behind the wheel of a car.

We did an exhibition in Manchester about five years ago and he'd pulled the short straw and had to drive. I was happy as it meant I could probably get my head down on the drive back to Surrey. No such fucking luck.

There's been talk of him doing Formula 3, which he'd absolutely smash – and I don't know if it was me being cocky in the passenger seat or what but I've never been on a journey like it.

We were in his Mercedes and he did what felt like 300mph all the way. I was absolutely shitting myself. He was going so fast I couldn't look out of the window – it was too scary.

"Fucking hell, steady," I told him, but he never listened, he was too busy enjoying how green I was turning.

I was back in my driveway, from Manchester to London, in about 90 minutes. He had to chisel my white knuckles off the side of the seat. So much for my relaxing sleep. "See you then Jimmy," he said, as I wobbled up my drive.

He'd driven that quick that I couldn't get my key in the front door and when I did I had to sit on the floor in the lounge for about 20 minutes to try and stop the room from spinning. I don't think I'd ever get in a car with him again.

He might be the greatest snooker player ever and a fantastic driver but that doesn't mean he's perfect and credit to him, he'd be the first to tell you that himself.

He's caused the game a few problems over the years and not always done himself favours. For example, when he first played left-handed against Alain Robidoux at the World Championship in 1996 I wasn't very happy and said so. I just thought he was taking the piss out of his opponent and that there was no need for that. Robidoux clearly agreed and when he should've conceded the frame to O'Sullivan because he was about 50 behind with nothing left on, he kept the frame going – his way of saying he wasn't very happy either.

I thought at the time it was disrespectful and stupid of O'Sullivan because he was playing every shot left-handed in the end.

Looking back now, my attitude was wrong and I was clearly stuck in the past. Ronnie hadn't done it to really upset anybody, he'd done it because he could. Which player would not love to be as gifted and as talented as that? What an asset to have. Dennis Taylor could roll the odd ball in with his left hand and Matthew Stevens has also done it from time to time but neither of those would pretend to be in the same league as O'Sullivan off their wrong hand. He'd be a top 32 player overnight if he played as a left-hander and for me, that sums up his genius perfectly. Imagine if Roger Federer walked out at Wimbledon and started serving up left-handed. The world would think he was something incredible and O'Sullivan is no different.

I really do love the kid. We get on best when we don't talk about snooker. A lot of special people are like that. Artists and sportsmen and singers and whoever else are surrounded, day in and day out, by the thing that they love and they're constantly being asked about it and interviewed about it and sometimes – no matter how much you love snooker, or singing or painting – you just want some time away from it all.

If me and Ronnie go to a nice restaurant for dinner, the last thing we'll talk about is snooker. He will ask me about the family or what I'm up to and I know that I only have to mention running and he is happy to chat and discuss it until the sun comes up.

One of the best ways O'Sullivan deals with what goes on in his life now is by putting on his running shoes and going for a 10k. That's where our friendship ends because I think the last time I did any running was when I broke my foot at Tooting Bec Tube stop. But he's a top-class athlete and he can run five-minute miles for fun. If he's running and seeing his kids and he's happy then other players can just forget it.

One night I remember a while back was when we were in Bangkok, staying in the Dusat Thani hotel, overlooking Lumphini Park. We had Rod Stewart's suite because Rod had gone home early. The manager liked us, knew we were mates of Ronnie Wood's, one of Rod's oldest pals, and he just opened the door and let us in. This suite had about four beds with a Jacuzzi in the middle. Not bad for two lads from London. It was boiling hot in Bangkok (when isn't it?) and I decided that a few drinks were needed to quench my thirst. "Come on," I told Ronnie, "let's nip out somewhere and see what's going on."

Ronnie had mixed memories of Bangkok as that's where he was in 1991 when his dad got arrested for murder. He was over there competing in the World Amateur Championship and the news obviously knocked him badly and he lost in the last 16.

I decided then that it was my job to paint a more positive

picture of the place so we went out, chasing around on tuk-tuks, drinking until all hours in Patpong and Sukhumvit and generally having a great time until we somehow staggered through the front door of the Dusat Thani. The concierge took one look at the pair of us and helped us into our suite where I collapsed in bed.

The next day I woke up to find Ronnie absent. Then my mobile rang. "Jimmy, I'm at the airport," he said. "I'm going home. That place is too much for me, I had to get out of there."

He must have been in shreds on that flight because even after I had a sleep I was still in pieces myself. That cannot have been a good 15 or 16 hours for him!

As well as being mates, O'Sullivan has said before that I was one of his heroes as a kid and that means a lot. I think he has respect for my game and I think he admires the way I've always tried to play and entertain the fans. However, the big difference between us is that I want to make people smile and win whereas he just wants to win. That's probably the reason he's got five World Championships and I'm still after my first.

Looking at it sensibly, he went the right way about it – he put the flair shots away and just wants to win snooker frames. He does that in an exciting way anyhow so it's the best of both worlds for him.

If there's one thing I'd change about Ronnie it's the occasional outbursts from him about not wanting to play any more.

Over the years he's made a few of those comments and he also quit a match against Stephen Hendry at the UK Championship in York when he was only 4-1 down, which was just fucking stupid. It was 2006 and there wasn't that much in the match but O'Sullivan just wanted to get out of there, find some mates and get on the piss. He missed a red and that was that – he walked over to Hendry, shook his hand and walked off.

If you watch the interview with Hendry afterwards, you've never seen a more shocked snooker player and I can't blame him. He deserved better than that. Hendry and O'Sullivan are big mates and to leave him standing in the middle of the arena like that was not on. But that is Ronnie for you; when he's flying and feeling good he's unstoppable, then occasionally the game gets too much for him and he needs to escape.

What a lot of people don't know about that episode is what O'Sullivan did next. After quitting, he was hanging around the venue and he started getting a bit of grief from people who were moaning about their tickets, claiming he'd short-changed them. A man who hates the sport and hates the fans would've told them all to fuck off. What did O'Sullivan do? He took about 50 people out to dinner, all expenses paid, to make up for it. He also issued a formal apology. His head just wasn't right at the time.

He's a super-generous guy and we both have that fault of paying for everything. He's a streetwise lad, too. Higgins was tough but wasn't streetwise at all whereas O'Sullivan, like me, knows his way around, he thinks quickly on his feet and can look after himself.

When he first started saying he wanted to pack in and retire, I used to get on the phone to try and talk him around. "Look Ronnie, you'll want to play again soon," I'd tell him. "Why are you saying stuff like this?"

I think it's more to do with him being away from his kids rather than him not wanting to play.

I hate it when Ronnie does it but in his defence, he's not

making it up. He knows he'll attract criticism for saying stuff like that but it's only how he feels at the time. He wears his heart on his sleeve and always speaks honestly.

Deep down inside, O'Sullivan needs snooker and snooker needs O'Sullivan. When he took some time out of the game after winning the World Championship in 2012, the public and press wanted to know my thoughts on it and whether he would come back as strong as he once was. I had no doubt that he would and I thought he'd defend his title with no problems at all.

Before he announced he was going to come back to play, Ronnie asked me to come to his press conference to deflect some of the questions and keep him relaxed. We both have a business interest with ROK Stars Oval Vodka so he called in the media and used that as a bit of a publicity drive for them as well. (Don't worry, the irony of me helping a vodka company out hasn't been lost by the way. I should've been given the keys to the distillery about 30 years ago).

At that press conference at the Hilton London Metropole, he spoke beautifully about how he'd missed the game and how he couldn't wait to get back.

The questions still remained from the press about whether he could possibly compete after letting his cue gather dust for 12 months but I soon set reporters straight and I meant every word.

"Not only will Ronnie compete," I said. "He'll leave with the trophy." I got on the phone and told all my friends to back him at 12/1 because I knew he was feeling better, fresher and his confidence was high and when he has that kind of mindset he's unplayable. He beat Marcus Campbell in the first round and I knew I'd be proved right. He easily beat Barry Hawkins in the final for his fifth title.

What other sportsman – in any sport ever – has taken 12 months off from playing and then come back and won the world title? I'll tell you that the answer to that is none. The man is just incredible.

Ronnie is friendly with Hendry but a lot of other players aren't comfortable around him because they're in awe of him. They know that they're in the presence of a proper genius and that puts them on edge. They probably also look at him and know that he's the single biggest thing stopping them from winning world championships because he is just that good.

When O'Sullivan is at his best he has a similar impact to somebody like Mike Tyson. When Tyson was in peak form, boxers knew they were beaten before they'd even got in the ring with him and O'Sullivan can have the same effect.

In the 2014 World Championship final against Mark Selby, I think O'Sullivan should've been 10-5 up but he missed a couple of easy balls and lost his focus. I, more than most, can tell you how that feels and how easily it can happen, but fair play to Mark Selby, who I like and is a nice kid, he did a fantastic job to turn the match around and win. I'm proud of Mark and his career and what's he's done but I didn't want to see him beat O'Sullivan. He stayed snapping at Ronnie's heels and eventually took over. That takes a massive amount of effort and skill, so good luck to him.

I beat O'Sullivan in consecutive years in the Masters in 2001 and 2002 and I was proud of that. To beat him you have to be at your very, very best and hope that he's having an off-day because if he's firing then you stand almost no chance.

Over the last few years he's joined the Snooker Legends tour and he seems to really enjoy it. We've had some great battles in that – battles that have helped convince me that I have no need to retire quite yet.

During one season we played 10 venues up and down the country and although they were only exhibitions, we were both trying to win. The 10-match series ended 5-5, including me beating him 7-1 one night in Reading and I think I showed him that night that I still had the skills. He knows that it becomes harder to win when you're older, so he respects the fact that I'm still out there playing and I showed against him that I can still string it together when it counts.

Proof that playing O'Sullivan always brings the best out of me came that night at Ronnie's house when we traded centuries for fun, but we went one better than that in Ireland a few years back.

In 2009, me and O'Sullivan were scheduled to do an exhibition together in the Knightsbrook Hotel, Trim, County Meath.

We played each other in front of about 700 fans. It all went well and then the last frame of the night was raffled off. For about 600 euros, these two fellas got the chance to play me and O'Sullivan at doubles.

Six hundred euros is a lot of money but these two lads were delighted and off we went. I broke the balls and left a long red on for O'Sullivan and before you knew it, he'd cleaned the table up! A 147 in no time at all.

This hotel was going absolutely crazy. I felt for these two lads, they'd not had a shot. As we were all shaking hands, O'Sullivan turned to me and went, "Let's give them another frame Jimmy, they've not had half a chance here." I didn't think we could get much better than ending the night on a 147 but I agreed with it and the two lads we were playing with couldn't get enough of it either.

Sure enough, this time O'Sullivan breaks off, leaves me a long red and I clear up...a 147 as well!

Two back-to-back 147s. Anything O'Sullivan can do...

I've played in front of massive crowds at the Crucible, the Masters and I've had my name chanted in Hong Kong loads of times but the noise in that hotel that night was up there with the very best receptions I've ever heard. It was absolute bedlam as me and O'Sullivan shook hands, started grinning and turned to the two lads. "What can you do?" I said and they both laughed. They've both got a story for life as well: the day they paid 600 euros for two frames against the Rocket and the Whirlwind and they never potted a ball. Good lads and a great, great evening.

Personally speaking, I'm just so happy that there's someone in snooker still wanting to play the way Ronnie does. Watch one of his five-minute 147s and tell me that's not an incredible sporting achievement. People talk about the speed and excitement of Judd Trump's game and I hope he continues to come through and keep the audience excited but, for now, there's nobody like O'Sullivan.

Snooker needs these special players and O'Sullivan, thank God, will keep the sport going.

He attracted a bit of criticism again when he originally refused to pot the black for a 147 against Mark King in the 2010 World Open but on this occasion I agreed with him. O'Sullivan wanted to make a point to Barry Hearn that there wasn't any prize money for achieving one of sport's hardest tasks. The crazy thing is, O'Sullivan knew he was on for a 147 as soon as he potted the first red and black and he asked referee Jan Verhaas, "What's the prize for a max?" THAT is the level of genius I'm on about. That's like Rory McIlroy sizing up a par-three and turning to the course steward and asking him if there was a prize for nailing a hole-in-one or Phil Taylor chucking one treble 20 and then asking what he'd get for a nine-darter. Only O'Sullivan could think of asking for that and only O'Sullivan could back that up by actually doing it – even if he didn't really want to.

After potting the pink to the middle pocket, he walked away from the table as if that was it but a quiet word from Jan, "The fans Ronnie, do it for the fans", soon convinced O'Sullivan to come back to the table and finish off and that sums him up.

He loves the game and he loves the fans, even if that love affair is sometimes a bit bumpy.

As for O'Sullivan's future, I can see absolutely no reason why he can't win 10 world titles. He has five (which could easily have been six or seven) and there is nothing or nobody to stop him, if he feels like it.

And that's my main point about O'Sullivan really; he is unstoppable for as long as he wants to be unstoppable. Nobody can beat him – he's a complete, genuine, one-off who can do whatever he likes.

Saying that though, I wouldn't be surprised if he takes his time getting to 10. I think he'll win a couple, take a year or two off, win a few more, take another break and so on.

But I have no doubt that he'll leave a milestone that will never be beaten.

11

Jimmy Brown

My credit card wouldn't work at a petrol station one day because Jimmy White didn't exist any more, and I had to do loads of other paperwork changes – just for the sake of one week and one tournament! I could've done without the hassle but I was signed up by now and that was that.

After moving out of our place in Oxshott, I stayed in a couple of flats in London, until I settled again in Epsom, in Surrey, a lovely, friendly little town that is still my home now. Me and Maureen got divorced and our beautiful place went with it as the lawyers' fees swallowed up what it was worth.

Life was now a lot calmer, it felt great to no longer be in the grip of booze or gambling and I wanted to concentrate on trying to regain a top 16 place and to win some tournaments. In other words, I'd just grown up.

I would still go out for a drink every now and then but it wasn't night after night, week after week, as it had once been. For starters, when you hit 40 your body just isn't able to do it any more. As a kid I never suffered from hangovers so I could happily drink all day, every day but when you slow up, that all changes and although it took a while to adjust to a slower pace of life, it also made me happier.

The gambling was the same. I could still go out and have a flutter. I loved nothing more than a day at Ascot with some pals but where I'd once have put thousands on the outcome of a horse race, I'd go there and bet £100 a race, tops. The £20,000 days were long gone, believe me, and life was all the better for it. In fact, I even managed to get involved in one gambling event that rewarded me with some very handsome winnings, without a single penny being laid down in stake money.

In 2003, Barry Hearn knew I liked the cards so asked me if I wanted to play in his Poker Million event, held at the Sky studios in Middlesex. "Sure Baz," I told him. "Can't hurt can it?" Barry invited me, Davis and golfer Sam Torrance to take part to add a bit of sporting celebrity to the event and get people talking about poker.

We were supposed to be easy meat and I was a massive dark horse. What would me, a snooker player, know about going all the way in the Poker Million? I could understand those people who didn't fancy me for the title but I've been playing the game a long, long time. I've always enjoyed playing poker or kalooki and the lads on the tour would sometimes get around a table for a tournament. There is a lot of spare time when you're away from home so a game of poker with the other players is a good way to spend the time and not get too bored.

Davis, Hendry and Ken Doherty are all decent players; there are a lot of similarities between snooker and poker. You have to remain disciplined at both. If someone produces a fluke shot or a fluke card then you can't let it bother you too much and you also have to know when to defend and attack. I've always enjoyed playing so to be asked to take part was a real bonus for me, especially as I knew that although better players would beat me over a week, on my day I could beat anyone.

The final was held in March but the heats for the event had started back at Christmas and both me and Davis managed to win and get through to the televised final.

Mine and Davis's wins caused a bit of a kick-off among some of the professional players there because some felt we proved that the game was just one of luck, not one of skill. That was bollocks. The pair of us had worked hard to get to the final, regardless of what anyone else thought.

In the final there was me, Davis, Joe Beevers, Tony Bloom, Guy Bowles and a geezer who did Elvis impressions called Bruce Atkinson. I was the 8/1 outsider and apparently stood no chance.

It was a mad event because our hearts were wired up to these monitors so viewers at home could see how stressed we were getting and the glass tables meant everybody could also see what cards we all had. It was a classic made-for-telly kind of tournament and I settled my nerves with a big early win – even if punters at home were being told my heart rate was 140!

Davis was soon out and admitted afterwards that his head had gone under the pressure but I just kept hanging in there. I got some lovely cards, I stayed nice and calm, played and folded at the right times and sat back and let some of my opponents destroy themselves.

Inside, I could feel the excitement rising. 'You can win this Jimmy,' I told myself. 'Just keep steady and then attack when you get the chance.'

In the end there was nobody left but me and Beevers, who had been the favourite from the start.

I was heads-up with one of the best players in the world but poker is a funny old game and I edged him out with a pair of aces to his pair of jacks.

Joe really couldn't believe it and I wasn't that far behind. It wasn't quite a ranking tournament but winning is winning and it was fantastic to prove quite a few people wrong.

The Poker Million was actually 'only' worth £80,000 to the winner but I wasn't complaining and the most satisfying thing about that win wasn't the crowd going mad, or the spotlight, or gaining the respect of the poker professionals; the most satisfying thing was what I did with the money. I banked it...

•••••••

I don't know if it was the little confidence boost from that poker win or my attempts to settle down but the 2003/04 season that followed soon after was my finest in over a decade, including my first ranking event win since 1992. It seemed like a long time ago (that's because it *was* a long time ago) but everything felt like it was clicking again. I was cleaned up, I was concentrating, I was focusing and practising harder than ever and my love for snooker was as high as it's ever been.

The signs that I was getting back on track were there at the UK Championship, where I got to the semi-finals and then the Masters in February, 2004. I eventually lost to O'Sullivan in that last-four match at Wembley after I'd been given a wildcard for the tournament. The Masters has always been special and I felt I could've gone on and won it that year and although it wasn't meant to be, I proved I was still good enough to beat the likes of Neil Robertson (who was just a kid but already showing signs of being a fine player), Hendry and Peter Ebdon.

The Hendry win was particularly satisfactory because it was my first ever victory against him at the Masters, even if it was overshadowed by the behaviour of quite a few people in the crowd. The Wembley spectators have always treated me very well – I suppose it's my version of a home match – but the crowd booed Hendry that night and it was totally out of order. In fact it pissed me right off. Fair enough, the fans wanted me to win but Hendry was a seven-times world champion, a modern great, and he didn't deserve that. In fact, nobody deserves that, not over a snooker match.

I kept having a word with Colin Brinded and tried to help him settle the audience down. "Colin, we've got to do some-thing here," I said. "Put a message out over the tannoy or some-thing telling them that I want people to shut up and respect Stephen." It was idiotic because there were some dickheads sat there coughing, clearing their throats and opening sweet wrappers; anything to put Hendry off.

If the Masters gave me an inkling that I was back in form, I felt even better in Malta about a fortnight later when I got to the final of the European Open. I again beat Hendry, 5-3 this time in the last 16, before beating Neil Robertson and my good mate Tony Drago in the semi-final. Beating Drago on his home turf was not my most popular ever move but I was thrilled to be back in contention even if I didn't really get going in the final. I played Stephen Maguire who blew me away early on. He took a 6-0 lead in a first to nine match and there's not much chance you're going to pull that back. I was feeling great though, the press were starting to make noises about the season I was having, the game felt suddenly easier than it had done for a while and all was well.

That was until something happened to spoil it all.

I got nicked.

•••••••

How's this for taking the piss?

I did cocaine for God knows how many years and never got my collar felt once for it. The closest I'd been to bother with the police was when I was rightly done for drink-driving and for dancing with a shop dummy during the riots years ago.

And then, when I'm as clean as a whistle, I go and get done for cocaine possession, just weeks after playing Maguire and halfway through my best season in years.

I was totally, totally innocent.

We were in a Holiday Inn in Preston before an exhibition match against Higgins and a couple of lads who were with me – mentioning no names – were on the coke. Higgins announced his arrival at this hotel by standing around openly smoking a spliff in the lobby and I tried to get him to stop. "You can't just stand around smoking fucking dope in front of everyone," I said, but he wasn't having any of it. "I fucking can," he said.

"It's good for my throat after the cancer." He reckoned it helped the pain, so in the end I let him get on with it.

Anyway, the police were finally called because the hotel reception started smelling like an Amsterdam cafe. As these coppers raced through the Holiday Inn doors, one of the lads threw this wrap of coke on the floor, it skidded along the tiles and landed near me.

'Oh that's just fucking great news,' I thought...

Before you know it, I'm in handcuffs, the lad who has landed me in it is crying and I'm on my way to the nick.

I got there and immediately started telling them that I'd not done anything. I was up all night in the cell trying to tell them to test me, sat on the edge of this dingy bed, no shoes or belt, begging to be tested.

"Take some blood or let me take a piss," I was shouting, well happy to do it because I'd done nothing wrong. They weren't listening and in the end I had to take a caution. It was the quickest and simplest thing to do.

I came out of this nick and there was no press there at all. I was grinning, thinking 'I'm absolutely home and fucking dry here.' Then, as I'm at the airport flying home, my nephew rang me and said, "Uncle Jim, you're on Sky News." So that was that. Chaos.

You win some, you lose some but I've never had a problem with media attention. I've always given a quote when I've been asked to. I get on with reporters and I get the fact they've got a job to do. Speaking to them under tense circumstances wasn't ideal but that goes with the territory.

At least about a fortnight later I was speaking to them for a happier reason. Finally, after 12 long years, I was back as a ranking tournament winner when I won the Players Championship in Glasgow.

Some snooker players' careers don't last 12 months, never mind 12 years, so to still be around, challenging, competing and winning was just the most fabulous feeling.

I'd been through the wars mentally, physically and emotionally. I'd seen world titles ripped out of my hands, I'd lost my dear brother and mum, I'd been hit with cancer and scarred for life by shit surgeons, I'd pushed through drug, gambling and alcohol issues and I was still there, still putting myself up there to be shot at. The thousands and thousands of miles of travel, the hotel rooms, the first round losses to some young kid who barely knew who I was, the qualifying rounds in the middle of nowhere, the arrests and the divorce and the chaos and everything else. And yet I was still throwing punches.

That week in Glasgow was fantastic. I was rock-solid all week. I won't say it was my best ever snooker or that the crowd were left in awe by some of my play but it just all came together nicely. My positional play was superb, my safety game was in good condition and I felt great. My confidence was obviously up after the season I'd been having and I wanted to prove I still had a ranking win in me; to prove that I still had some power in my game.

The win took me to double figures for ranking title victories and there ain't many players out there who can say that. If you look at that tournament, I beat Shaun Murphy, John Parrott, Ian McCulloch and Peter Ebdon before I faced Paul Hunter in the final. None of those players are walkovers, all of them give you a hell of a match but I still had enough to win.

It was the kind of victory I'd been striving for and it was a tournament where everything came together nicely for me, just when I needed it to.

Against Ebdon I was 5-3 down, including a long sit-down as he made a 144 break, before I went on a great run to beat him 6-5. The Glasgow crowd were loving it, almost as much as I was. In that last frame I took on a tough green that I had to double if I wanted to stay alive. 'Here goes,' I thought, and I nearly closed my eyes as I attempted this shot to the middle pocket. It flew in and I went on to clear up. "Well played Jimmy, best of luck for the final," Peter said, as we shook hands. Ebdon is one of the hardest competitors in the game's history. His style of play isn't my cup of tea but snooker has a rulebook, not a style guide and it's certainly paid off for him.

In the final I played Paul who'd been red-hot in the rounds coming up to the final. I just wanted to compete with him and seize on any errors. I just wanted to prove I still belonged among the best in the world.

But I messed up early on. There were loads of errors, I couldn't find any fluency or form and I started to think the worst. The semi-final against Ebdon had lasted for what felt like six months and maybe I was knackered from that. Fortunately for me Paul didn't twist the knife like he could do – he was such a naturally gifted, wonderful potter – and it was still 4-4 after the first session.

I had a serious word with myself during the interval and then everything clicked. I hit some solid breaks, including a 76 to put me 8-5 in the lead.

I just needed one to win, one frame to end 12 years of waiting.

Paul, though, never gave you anything and was a born fighter. He got it back to 8-7 including a great pressure clearance to win on the black and I must admit, the old memories of the Crucible did start to surface. I knew the press and the commentators would be talking all about my past, and the tight matches that I'd lost.

But I wasn't going to be denied this time.

In the 16th frame I made a 49 break before missing a simple red over the middle pocket and that gave Paul half a chance. We then traded a few chances each, both going for our shots before Paul left me a very tough red into the top left hand pocket. The cue-ball was near the brown but, after 25 years of taking on these kinds of shots, I was hardly going to turn it down.

Yes, I was a new Jimmy – but there was still enough of the boy from Zan's in me to take on the impossible shot when I fancied it.

The red didn't touch the jaws as it disappeared and as the crowd started going crazy, I knew I was on the way to ending my long wait.

The crowd applauded every shot until Paul conceded. He came over to me straight away, gave me a big hug and we had a few words. I knew he was delighted for me because we were mates and the boy oozed class. My win meant Paul lost out on about £50,000 based on his season's ranking-event performances. That didn't bother him for a second and his grin was almost as wide as mine when I lifted the trophy.

It was such a sweet victory but it came at a price. It probably cost me about 10 days later when I lost to Barry Pinches in the first round at the Crucible. I had a shocker, from start to finish and Barry – who'd never really progressed past the first couple of rounds in any tournament – did enough to beat me. Fair play to him, he deserved it but I felt upset that I'd never got going and capitalised on my wins in Glasgow. If anything, the Players Championship win had sapped me of my mental and physical energy – proof, if I needed it, that although snooker is played in a suit and doesn't look like it takes much out of you, it is actually very gruelling at the highest level.

I was upset to lose at Sheffield under those circumstances but, as always, I accepted it quickly, realising that worse things happen in life.

Don't forget, I now knew what it felt like to not be at the Crucible during the best 17 days of the year, so although a first round loss left me gutted, it was better than being sat on a beach somewhere, pretending Sheffield didn't even exist and, anyway, I would soon have far more serious things to worry about.

•••••••

About eight months after losing at the Crucible, I was on the way back from Dubai where I'd been taking part in some private exhibitions. I was sat on the flight and I couldn't sit still; I was jumpy and couldn't fall asleep at all. Flying doesn't bother me and I must have travelled a million miles by air over my career but on this occasion I just couldn't settle. I was shuffling around and generally not having much fun. Ironically enough, once upon a time I'd would've just got smashed and fallen asleep but the new me didn't do that any more. When I look back now, it would've been far, far better if I'd had a drink and passed out instead of what actually happened.

Next to me on the plane was a pilot, on his way somewhere for his next flight. He was a great bloke, your classic-looking, clean-cut pilot and we got chatting about jet-lag and our jobs and so on. He knew who I was and we got on really well, plus he knew all about spending hours cooped up on a plane. He did it for a living, after all.

I happened to mention to him my problem with going to sleep and his answer made sense at the time. Little did I know it would fuck me, good and proper.

"Jimmy, mate," he started. "You want to go to the doctors and get some proper medication, they can give you stuff to help you sleep."

At the time it sounded really tempting. I got back to Epsom and went to see a doctor and told him what was up. Twenty minutes later I walked out of there with a prescription for Temazepam.

To start with, there was nothing wrong. These pills helped me get to sleep and it was all fine. Then, before you knew it, I could feel myself getting into bother.

When I went out and had a few drinks, I might have expected to drop off in front of the telly when I got home, like any normal bloke. But that wasn't happening. It didn't matter what I did, my brain never let me switch off until I'd taken my tablets.

I'd always remember to take my pills and they went from helping me to hurting me in no time at all. I realised I was gone. Gripped again. It just kind of crept up on me. One minute you think you're fine and the next it hits home how much these pills have you by the balls.

I remember one time I said to myself, 'Right, no more tablets.' That lasted about 48 hours before I was back down the doctors. 'Fucking hell, this has got hold of me big time,' I thought. I wasn't wrong and in the meantime I was really aggressive and short with everyone and in a really bad mood.

That was a turning point for me.

Finally, I decided that enough was enough and I decided to go cold turkey in my house in Epsom. It was time to do something about this. I cut the drugs out completely and prepared for the worst.

But preparing for the worst and actually going through it are two different things. If I'd had to battle in the past to get off crack cocaine and then wean myself off powder, it was nothing compared to giving those sleeping pills up.

I can honestly say I went through the worst 11 days of my life as my body let go of those drugs.

I didn't sleep properly for any of it. I'd grab 15 minutes here and there throughout the day and that left me like a zombie. The pills were truly destructive and frightening – and don't forget that half the world is on them.

As I already knew through crack, sometimes you have to put yourself through the mill and just stare a drug down if you want to get off it and slowly it got better. I stopped being a lunatic, screaming at anybody who came near me and I finally managed to get it under control.

When I came out the other side, the most satisfying thing was knowing that I'd had the strength, again, to do it. Anyone who has gone cold turkey on any drug; crack, coke, booze, fags or anything, deserves massive respect because you won't do anything harder in your entire life. I should've gone to see a therapist or got some help but I didn't bother because when I set my mind to it, I can be as strong as anybody.

Just before I decided to give up, I also had a line of charlie, the first in quite a few years by this point. I don't know why I did it; temptation again, I guess, but it happened. Turns out it was the best thing for me because it made me realise that I was missing fuck all.

I was so thrilled to finally ditch those pills as my game had slipped while I was addicted and I'd really struggled to make any impact in ranking tournaments.

The game itself seemed to be in decline as well. The 1980s were a long, long time ago and snooker's heyday seemed well and truly gone. The game needed some publicity, it needed some fun and some humour.

It needed Jimmy Brown.

•••••••

Before the 2005 Masters, I was approached by a PR company doing work for HP Sauce, who'd decided to sponsor the brown ball in the tournament to the tune of £100,000.

I've heard some mad ideas in my time but this one was the best yet. "Jimmy, would you consider changing your name to Jimmy Brown?" I was asked. And the answer was, obviously, "No" at first. However, I got thinking about it and as far as I could see it was a way of getting snooker back into the headlines and under the spotlights.

The game was in a real mess, the prize money was poor, there were only about six decent tournaments a year and players were getting bored, restless and earning bad money. I thought that this little stunt might raise a laugh or two and remind the British public that snooker was still around and still something worth getting involved in.

In the end I agreed to do it and it was a bit of a laugh. I wore a brown tuxedo rather than my normal black one and it made all the newspapers and TV news channels, just as we'd hoped it would.

If I'd have won the Masters that year, I would've genuinely wanted the name Jimmy Brown engraved on the trophy, even if snooker's bosses did not see the funny side. The BBC, Eurosport and World Snooker all declared that I'd be known as Jimmy White throughout the tournament and I'd be introduced to the crowds by my 'old' name as well. It all seemed a bit pompous to me; it was only a fucking joke after all.

What wasn't as funny was the hassle you had to go through to change your name. Girls, you have my sympathies because if changing your surname is always such a pain in the arse then I'd never want to get married in the first place!

I got it done by deed-poll and then before you know it there's loads of aggravation, everything stops working, including your credit card, and loads of paperwork needs sorting out.

On the table, Jimmy Brown performed far, far better than Jimmy White had been doing, coming from 5-1 down against Matthew Stevens to beat him 6-5 before eventually losing to O'Sullivan in the semi-final.

Hearing Wembley roar after a close win, especially the victory over Stevens, was as thrilling as ever but, overall, the season was a disappointment as I couldn't get past the last 16 in any ranking tournaments and eventually, the season after I changed my name, I dropped out of the top 32 altogether. I couldn't buy a win all season – and lost to David Gray in the first round of the World Championship.

The only point I'd make about that year was the tables were a total joke – that's not sour grapes either as loads of players complained but, equally, you can't go into the Crucible on the back of such a bad season and expect to produce a miracle. David was solid enough to beat me fair and square and you could feel the Crucible disappointment when I walked out of the arena. I lifted my cue to say thanks and acknowledge the crowd. That was my last World Championship visit. For now.

The press the next day was full of chat about it being the end of an era and I was obviously gutted to fall out of the top 32 for the first time in 25 years as a professional but you get what you deserve in this sport and my game had just gone, completely.

Dropping out of the top 32 also meant I'd now have to qualify for major events, spending hours in Prestatyn in front of nobody, trying to make it into a tournament's later rounds. Sometimes people ask me what that feels like, to have gone from playing in front of thousands to playing in front of, literally, two punters and I genuinely have no problem with it whatsoever.

Every player there is scrapping for their professional lives. They've all put the work in, they've all got their own hopes and dreams and just because my track record at the very top of the game is so long doesn't mean I haven't got massive respect for those lower down the sport.

If anything, I respect them even more.

It's easy to play snooker when the limelight is on you and when the fans are on your side, you're making great money and you're famous. But you try getting out of bed every morning and practising for six hours a day when nobody gives a shit who you are. The players who do that (and there are hundreds of them) are the players who really love the sport and I consider myself in their camp as well.

Qualifying in Prestatyn wasn't 'beneath me' because I've never been a snob. I've always treated every opponent and every frame with respect and, when all is said and done, all I've ever wanted is a table, 22 snooker balls and a cue. I'd play the game in the dark, on my own, if I had to because ultimately it's the sport I love, not the circus that comes with it. Plus, life very often has a way of reminding you what actually matters. And it ain't snooker, not really – not when it comes down to it.

The things that matter, that actually count, are your family, your health and your mates.

Mates like Paul Hunter.

•••••••

I thought I'd felt enough grief when it comes to cancer but the death of Paul in October, 2006, was another unwanted reminder of just how cruel the world can be. I don't think I'll ever suffer anything as devastating as Martin passing away but Paul's death comes close. Me and Paul were a fair few years apart but we got on like brothers.

He was my little mate and I loved him to bits.

From the minute he came onto the tour he had that charisma and character and we were just drawn to each other immediately. He had that glint in his eye, he liked a party, women absolutely adored him and life was exciting with him around.

The first time I got to know him properly was when we went to Thailand for the Thailand Open in 1996. Me and Maureen were split up at the time – surprise, surprise – and Paul sat next to me on the plane. He was so excited.

Paul was a beautiful looking boy, about 18 at the time, and already full of life and adventure. He used to call me 'Toucan' because of my hair – he was the only one who dared call me that and I didn't mind because I loved the kid – and he wouldn't shut up about how much he was looking forward to Thailand.

"What's Bangkok like, Toucan?" he said.

"It's fucking magic mate," I said. "You'll love it."

Well, anyone who's been to Bangkok will tell you that the place is insane and all the girls on the street corners and in the bars go crazy for tall Western boys – especially tall Western boys with a pocketful of cash.

I thought I'd take him out and try and shock him but Paul took it all in his stride. We walked past street after street of bar girls and strippers trying to entice us in for a drink. At one point Paul had an endless stream of girls following him, telling him that rather than paying for their 'services' he could get whatever he wanted for free! He just grinned and we had a wild night. He wasn't married at the time and took a few girls home for company, swigging back some bottle of Thai spirit and having the best night of his life.

The next day at about 1pm, there was a little knock at the door.

I opened it and there was Paul, with this lovely big smile on his face.

"Morning Toucan," he said.

"What do you want?" I said, half-asleep.

"I don't want 'owt," he said.

"I just had to tell ya I can't wait for tonight. I just can't wait."

So, from then on, I nicknamed him 'Can't Wait.'

He was a really lovely bloke who lived his life to the full. One of the reasons for that was he always had a bit of a downer about his life prospects. It was weird but somehow he always felt that he wasn't destined to be around for a long time. He always thought he'd get something terminal and maybe that's why he lived for the day.

It was sad that he thought that way and even sadder when it came true.

He was also a tremendous player. He was a pretty boy but he had a backbone as well. Tony Knowles was the pretty boy of the '80s but Paul became the ultimate pretty boy of the 2000s.

I stay in touch with Lindsay and Paul's daughter Evie Rose. I get in touch with her on a birthday and she sent me her first letter this year, which was very touching. Hopefully when she gets to 18, I can tell her what a beautiful guy her dad was.

Paul had the potential to be the world champion but he was also a full-blown party animal. He really liked a drink and a night out. We only had one rule: we went for it until one of us passed out. That was what Paul was like; and, believe me, I struggled to stay close to him some nights.

Don't get me wrong – there was more to Paul than making headlines and liking a drink. If you got on the table with him he'd try and beat you, plain and simple. He was a fabulous talent and he could get into a zone where he wouldn't miss a ball. If he got going you might as well hang your cue up and ring a taxi because he was close to unbeatable. Paul won the Masters three times and you can't be a mug and do that. He would also have gone on to win the World Championship for sure.

Paul had a really rare form of cancer and suffered from neuroendocrine tumours that attacked his stomach lining. Only about 3,000 people a year get hit with it and he fought so courageously to try and beat these tumours but there were too many of them.

One of the bravest things I've ever seen is Paul's performances at the World Championship in 2006. He'd undergone so much treatment by then but he didn't want anyone to feel sorry for him. He just didn't have the strength to compete as he once could and Neil Robertson beat him 10-5.

That was his last match.

See what I mean when I say something like a snooker match isn't worth getting upset about?

I'd gone to see him during his treatment and it left me heart-broken. Anyone who has seen cancer close up knows that the treatment for the disease is truly painful and agonising in itself and Paul was no different. He was so weak and he knew it.

"Toucan, I can't practise," he said. "And if I can't practise, I can't win." He was right but he went to Sheffield that year and still tried his heart out like the champion he was.

We were praying for a miracle because of his age and his strength but it wasn't to be. I was playing an exhibition in Bredbury Hall when I heard he had passed away. A casino in Stockport had bid quite a lot of money for some of its members to play me with all proceeds going to Leukemia Research. Paul got married at Bredbury Hall so it felt a bit strange to be there when I heard he'd died.

I was with Kevin Kelly and as I was playing, Kevin took the phone call. You could literally see him turning white. The blood just ran from his face, I knew something was up but I was trying to entertain these people so I carried on potting. Finally, I went over to see what it was about and Kevin dropped the news on me.

"It's Paul," he said. "He's gone."

I had to finish the game. I was in the room with 40 strangers who'd all paid good money so I wanted to make sure that the exhibition went as well as it could but I couldn't wait to get out of there, couldn't wait for some privacy. When me and Kevin did manage to escape we cried our eyes out, two grown men, for about an hour. What a terrible, terrible tragedy and liberty – a young man as talented and as lovely as Paul, gone.

I think we stayed at Bredbury Hall that night – I can't really remember – and we just went to the room in total and utter shock. We knew he'd been very poorly but you can never prepare for that moment when you hear something as dreadful as that.

At the funeral in Leeds Parish Church, all the snooker players stuck together. There was me, Ronnie O'Sullivan, Steve Davis, John Parrott, Willie Thorne, Dennis Taylor, John Virgo and Joe Johnson there, as well as a few others.

I was the first to start crying in the church because I just couldn't hold it in any more. I'd had a good cry before the service started but managed to get control again until he was carried past me and that was it. I set everybody off. We were all sobbing by the end, all crying for our mate, a talented boy we all loved and still miss.

His missus, Lindsay, is a strong woman. She was like a rock during that time – an amazing effort under the circumstances – and the sheer unfairness of life hit me right between the eyeballs, again.

Paul had done nothing to deserve what had happened to him and yet we were watching his coffin being carried in. That day will live with me forever, as will my memories of 'Can't Wait', one of the finest talents, and loveliest mates I've ever had.

•••••••

A year after Paul passed away, I lost my dad too.

What can I say about my dad? Tom White was a great, great man – and not because he let me come to The Duke with him on a Friday.

He was one of the biggest characters I've ever known, a lovely, generous, genuine fellow – quick to buy you a pint and crack a joke.

At tournaments during the height of the rivalry between me and Davis in the '80s, if you wanted to know where Tom White was, all you had to do was ask where Bill Davis was. While me and Davis were slugging it out on the table, my old man and Davis's dad would be in the lounge, sharing a beer together and having a laugh. Both men obviously wanted their boys to do well but they had a great friendship and that summed up how much class they both had.

Dad used to have me in stitches and he followed me around on tour for 20 years, always offering support, lending a hand and usually making people laugh.

One year at the Crucible, he had a thing for the drama series Boys From The Black Stuff. He thought he was Yosser Hughes and he kept walking around the Crucible to every member of staff going: "Gizza job. Go on, gizza job, I could do your job." Everybody was falling about pissing themselves and all the other players in the snooker world loved him.

Dad would go and dance the Charleston in the Crucible foyer some years, made up that I'd won. He'd be in all the bars with the WPBSA guys or just with the public, holding court, making people smile and having a good time. He wasn't just there when I won, if I lost he was still out and about with people, enjoying himself.

JIMMY BROWN

We only had a cross word once. One year I lost one of the finals at the Crucible – I can't remember which one – and he said, "I might not be here next year" and I got the hump with him for that and didn't speak to him for about two months. That was the closest we ever got to an argument because he was as proud of me as I was of him. He'd been a wonderful dad in his own, old-school way.

I remember being in the Balham United Services Club one time when I was about 10 and I had a black eye. Some kid at school had beaten me up (nothing good ever happens at school does it?) so I was a little bit down and Dad turned around to all his mates and he did his best to cheer me up.

"There's my boy," he said, pointing at me.

"He got beaten up today but he gave it everything he had and I'm proud of him for that."

When you're a young kid, a bit of praise from your dad goes a long way and he restored my pride with that little performance. I've never forgotten it.

He lived with me for the last seven years of his life. At 80-odd years of age, he'd be out until midnight every night, he'd come back and then take the dogs for a walk. He was a livewire and he got well known in Epsom because he'd nip in everywhere during the day to say hello.

Every day would be the same. He'd put on a suit, the Racing Post tucked under his arm, and he'd pop into all the shops and pubs, just to see how everyone was. He still loved a pint and I'd have drivers looking for him everywhere but he'd give them the slip, so he could nip off for a beer. He used to worry me but I knew he was happy and that people were looking after him. I used to get texts from people all over Epsom saying, "Your dad's in the British Legion, he's okay" and that would put me at ease. He'd then usually come back in at all hours, get some frozen chicken out and try and fry it; he was fucking nuts!

One day, though, he was in Wilkinson's and some kid who worked in there banged into him heavily with a trolley. It was a total accident and the kid never meant it but it totally knocked my dad for six and he went downhill from there.

You could see him slowly slipping away. He got angry about it in the end because he hated not being able to do the things he loved, like going out and speaking to people, having a pint and a flutter. In the end he went to my sister Jackie's, just like my mum did, and he was nursed there until he eventually passed away in Epsom Hospital.

Dad had always loved being the President of the Balham United Services Club and about 400 people turned up at his funeral at Lambeth Crematorium, including Higgins, who flew in from Ireland for it. It was a lovely tribute and the number of people there was a testimony to what a character he'd been and what a life he'd lived.

Unlike when Martin or Paul died, and to some extent Mum, there was no anger or bitterness when dad passed away. He'd lived a fabulous life, raising five kids who totally adored him, he had friends all over the country and the world and he'd spent 20 years with me, enjoying every moment of my career alongside me. He'd had a ball.

By the time Dad died, I was becoming a stranger to the later rounds of tournaments, barely making the last 32, consistently losing out when it came to getting to the World Championship and my ranking continued to head south.

But you know what?

JIMMY BROWN

It didn't bother me.

Of course, I still wanted to be playing winning snooker, I still wanted to the world champion – I still do – but I was playing the game for the thrill it gave me, the same as always. The snooker world had moved on and we were now in O'Sullivan's era as me, Davis and Hendry all struggled to hit our previous heights.

Snooker had given me the opportunities to do something with my life, to let me see the world and it had given me the opportunities of a lifetime, one of which included a trip to the jungle.

•••••••

I first got asked to go on 'I'm A Celebrity...Get Me Out Of Here' back in 2006 but I didn't really fancy it. I was happy playing in tournaments and doing exhibitions and life was okay. I didn't need the money and I certainly didn't need to sit in the middle of the Australian jungle for a fortnight, doing fuck all.

However, by the time they asked again in 2009, snooker was starting to look like a shambles. Barry Hearn hadn't got involved yet, there were only about six tournaments a year and it was all so boring. The game was in serious danger of going bust. You'd play in a tournament and then have to wait about six weeks for another one. I was just getting so fed up with not playing that when the phone went one day and they asked me if I fancied getting involved I thought, 'Fuck it, I'm off.'

I thought it would be fun and, of course, everyone goes in there for the money. I got a sum that I couldn't really turn down.

Until you actually get in the jungle, ITV treat you very well and I was given a business class ticket to Brisbane. It was all going nicely, a glass of champagne here, a canape there, until

I realised I might have to do a parachute jump to get into the jungle, full of snakes and fuck knows what else.

I looked out of the window at Brisbane Airport and it all dawned on me what I was being asked to do.

'What the fuck have you done here Jimmy?' I said to myself, grinning. 'You've been in some spots and made some moves in your time but this is the best yet.'

I didn't parachute into the jungle. I went in on a horse called Paddy. Being thrown out of a plane didn't sound like my cup of tea but then after 10 seconds on Paddy I would've happily thrown myself out of a plane, parachute or no parachute.

It was boiling hot and Paddy didn't seem to want to follow the same script as everyone else. We had to get on these horses and descend into this big deep ravine, surrounded by rainforest and animals on all sides.

The jungle was moving with life and dangerous creatures that I didn't recognise – a bit like Zan's really – and as we were going down this ravine, with big 100-feet drops all around us, Paddy, God bless him, did not fancy it. This fucking donkey kept stopping and panicking and I eventually got told that the reason he was so nervous was because he had a cataract in his left eye and couldn't see.

"Sorry," I said. "I could've sworn you just told me I've got a half-blind horse." Terrific. That was just what I needed.

Here's me, sweat pouring from everywhere, a boy straight from the concrete jungle, stuck in the middle of a real one with a one-eyed horse. 'Well, well, well Jimmy, you've done it here son.'

Paddy didn't want to know, wouldn't listen to what I was trying to tell him to do and it took us forever to finally get down into the camp. I've backed better donkeys than Paddy – and that's saying something.

With a show like 'I'm A Celebrity', you don't know how you're going to get on with everyone and whether or not someone is going to do your nut in or act like an idiot. Luckily enough for me, I got on with pretty much everybody in there.

As far as I could see, we were all there to try and help each other through it and to try and have some fun and be entertaining along the way.

I knew Sam Fox from the '80s when we'd had a few drinks and knocked about in the same circles in the West End and I was also a big fan of George Hamilton. Through Ronnie Wood I was a fan of the Small Faces, and Rod Stewart had married George Hamilton's first wife, Alena, after they'd split up. I couldn't really believe he was on the show because to me he was a big American film star but we got on really, really well. I asked him why he was stuck in the middle of the Aussie jungle with the rest of us and he told me the honest truth, which I respected. "Jimmy," he said. "These days I come to London and nobody recognises me any more. That feels strange."

The show was his way of getting back in the public eye and he was a really funny, charismatic guy who charmed all of us.

Jordan was also in there with us and she was a fantastic girl. I really got on with her. She's fiercely clever, she takes no shit off anyone and knows exactly what she's doing. Jordan came in the jungle after she'd split up with Peter Andre, so the public were out to get her and she got elected to do trial after trial.

She just laughed it all off though and wouldn't let it bother her until, about nine days in, she'd had enough and pulled out. "I'll send that hotel crazy," she said and that is what she did. She started this big media circus at the Palazzo Versace Hotel where we were staying and probably made a ton of money from it as well. She's the kind of girl who should never be underestimated, no matter what people think or say about her.

Me, Gino D'Acampo, Justin Ryan and Kim Woodburn all got really close during the show.

Me and Gino had a bit of a system because as an Italian chef, he wanted to do all the cooking. You know what the passionate Italians get like and he saw the kitchen area as his territory.

He came to me one day and made a plan. "Jimmy, when my voice goes higher at the end of a sentence, get the kitchen cleared out." From then on, whenever Gino fancied doing some cooking without hurting anyone else's feelings he'd just shout "Jimmy, JIMMY," and that would be enough. I'd get the kitchen ready and he'd get on with cooking our food which was usually beans. I think I ate every type of bean on Earth during that fortnight and I'll never touch another one as long as I live.

The thing was, the ITV producers were devastated because they love a bit of a kick-off during the cooking each night to boost ratings but Gino's high-pitched voice and my efforts to make sure he could always cook meant that everybody always got on pretty well. The only person I wasn't that keen on was the Australian boxer, Joe Bugner.

Bugner was a bit aggressive towards a few people and he still thought it was the 1970s at times. I took the piss out of him a bit and it kept going over his head until one day, the penny must've dropped and he turned. "What the fuck did you just say?" he said. That was me done. I never said another word because I knew there was nowhere to hide.

It was a great laugh but it was also very, very tough. Weight fell off me and it was so hot and humid for most of the time but I wouldn't swap it for the world.

I thoroughly enjoyed it and when Davis came up to me about 18 months later and asked me whether he should go on it or not I didn't hesitate. "Jump at it mate," I said. "It's brilliant and it will change your life."

I really meant that as well. I was lucky to be involved. I got plenty of column inches and I came third but it didn't change my profile at all.

The phone wasn't ringing off the hook all of a sudden so I got the best of both worlds – it was nice to know I still had plenty of fans out there but it didn't lead to a manic three months of interviews, so I was more than happy.

I did get offered the chance for a couple more celebrity shows but that was me done. There's no way I want to see me dancing on a Saturday night, never mind half the country, so I drew a line under all that.

•••••••

At the same time as I was messing about in Australia, I also got involved in a venture that has given me another lease of life and means I still get to entertain the public, have a laugh with some of my old pals and travel the country; three things I've always loved doing.

I got booked to do a presentation in Reading one night for the Reading and District Billiards Snooker League. I was late getting there because of traffic trouble but I finally managed to make it and as I was handing out awards, a complete stranger called Jason Francis saw a chance and couldn't resist it.

"Jimmy, I could put exhibitions on at the Crucible with you and Alex if you want," he said.

Yeah, right, course you can.

I didn't know who this geezer was and he stood in front of me and started promising all these events and exhibitions and everything else. I've spotted enough charmers and chancers in my time and thought Jason was just another one.

However, what I didn't know was that he could actually back up every word.

In 1997, he'd set up a company that produced children's theatre shows up and down the country so he had contacts all over the place. Jason was a massive snooker fan, Alex was his all-time hero and he dreamt of getting some of snooker's old school back together.

I was still sceptical but Jason got back in touch over the next few weeks and slowly it all came together and the Snooker Legends tour became reality.

He even delivered on his promise of getting us back in the Crucible, something I'd never dreamt he could really deliver on. The Crucible was only supposed to host the World Championship – no other snooker was meant to be played there – but because Snooker Legends had no prize money and wasn't a professional tournament, Jason managed to get around that loophole.

Jason's biggest challenge had been trying to get Higgins on board but he finally agreed to meet in a Dublin hotel and Higgins walked in, kissed Jason full on the lips and then gave him a receipt for 60 euros for the taxi ride, all written out on the back of an old bookies slip. "Babes, let's do it," Higgins said, and we were up and running.

The first Legends show was a sell-out in 48 hours. It really caught the public's imagination and all was going well until five days beforehand when Higgins went into a Belfast hospital with pneumonia but, true to form, he checked himself out and turned up in Sheffield still wearing the hospital wristband.

"I had to bribe a doctor babe," he told Jason. "It cost me 600 euros to get him to release me. You owe me that money I'm afraid." Jason had no choice but to cough up, even if he thought Higgins was pulling a fast one.

For that first exhibition there was me, Higgins, John Parrott and Cliff Thorburn while Jason also pulled off the masterstroke of getting John Virgo on board as the MC and Michaela Tabb in as the referee. JV is great at his job, taking the piss out of himself and all the players and putting everyone at ease while Michaela is a very popular referee so it worked really well.

Unfortunately, Higgins didn't. He wore the hat and the green shirt he'd worn back in his heyday but he had no strength, no cue power and it was clear that he couldn't play at the level we needed him to.

I soon fell out with Jason when he decided to let Higgins go after just one exhibition because I felt that was the wrong thing to do but he was replaced by Dennis Taylor – another crowd pleaser – and the events just went from strength to strength.

It gave me so much pleasure to be playing on great tables, against great mates, reliving some of the wild times of the '80s, in front of crowds who just wanted to be entertained.

In 2010 we did 18 shows, all with me, Parrott, Thorburn, Dennis, JV and Michaela. We played a format where there would be one winner and even though it was an exhibition it was amazing how quickly it became competitive between me and Parrott over who could win the most. John had only just retired so was still sharp and over the short distance he was capable of beating anyone.

You never lose that will and the desire to beat other players, even when there are no ranking points at stake. Good old fashioned pride is enough to play for and me and John were always trying to get the better of each other.

As the Snooker Legends tour grew and grew, we started to get guest appearances from Ken Doherty and Mark Williams also joined us for one in Wales.

It was good, competitive snooker but always with a smile and a joke – usually at my expense when Virgo had a microphone in his hand. It also kept me sharp, kept me practising well and focusing on still trying to improve.

Playing professionally on the tour will always be my number one ambition and motivation. I was still travelling all over the country and the world to play in events – even if I rarely made the last 32 – and the Snooker Legends tour benefitted from me still being competitive while my professional career benefitted from me playing so regularly under pressure with Snooker Legends, so it was win-win really.

One of the early highlights came in May, 2010, in Redhill where I hit the Snooker Legends' first 147 break and then followed it up with a 134, just missing the pink into the middle pocket, which would have given me back-to-back maximums.

As that proved, I was still good enough to be competing and still hungry enough to want to be the very best, even if my tournament play and ranking were not where I wanted them to be.

In 2011, we played 28 dates and the carrot that got everybody involved was playing at the Crucible again. I don't know what it is about the place but when Jason mentions it to any of the old players, their eyes light up and they sign up on the spot. It's the home of our game and most of the guys on the Snooker Legends tour have long since given up trying to get back there. Most have tasted glory in that arena so I suppose the chance to take one last, long, look around the place, to walk down those steps and to hear the crowds roaring your name one more time is too tempting to ignore.

And in 2011, it was certainly enough to bring Kirk Stevens back over from Canada.

Coke had ruined Kirk's life but he'd worked so, so hard and turned his life around entirely. After leaving the tour 20-odd years ago he'd gone back home, worked as a car salesman and loads of other things and cleaned himself up. I'd booked into the Jury's Inn in Sheffield and thought Kirk wasn't arriving until the day after so, after ditching my bags in the room, I got back in the lift and went back down to reception. As the doors opened there was my old mate, stood right in front of me, looking as healthy and as happy as you can be.

You know what's it's like when you see old friends, the years just drop away in a split-second. "Hello mate, how are you?" I spluttered out and there were tears in my eyes as well. We hugged and laughed and it was as if 20 years had never happened. It was a very, very emotional moment. I knew all the other players were the same when they saw Kirk again.

You've got to remember that me, Kirk, John Parrott, Virgo, Dennis, Cliff had all spent the very best, funniest, greatest years of our lives together; travelling the world, going to nightclubs and bars all over the place, getting in and out of scrapes and having a ball.

We'd been on top of the world while snooker was on top of the world and the ride had been something else.

The chance then to see that Kirk had not only survived all those scrapes but come back a better and stronger man for it was wonderful. I loved him when we were both kids and I feel no different now.

Over the years, other legends like Tony Knowles and Doug Mountjoy have joined us and O'Sullivan and Hendry have also become regular competitors so the standard of play is higher than it's ever been.

We've also started branching out and involving competitors from other sports and John Terry, the Chelsea captain, joined us in Guildford at one event.

I'm a big Chelsea fan and it was great to have him on board. I've known John for quite a while and he is a fantastic guy and a real credit to Chelsea and to himself.

On this night in Guildford, he was on Hendry's team while I played with a raffle winner. As we were waiting to walk out into the tunnel, he was literally shaking.

"Jimmy," he said. "I'm more nervous walking out here than I've ever been playing football. How do you cope with this all the time?" I just laughed and couldn't believe what I was hearing.

This is a bloke who's played in a Champions League final and has captained his country and he was terrified!

We soon put him at ease though and he hit a 30 break so he can definitely play a bit. He really loved it and grew into it. I see him in the Surrey area a fair bit and we always catch up and have a coffee together when we can.

I hope the Snooker Legends tour continues to go from

strength to strength. It's a fantastic way to get out there, meet new people, try and beat my oldest rivals and have a laugh.

I suppose my only regret is that Higgins, my best friend, is not around to be part of it.

12

Higgins

On July 24, 2010, a lovely lady by the name of Ann went to check on her brother's address in Belfast.

She thought he was in Marbella getting some badly needed teeth implants and wanted to make sure his flat was in nice shape for when he returned.

She turned the front door key and immediately knew something was up. She walked into her brother's room and found him lying there, dead in bed.

Ann had just lost her beloved Sandy.

I had just lost my best friend, my inspiration and a man I worshipped to the end.

The snooker world had just lost the greatest shotmaker of them all, Alex 'The Hurricane' Higgins...

HIGGINS

To be honest, I didn't know how to deal with the subject of Higgins (I rarely called him Alex) because of the size of the impact he has had on my life. In the end I thought that the best way to do him justice would be to try and put most of the laughs, the madness, the thrills and the danger of being his best mate into one place. So here goes...

Being close to Higgins meant you were constantly in a world of chaos. Utter fucking chaos. But it also meant you were in a world full of excitement and drama. His life was the maddest soap opera ever. He could be the kindest soul on the planet, speaking in a tiny whisper, or he could be a maniac, roaring and ranting at anyone in his sights – scaring fans, fellow players, sponsors, snooker officials and anyone else who he decided, on the spot, had done him an injustice. Alex had two sides to him. Often you saw both of those sides within 30 seconds of each other.

He was the most enigmatic, charismatic, energetic, fantastic man I ever knew. When you were with Higgins, you weren't a passenger in life – you were living it to the maximum and, yes, living on the edge often meant he fell off. He took me with him a few times and there have been moments in my life when his vanity and insane behaviour truly pissed me off.

But Alex was Alex.

The first glimpse I got of him came from the television show Pot Black. It seems crazy to think it now but Pot Black was invented, apparently, because the bosses at BBC needed shows that could promote colour telly. For snooker it was the perfect fit because back when Pot Black started in the late '60s, snooker only had a handful of tournaments and was still only popular in social clubs up and down the country. So snooker needed the publicity and the BBC needed the viewing figures – the perfect match.

I was sitting at home one night with Mum and Dad and Higgins was on the TV. I can't remember who he was playing but I'll never forget one particular shot he played. There was a straight red and a black over the middle pocket. It was just a case of potting the red and then sending the white up and down off the top cushion. Ten out of 10 players would play it nice and simple but Higgins always wanted to entertain, not to play safe. He hit the red ball with tons of check-side and came straight back up the table for the black. It was an amazing pot, a shot that at the time nobody else in the world could've dreamt up, let alone attempted. I was learning, right there and then, that there might be a million snooker players out there but there was only one Higgins.

I fell in love with his style from that moment on. It was just everything about how he played and the swagger with which he did it. He hated all the stuffiness and the dickie-bow world of snooker. He hated playing with a formula or a plan. He was just a born genius; a man who lived by instinct alone and who survived on the snooker table by being more attacking, adventurous and skilful than the rest of the sport put together. Sitting there, watching him perform on Pot Black on our little telly, was one of the most important few moments of my early life. I knew right then that he was the man I wanted to play like.

I first met Higgins when I was about 13 when my dad put an exhibition on in the Balham United Services Club. Back then, exhibitions were the main way for a player to make any money. Now, of course, there is a tournament somewhere in the world every five minutes but in the 1970s, the snooker world had no real structure to it. You were on your own. So players like Higgins trawled up and down the country to play in exhibitions to earn a few quid and entertain the fans. He turned up at Dad's exhibition for something like £90; amazing when you think about it. Imagine the same thing happening today. Imagine Cristiano Ronaldo turning up for a five-a-side match for that. It just wouldn't happen.

The club was packed that night, dense with cigarette smoke and with the paying punters only a few feet from the players. Often, a player would have to ask a punter to shift in their seat, one way or another, so they could play their shots.

Players quipped and laughed with the audience and they shared the ups and downs of a match in a way that doesn't happen now. Snooker fans are still close to the action compared to a lot of sports but during those exhibition nights, a player would barely have to move an inch before he was sat in the front row himself. He could nick a punter's fag without them even knowing it.

Alex was the big draw that night but Dad was sceptical about whether he'd show up and he'd also booked Willie Thorne, just in case. It was good thinking from my old man because Alex going AWOL wasn't exactly a rare event.

However, word soon raced around the club that he had arrived and was outside. You could feel the tension and the excitement rise, the punters spoke louder and faster, jockeying for position to see Higgins' entrance.

He finally waltzed into the room in this big, flash fur coat.

As always, he seemed determined to entertain and cause a stir. He oozed charisma and when he was in the spotlight he seemed to change and grow somehow – as if he was born to be there and to do it. I saw it that first night with my very own eyes and he did it again on thousands of occasions. Like a rockstar or a comedian who needs the cheer of the crowd, Higgins came alive when all eyes were on him.

Higgins never drove anywhere and he had turned up on his own, as he always used to do back then – until we became friends and used to travel far and wide together.

He might have arrived on his own but he was determined that he would be leaving with some company as he settled into a bit of patter with a girl in the audience who he was sure he could convince to go home with him. The only problem was, the girl was my sister. Higgins gave it all the Blarney Stone charm he could muster – which wasn't much, he was terrible with women – until, eventually, my eldest brother, Tommy, decided enough was enough and wanted to knock him out. But that was what Higgins was like.

It was an early and up-close lesson in the man himself. He had no sense of timing and no understanding of circumstances. His whole life was a rollercoaster. He was a man who couldn't be contained, a man for whom the normal rules of life – just like the normal way of playing snooker – meant absolutely nothing. I remember being so excited about meeting him that I didn't sleep for the week before he turned up.

I can't remember that first conversation but it was probably filled with "babe" – his favourite word (he called men that, too). It was the start of a friendship that would become the most important in my life.

In between trying to pull Jackie, I played a frame against him and won. I couldn't believe it. Higgins was totally gracious and the complete gentleman, telling my dad that I was a star of the future. I was that stunned, and that shy, that I just stood there in silence and in total awe.

One of the reasons Higgins was a genius was because he could play on any table. When you travel the thousands of miles he did throughout his life, playing exhibitions in bad clubs and pubs across the country, you become tuned in to how to play on tables with bad cloths and tight pockets. The best modern player would walk into a working man's club these days and be clueless on the tables because they can be so bad. But that was the world Higgins knew, the world he had come from and the world he was most comfortable in. It was the world I was most comfortable in as well. He had learnt his trade in The Jampot in Belfast, me in Zan's. From that point of view we were snooker soul-mates.

When I saw him play in that exhibition put on by Dad I knew it was his style I wanted to copy. He made the audience gasp and applaud like crazy and that is a very addictive sound and feeling. It was a feeling I wanted and loved as much as Higgins himself.

Sit him in a cramped, dingy, dark, smoky club, on a shit table in a tense environment against someone who wanted to beat him for money, or, even worse, for bragging rights, and the man was unstoppable and unplayable.

A fag burning away in an ashtray, a large vodka and orange waiting to be necked, a waistcoat sitting awkwardly on his skinny frame, Higgins brought the danger, drama and glamour of snooker's darker side to the wider public. He made it exciting and thrilling and that was the reason he was loved. Yes, he was hated by a fair few people as well – he was no angel – but he was unmissable and unforgettable.

JIMMY WHITE

A few years after first meeting him at Dad's event, in 1977, me and Tony Meo travelled to Pontins in Prestatyn to play in a snooker tournament there. The Pontins Spring Open was a great chance to get pissed, meet girls, try and win a few quid and play against the handful of professionals who were paid to show up and give the event some importance. There was also a professionals-only tournaments that ran alongside it but that year, Higgins, surprise, surprise, hadn't been invited to play as a professional because he'd threatened to walk off Pot Black after the first day of filming and Ted Lowe, who used to organise the players for Pot Black and Pontins, didn't want him there. He'd gone to Prestatyn anyhow and entered the amateur competition as just another player, determined to prove everyone wrong.

After walking around the Pontins site, past God knows how many chalets, we finally worked out which one Higgins was staying in. This was too good an opportunity to miss. By then, me and Tony had both really fallen for Alex's swagger and style of play so the chance to meet him again was driving us mad with excitement. Meo was so in awe of him he had been working on an impersonation of Higgins while we'd been going up and down the country with Dodgy Bob. He could take him off brilliantly and if you didn't know it was Meo, you would swear it was Higgins himself.

We poked our heads around this corner, and I remember we still had our cues with us and we were chalking them! You chalked your cue every 10 minutes back then, even on the train, as we tried to pluck up the courage to go over to him and speak.

Finally, we sneaked up on him and opened our mouths. He was sitting there in a deckchair on the grass outside his chalet, just a damp towel around his waist, his nuts hanging out everywhere and asked us what we'd been up to. "Hello boys, how are you both?" he said. We could barely listen to a word he was coming out with because of what he was doing.

Laid out in front of him were two loaves of bread and loads of knives that he'd taken from his chalet.

He was lobbing this bread about, the seagulls were swooping down on it and then Higgins was chucking these knives at the birds. These knives were that blunt they had a better chance of knocking the birds out if anything! He's firing them everywhere and cursing as they're missing. "Excuse me," I said. "But what are you doing?" "Young man," he replied, "I'm trying to find my killer instinct."

We legged it and laughed it off, thinking he was mad and then, before you know it, he'd come through a competition of about 1600 people and beat Terry Griffiths 7-4 in the final, playing some unbelievable shots. Only Higgins would have the courage and nerve to show up AND then back that up by winning. Nobody tried harder than him and nobody wanted to win more than him, especially if he felt he had something to prove. Maybe those seagulls did teach him a thing or two...

•••••••

By the time of the World Championship semi-final in 1982, me and Higgins were firm pals. We'd been across to Ireland on many occasions to exhibitions and we both loved the same things: playing dangerously, gambling and boozing. We were made for each other but at the Crucible we had to put our friendship and respect for each other to one side. Yes, we were great mates but the fact is, we both had a match to win and we both wanted to get into the World Championship final.

As a result of Higgins's urge to repeat his World Championship success of 1972, he decided to give it plenty of verbals. During one session I was drinking milk and Higgins jumped on that, telling reporters, "Young James might have the milk, but I have the bottle."

Shocking isn't it? I mean, who drinks milk when they're playing snooker?

If you watch our handshake at the start of the match, I refuse to look at him. Take a look at the picture and see for yourself. The glowering stare from Higgins was his way of trying to unsettle me, of making me realise that although we were good pals that meant nothing for the next 30-odd frames.

That semi-final was epic and ranks as one of the hardest and most gruelling matches I've ever played in. In one sense, I was just thrilled to be playing him. Who gets to play their idol in any sport, especially in a match as important as a World Championship semi-final?

At 15-14 up, I was leading 59-0, and I was only two reds away from finishing Higgins off. The match was there for the taking but I overreached for a red, using the rest, and it rattled the jaws and bounced out. Who knows why I missed? That is what snooker is like. You're always on the tightrope, you're never safe until the frame is completely won.

My shoulders slumped as I returned to my chair while Higgins was out of his in no time at all. I wasn't too worried though, because I thought no one could win from there. The position of the balls and the pressure of the match meant that winning the frame was an impossible job. 'There's no chance he'll clear that lot up,' I thought to myself. But this was Higgins we were on about. And nothing was impossible to him.

What happened next has, of course, passed into snooker folklore. His break of 69 won the frame and from staring defeat in the face, he turned the semi-final back in his favour.

When you watch that break back on the internet it seems even more unbelievable now than it did then. It is a break from another world. I didn't think he had a prayer but, as one commentator said at the time, "every shot was a trick-shot." He almost missed the first red and overshot, so missed position for the pink. Instead, he took on a risky green and nailed it but again he failed to find the right position. The reason the break is so wonderful to watch, and still quite nerve-racking, is because it was anything but perfect. That's what gives it its magic. Technically speaking it was bad snooker; Higgins never gets into the right position and never looks comfortable. But isn't that what made him so amazing? Isn't it that unpredictability that made him so interesting to watch? If he'd have got out of his chair and gone 'bang, bang, bang' and made it 15-all, nobody would've remembered it. But that frame was Higgins flying by the seat of his pants – it was him and his life in a nutshell. It was blind instinct. It was amazing. He potted about four incredible shots in that clearance that nobody has ever done before or since.

As much as I really wanted to win, I was also, secretly, still in awe of him. He was my hero and, in a weird way, during that match I wanted him to actually pot the balls as well, even during that frame when everything was at stake.

Just as he was getting going, he took on one black that went from near the yellow spot down to the top right hand pocket.

You can almost hear the tension in the crowd and then the stunned relief when it rolled in. If you played that in practice you would be happy; to make it in the semi-final of the World Championship, with everything at stake, was just nuts.

I can still see him now, grinning his way around the table, smirking into the commentary box as he slowly found his touch and at 59-13 down, he potted a blue that remains the greatest single shot I've ever seen.

If he missed it, the match was over.

I would've got out of my seat and cleared up. Higgins knew this but that gambler's mindset took over. He got into his usual awkward position – he was constantly twitching and moving when playing – and he thumped the blue into the bottom pocket before then potting a wonderful long red. Still, he couldn't get into decent position and it kept feeling like it could go badly wrong at any moment.

As I sat there, I was just waiting for the one shot that would miss because I knew something most others in the Crucible didn't.

Higgins was totally and utterly pissed during that break. I mean properly pissed, gone, gripped.

Just behind the BBC commentary box, me and Higgins used to have a mate called Martin and his job was to keep Higgins topped up. Throughout that session, as the tension grew, Higgins made more and more nods and winks in the direction of Martin, who did his job wonderfully, keeping Higgins well oiled on large vodka and orange.

When Higgins asked for an orange juice, he actually meant a vodka and orange and when he asked for a vodka and orange he actually wanted a huge one. That was his little code and by the time the match got towards the end he was smashed but he still had enough brilliance to make that break and finally, eventually, after what felt like years, he found his touch and cleared up. To be able to do that sober would've been great; doing it pissed was unbelievable.

After making me sit in my seat for about 30 minutes, I had no touch or feel in the last frame and Higgins beat me comfortably to make it into the final. To be honest I can't say it bothered me that much. In fact, I barely gave a shit. I was not yet 20, a surefire champion of the future and I didn't give a fuck about anything at all, except where the next drink or next bet was going to come from.

Looking back, and I've said this publicly before, I think that if I had won the world title in 1982 it would've killed me. Seriously. Life was fucking insane back then.

I might've had a wife and daughter at home but I barely knew where my own front door was, never mind how to act like a responsible husband and parent so if I'd added the world title into that madness, I'm pretty sure I'd be dead by now.

Maybe Higgins did me a favour.

In a funny way, when he went on to win the world title that year, beating Ray Reardon in the final and winning it in style with a 135 break, maybe he saved two lives; probably his and definitely mine.

If he hadn't have won that final, his self-destruction would have happened earlier. Yes, he died too young as it was but he was so crazy at times that losing in 1982 might have killed him quicker, especially as he'd also lost the 1980 final against Cliff Thorburn, a man he'd had several punch-ups with over the years.

As for me, if I had won then the fame, fortune and insanity of it all would've seen me off as well.

I hadn't quite made it home from the semi-final by the time he beat Reardon; I was out and about somewhere, enjoying myself, but I was genuinely thrilled and happy for him. It was the best thing for both of us.

Also, don't forget that Alex started a sporting trend that has continued to this day after beating Reardon, when he called for his then wife Lynn to bring him his baby girl Lauren. The most famous image of the 1982 World Championship is definitely Higgins crying with little Lauren in his arms. You can't go to an FA Cup final or a golf tournament these days without the players walking around with their kids. Higgins started all that.

●●●●●●●

He called his 1982 victory 'the 10-year itch' and he was now more in demand than ever. Nobody loved the public limelight like Higgins, so when he got the opportunity to parade the World Championship trophy around Northern Ireland, he jumped at the chance.

But, as always, madness wasn't far behind. He took me with him on the trip and we sold out every venue. He was the world champ, I was the best and boldest kid coming through – together we were a dynamite combination for the promoter of the tour, especially after our semi-final clash that had been the talk of snooker fans across the world.

We started out in this caravan provided by the promoter, which had a driver so we could sit in the back and get pleasantly smashed whenever we felt like it. The promoter insisted that Alex took the trophy with him wherever he went. Higgins wasn't happy about this. "I don't need a trophy to prove I'm a star," he would say. "People come to watch me because I'm Alex Higgins, not because I'm world champion."

We began making our way around loads of venues in Northern Ireland. The laughs and drinks flowed, as they do in that fabulous country, and we were having a great time trying to pot balls in off the lampshades and put on a good show – with Alex's trophy always on show.

I thought everything was going great but eventually Alex got pissed off about living in a caravan saying, "I want a hotel room and a bath and a proper bar." Eventually he had enough and demanded that we stay in a hotel one night in Derry. We checked in, had a few drinks in this little place, a lovely spot right on a river, and thought no more of it until our peaceful trip was shattered when we got up the next morning and discovered that the promoter had done a runner with the tour takings.

You can imagine how happy me and Higgins were about that.

To make matters worse, although we had checked into the hotel, we'd left our cues in the caravan with the driver. And the World Championship trophy was also still on board.

World War Three was around the corner.

The caravan driver was just as skint as we were now that the promoter had run off and he was even more pissed off than Higgins was.

BANG! BANG! BANG! A half-dressed Alex knocked on the side of the van. "Open this door right now, I want my trophy," he barked. But the caravan driver wasn't having any of it. "You'll get your trophy when I get paid for this tour," he said.

What followed was a Mexican stand-off, Irish style...

Higgins started getting redder and redder until he looked like he would totally explode. "OPEN UP THIS INSTANT," he said as I stood by, clueless as to what to do. "I will have him fucking shot," was all he kept repeating to me.

Eventually, news got to the local police force that Higgins was on the rampage in a hotel car park in the area and a policeman turned up on his ancient bike, ready to sort it all out. The constable recognised Higgins straight away and tried his best to calm him down.

"Open this door in the name of the law," he shouted to the caravan driver, a bit dramatically. "I demand that you give Mr Higgins his trophy back." Fair play to the driver, he was still not budging and told the bobby that the door would be opened the moment he got paid for his tour. He didn't care less if the promoter, me, Higgins or the bobby himself were going to cough up – he wasn't moving until he had his cash.

There was only one thing for it.

Me and Higgins retired to the bar to let tempers settle and let the bobby work his magic. So much for that. Before you knew it, he was at the bar with us. "A small drink is needed I think," the bobby said. His Sunday breakfast had been spoiled by this incident and he was determined to see that his lunch wouldn't go the same way.

Before long, one pint became two, until he got on the phone to his sergeant who soon joined us all to see what the fuss was about. Again, the caravan driver was not moving. He was blind and deaf to everybody's pleas.

Next thing you know, the chief constable had turned up. The fucking chief constable! All over a bit of handbags in a car park! Still, the caravan door stayed shut. Police cars were now arriving by the minute, blaring their sirens and beeping their horns, all trying to unsettle Ned Kelly in his caravan.

I watched all this from inside the bar, propped up on a stool, not knowing whether to laugh or cry. I did a bit of both and tried my best to keep Higgins sane by plying him with Guinness after Guinness until we went outside again, only to be joined this time by the local priest, fresh from Sunday Mass, and ready for a drink himself.

It was getting more out of hand by the second.

"He will listen to me, a man of the cloth," the priest said. "But before that, I think a drop of Guinness is needed, to keep my voice nice and strong." So off he went to the bar before joining us outside. There we were, stranded in the middle of the Derry countryside – me, the world snooker champion, a bobby who'd had two pints, his sergeant, the chief constable and now a priest, all stood around wondering what the fuck was going on.

The priest was loving it by now, chuckling away, and he loved it even more when two television crews and the press turned up, all looking to investigate The Great Trophy Robbery.

For fuck's sake.

"Alex, Alex, can we have a quick word?" shouted the reporters, not knowing that Higgins was definitely past the moment of finding the situation even vaguely funny. Next thing Alex is getting ready to go on television, straightening his shirt and combing his hair. "Ladies and gentleman," he said. "In 1966, a dog found the World Cup trophy. In 1982, a dog has nicked the World Championship trophy."

It was classic Higgins; hysterical, crazy and totally, totally genuine. He believed every word he was saying.

Before he had the chance to say anything else it became clear that the smells coming from the van meant that Higgins had well and truly lost.

The caravan owner had enough food supplies on board to keep himself happily safe and sound for days and days and he'd let that message be known by frying some bacon and letting the smell of it waft through the windows.

"Okay, okay," Higgins told the driver through the door, "You win. How much do you need to open this fucking caravan?"

"Ah, Mr Higgins, you're a real gent," he replied. "I knew you'd see sense in the end. I need £250 and I do take cheques."

Higgins got out his chequebook and reluctantly signed away the £250. That was far more than he was now getting from the tour because the promoter was long gone. He never stopped the cheque either and part of me reckons that was because he respected a pig-headed Irishman when he saw one.

Before you knew it, the trophy was back in Alex's arms and we were off to another exhibition that night, now completely skint and half-pissed.

But that was life with Alex. You try and get your head down in a nice Derry hotel and the next thing you know you're sipping Guinness with the local priest and half the bloody police force.

We got on so well at the time because we had completely the same outlook on life. If in doubt, drink it, smoke it and gamble it.

•••••••

Higgins's lifelong ability to get under people's skin and yet get back in their good books straight afterwards was legendary. My wife Maureen had her fair share of arguments and stand-offs with him but he always managed to win her over.

One time, when his life with Lynn took a turn for the worse, he stayed with me for a few days and asked Maureen a question that saw her hit the roof. Alex's daughter, Lauren, the tiny girl he'd held at the Crucible, was quite a bit younger than our own daughter who was, of course, also called Lauren. That didn't faze Higgins at all. "Maureen, babe," he said one day, propped up against our kitchen sink. "Do you think you could change Lauren's name to something else? I only want my Lauren to have that name." The cheek! Maureen, full of Irish blood herself, soon let Higgins know that he'd crossed the line but by the next day we were in tears of laughter over it. Only Alex would even dream of saying something as crazy as that, especially while he was staying with us.

Probably the most famous occasion when we got into bother together was, once again, when we went to Ireland (it was always Ireland!) for an exhibition.

I only took with me a pair of old jeans, a jacket and a suit. "I don't need anything else," I told Maureen. "I'm only going for the weekend."

I got back home six weeks later.

In the '80s the paparazzi never bothered you in Ireland. God knows why but they didn't. Maybe they didn't have the brains to get on a plane. So basically you could do whatever you liked in Dublin and get away with it and there were so many celebrities up to no good over there.

I've always loved going to Ireland because of the way the people greet you, how excited the crowds get and because, especially, how much going out and getting as pissed as possible was the number one priority for pretty much every person I met while I was over there.

Boozing, gambling and playing snooker all day, every day? Now that was my idea of what a country should be all about.

The guy who'd sorted this exhibition was called Warren Lusher. He ran a couple of businesses in Dublin and he made it known to us that he wasn't exactly short of cash. The only problem was that the exhibition was in Bray, which was too far from Dublin's bars and clubs for my liking.

"We need to be in the city centre," I told the guy. "What hotel can you sort for us?"

If I'd had any doubts about just how flush this geezer was, they soon disappeared when he booked us into The Gresham Hotel, one of Ireland's very best, and perfectly located for a quiet drink or 10.

I walked through the big grand front doors and could barely stop myself from laughing. 'Well Jimmy,' I thought. 'You've cracked it here.' The hotel was unbelievable and Warren pulled out all the stops.

The hotel was beautiful, by far and away the nicest I'd stayed in at that point and Warren was keen to make me as comfortable as possible. "Jimmy, I've booked you into the Elizabeth Taylor suite," he said. "Enjoy it."

The room had its own bar, about three bedrooms, a massive bathroom and its own butler, ready to bring me whatever (drink) I needed.

Warren wasn't finished there though. "What is your favourite champagne Jimmy?" he asked. I was definitely a Screwdrivers man but I'd been known to have a drop or two of champagne as well. "Erm, Dom Perignon I suppose," I told him.

"Okay," said Warren, before he rang down to reception. "Yes, yes, I'd like 24 bottles of Dom Perignon to Mr White's room every day," he told the concierge.

Twenty-four bottles a day? This was my kind of 'work' trip.

All was going well until Higgins checked into the same gaff the day after.

"I'll take my usual suite," he informed reception. "Sorry Mr Higgins, but a Mr White is already booked into that," he was told.

Higgins wasn't happy. Who was this little upstart stopping him, the two-time world champion, from staying in his favourite room?

"That's no trouble," he told them. "I'll just stay in his bathroom."

He fucking did as well. He constantly wore this white suit – Higgins thought he had to dress at his very best in The Gresham – and he slept in the bath, in this white suit, for three nights until he finally admitted defeat and moved to the floor below.

They were crazy days.

Me and Higgins used to sit at the bar in my suite and tried our best to empty it constantly. Steak, oysters, lobsters, champagne; you name it, we ate it and drank it. We lived like kings and it soon got around Dublin that The Gresham Hotel was hosting the party of the century.

We'd occasionally leave the hotel to play in an exhibition, the pair of us absolutely slaughtered, we'd give the crowd what they wanted and then leg it back to The Gresham to carry on.

At the time I knew Phil Lynott from Thin Lizzy and UB40 were also around the corner recording a new album so I thought it would be best if I invited them all round for a little gathering.

"Phil, come along as soon as you can, I've got all the booze you can drink up here," I told him.

"Jimmy, I've heard all about it – I'll be there tonight."

Phil turned up and the party just continued and went on and on and on. Days turned into nights and back into days and there was no let-up.

I was walking around this suite like fucking Hugh Hefner with a dressing gown on, emptying these Dom Perignon bottles as quickly as I could and the party grew and grew until you couldn't move in there for nightclub girls, croupiers, hostesses, UB40, Phil, Higgins and me; the great, the good and the very, very bad of Dublin.

The party carried on for 17 days. Mad times.

All this time Maureen was trying to find me but I wasn't interested in coming back to the real world.

The real world had bills and responsibilities and boring shit to cope with. I was sat next to my boyhood hero, sipping champagne and pinching myself. Why the fuck would I want that to stop? For as long as I was in my plush Gresham suite, the world couldn't get me and I was more than happy with that.

Sooner or later though it had to stop or someone would get killed.

At one point, Warren's wife came to the hotel to see me and I thought that was that and that he'd pulled the plug on our little Dom Perignon deal.

He'd been carted off to a mental hospital after having a breakdown and his wife wasn't too happy.

"Now then Mr White," she said. "You've been drinking all this champagne haven't you?" I told her I had been and was sorry to hear about her husband.

"These 24 bottles a day has to stop," she said, and I nodded my head, gutted that the fun was over.

She then pulled a rabbit out of the hat. "Now, now, I don't want you to think we're not generous so you can still stay at The Gresham and I'm halving the Dom Perignon to just 12 bottles a day. Is that good enough for you?"

Ha ha, we were back in business.

Every now and then I'd ring Maureen and tell her I was sorry and that I was coming home. "No you're fucking not," she'd scream down the phone, sick of my antics and disappearing act. She could give it as good as she got and she made it crystal clear that I was in real trouble.

In the end all the booze gave me alcohol poisoning and I stood at the bar and decided it was time for home. "I'm off lads, I've got to go," I told some of the stragglers still left.

I made my way to Dublin airport, flew to Gatwick and presented myself at our front door, ready to make peace with Maureen. I knocked on the door and prepared to cop it, big time. The second it opened I knew I was in trouble. It all kicked off and before I knew it, I was out of there again. 'Fuck this,' I thought and I told the cab driver to get me back to Gatwick as soon as possible.

Fast forward two hours and I was back in The Gresham bar. "Can I check into the Elizabeth Taylor suite reception?" I said to the girl behind reception. "You could do," she replied. "But you never checked out in the first place."

I'd been that pissed I'd completely forgotten to even do that.

It felt good to be back. I nipped into the bar and it was as if I'd never left. Someone shoved a Guinness in my hand and I was back with the lads.

"I thought you'd gone home?" Phil said.

"Yeah, never mind that," I replied. "Now who fancies a glass of Dom Perignon...?"

•••••••

As time passes, Higgins's on-off marriage to Lynn was dragging him down and it made mine and Maureen's relationship look calm and normal (which says a lot).

I got a phone call from him one day that summed up the drama. I was in London and he was at home in Manchester. He'd had an almighty tear-up with Lynn and the press were camped on his doorstep, smelling blood.

Every newspaper in the country wanted as many stories about Higgins as they could get and who could blame them?

He always had a quote or an antic or something going on in his life. The stories about Higgins practically wrote themselves and he was always giving reporters plenty of ammunition.

"James, my friend, I need you to come and rescue me, I need you to save me," he said. Oh great. Nothing too dramatic then. Me and Dad went up to Manchester and Dad was great with Alex, trying to calm him down. "Come on Alex, let's have a frame of snooker and a drink," Dad said.

We eventually went to the pub and it soon filled up with reporters, wanting to know the latest mad drama between Alex and Lynn.

He had apparently dragged her outside by her hair and the press had got wind of it. Higgins was going insane, blaming Lynn for the bad name he had with the WPBSA.

Dad was brilliant, totally taking the heat out of Higgins by remaining calm and trying to find the funny side of everything. After we returned to Alex's bungalow, Dad set up the table again as Higgins kept getting edgy about the press camped outside. "Forget them Alex," Dad would say. "They're freezing out there in the pissing rain while we're in here, with a bottle of whisky and a few games of snooker. What more could you want?"

Dad worked his magic and calmed Higgins down – but it was a sign of just how highly strung Higgins could be, especially over his relationship with Lynn, which eventually, and sadly, broke down for good.

Higgins had better luck in the Hofmeister World Doubles Championship in 1984 when we partnered each other and walked it. In previous years I'd always partnered Tony Knowles but I never felt like he was giving it his all so I decided to play with Higgins and we totally cleaned up.

I don't think I've ever won a tournament as easily as we did that one. We were phenomenal and that was because we brought out the best in each other. We put in about a month's practice beforehand because we really wanted to win it.

Me and Higgins were very much seen as the outsiders in the snooker world; the boozers and gamblers who abused themselves and took the piss. We were determined that year to show that there was more to us than that and that, together, we could shut everybody else up.

We certainly did that by smashing Cliff Thorburn and Willie Thorne 10-2 in the final. For me, it was just a pleasure and a thrill to play with my hero and someone who had become my best mate. Hanging around with Alex was fun. It was dangerous, madness, sometimes scary, but always hysterical.

The year after our World Doubles win sums Higgins up perfectly. We partnered up again and should've been contenders but Alex's private life meant we never stood a chance.

We were facing 'Dustbin' Danny Fowler, a former bin man, and Barry West in Doncaster. Higgins invited Siobhan Kidd, his then girlfriend, to come and watch. He'd split from Lynn by that point and was all over the place emotionally. As for what happened next, thank God it wasn't on the telly, that's all I'm saying.

Danny and Barry were good lads and decent players but me and Higgins should've won the match with our eyes shut. We lost 5-4. Why? Because Higgins wouldn't stop arguing with Siobhan throughout the match. I'm talking, literally, as he was getting down to pot balls, Siobhan would say something, Alex would flip and he'd be after her, into the crowd, looking to fight and scream and shout. It wasn't pretty and that threw us off our game.

But, again, that was Higgins. The fucking insane world of Higgins.

If it meant messing yourself up, there was nothing Higgins wouldn't do. Booze, gambling and drugs all played enormous roles in his life – and I was normally by his side getting stuck in as well. It was reckless, crazy living. We both had kids and families – but we just didn't care.

Alex smoked a lot of cannabis throughout his life and I think that had a massive impact on him. I don't think he realised how strong it was or how much it could affect him. He'd been constantly smoking these huge, strong joints and be out of it.

Being stoned meant he couldn't always practise properly which meant he couldn't then hit his usual high standards and

White T-shirts: I've always had great support from the fans over the years, which has meant a lot

Out and about: I'm always happy to do exhibitions. Here I am (above) putting on a show in Dublin. Left: Having a laugh at Newcastle Snooker Centre

The People's Champions: A special picture I have framed at home of me and Higgins. We spent some special times together. I still miss him

Three's company: Me with Higgins and Ronnie Wood. We had some fun times

True legend: Lining up at a Snooker Legends event (top) and (left) Alex pictured with me at a fundraising night in his honour. I shouldn't have had to say goodbye to him so soon. Below: At the memorial in Belfast

Still on tour: Lining up with the Legends at Plymouth in 2010. It's all good fun – and usually at my expense if John Virgo has a microphone in his hand!

The lads: Me with Ronnie Wood and my friend Tommy – we love catching up. Above right: Me and the two Ronnies. Ronnie Wood is wearing one of my Tommy Nutter waistcoats from 1985 which fits him now!

We meet again: Still playing Stephen after all these years, this time in the UK Championship in Telford, 2010

The Greatest:
Shaking hands
with Muhammad
Ali – another
mate of Ronnie's
– and meeting
another great
boxing champion
Joe Calzaghe
(above)

The Rocket's back: Ronnie
asked me along to the
press conference where he
announced his return to the
game in 2013. I'm so proud of
what he's achieved. He can go
on and on. Left: Pictured on the
red carpet at a film premiere in
Leicester Square – we've had
some great nights out

Soul mate: With my beautiful girlfriend Kelly. She's so special to me

It's only rock 'n' roll but I like it: I had a wonderful testimonial with Ronnie Wood and Mick Hucknall taking to the stage (right)

Jungle Jim: Doing 'I'm A Celebrity Get Me Out Of Here!' was an amazing experience which I'd recommend to anyone…but once was enough! Right: Sporting a 'tache for a good cause – Movember

So proud: My four beautiful daughters. From left: Ashleigh, Lauren, Breeze and Georgia

Happy days: With my son Tommy and grandson Sonny. Left: Me and Tommy fishing and (right) supporting Chelsea

The Tooting Kid: Still playing, and still dreaming. I'm the luckiest man I know

that would send him crazy. Add the paranoia that smoking weed brings into the mix and it was a combination that was always ready to explode.

You only rarely saw Higgins totally pissed. Like most people with a drink problem, he would get up and then drink slowly and steadily all day, every day. He didn't go for strong drinks early on, just a Guinness or two after his breakfast but then he would stay on that all day until the vodka would come out later on. Then his face would start showing the effects and he would get aggressive. However, on other days, he was the nicest, most generous man you could ever wish to meet and there was always, always, something going on around him.

One time, in about 1986, we went back across to Ireland and decided (for a change) to spend a day – and all our cash – in the pub and the bookies. We might have loved a bet but we were useless most of the time. Barry Hearn reckons he never saw Higgins win a bet and I was hardly Mr Lucky either. Anyhow, we went into this Irish bookies after studying the form and Higgins went and put the bets on. So far, so good. We retired to the pub next door and got ready to watch the afternoon's racing. I took one look down at the betting slip and my heart sank. "Alex, what have you done here? You've backed the wrong horses."

In race after race that afternoon, Higgins had got his wires crossed and we were fucked. We spent about 250 punts up front and it was gone before we'd even started. We should've been backing thoroughbreds but Higgins had accidentally bet on the donkeys instead. The first race began and all looked lost until, fuck me, this old nag that Higgins backed actually romped home from nowhere. "Amazing, amazing James," he was shouting, as we fell into the street to do our version of an

Irish jig. It was the start of an amazing afternoon when almost everything we backed turned into gold, or at least punts. Dodgy horse after dodgy horse came in, each victory more mad than the one before it. As the afternoon wore on and the more Guinness we got down our necks, we thought it was time to go and get our winnings.

We returned to the bookies, your typical smoky shithole, covered in old betting stubs, dim lights and old fellas who'd not had a winner in weeks, only to be greeted with bad news. A big sign behind the counter now read: 'NO PAYOUT FOR BETS OVER 100 PUNTS'. This crafty bookie knew how down he was and knew he was fucked after our miracle day.

Well, neither me or Alex were in the mood to be mugged off. Full of bravado – and booze – we stormed the joint until the bloke behind the counter admitted that the owner had legged it to the golf course. "Follow me James," shouted Higgins, determined to get our 2,500 punts.

We walked and walked until we found the bloody golf course. Nowadays he would've had a tip-off on his mobile phone but back then we had the element of surprise and I'd just about had enough of this shit. We finally found him and he knew he'd been collared. "Oi, you!" I screamed at him. "Good try mate but we ain't leaving here without our money." A bit of a crowd gathered and the golf society snobs started whispering about the scandal opening up before them. My attempts at diplomacy were swiftly followed by Higgins – and he was worse than me. "You've got two choices," he snarled at this fella. "You either give us our money or I use you as a fucking seven iron." That did the job and we got our money, headed for the golf club gates and back to the pub. Job done. It was a fantastic day and summed our lives up. Funny, dangerous and totally unpredictable.

On another occasion we were on the way to Australia and we stopped off at Bahrain and Higgins went missing, the minute we got off the plane. John Virgo was the chairman of the WPBSA at the time and we all thought Higgins had dashed off for a fag and a drink at the bar. As we were waiting for the connecting flight to Australia, we were all getting more and more anxious about where he'd gone. 'What the fuck is he playing at?' I thought. 'He'll miss his flight.'

Next thing, this bloke turns up and sits among us, dressed in the traditional Arab clothing. He's dressed head-to-toe in white garments with a pair of sunglasses on. I clocked him straightaway. It was fucking Higgins. Where had he got that from?! He starts talking to Virgo but Virgo didn't get it. "So then, who are you?" Higgins started, but Virgo didn't want to know. Eventually, after banging on for two minutes, Higgins whipped his glasses off and roared "Virgo, it's me you cunt!" Well, that was it. None of us – Virgo included – could move for laughing. We were a bit knackered from the first flight and probably all a bit pissed but that tipped us over the edge. We could barely walk through the airport to our departure gate because we were that far gone. Higgins had gone all that way just to get a laugh. That was how he was, hot and cold, a clown one minute, a devil the next.

He caused just as much chaos in England as he did overseas and how I didn't kill him on one occasion I will never, ever know.

I was in my house in Oxshott and he'd had a bust-up with Lynn or something so he was living with me for a bit. Maureen had gone out somewhere, so... bingo! We had an excuse to get into trouble. We had a little game of snooker in the morning until about lunchtime and then it was on. "What do you want to do?" I asked him. "What do you think I want to do James?" he replied. "Let's go out somewhere." So my mate Peewee came and picked us up in this Mini Metro I'd been given by a sponsor and we decided to go out on the piss around the Surrey countryside. You name a little country pub and we went in it. We spent all day getting more and more pissed until it was kicking out time. By this time, me and Alex were at each other's throats about something, God knows what, and Peewee had had enough. Higgins had probably been rude to someone over nothing, which he often was, so I'd had enough of his bullshit and wanted to get home.

"Mate, can you order us a cab please?" I slurred to the landlord of this pub, trying to be a good boy, but he was having none of it. "Jimmy mate, you won't get a cab around here at this time. It isn't London you know," came the reply. So much for good behaviour. 'Fuck it, I'll drive,' I thought. Peewee thought it was a half-decent idea as well and Higgins was too pissed to give a shit so we decided on it. I knew it was wrong – totally stupid in fact – but that's what booze does to you, doesn't it?

Next thing, it's pissing down and I'm behind the wheel of this motor and as we come to this corner, I've gone too fast and lost it. I crashed into this brick wall – and it was a proper brick wall as well, part of a country estate or something – and before I knew what was happening, the windscreen has popped out, followed closely by Alex, who sailed out of the front passenger seat like fucking Superman. Peewee and me had our seatbelts on so we were okay but Higgins was dead. He had to be dead. In slow motion, I'd watched him go through the front window and do a somersault and somehow land facing me. 'Oh fuck, I've killed Higgins,' I thought. 'I'm fucked here, good and proper.'

As I looked out into the pissing down rain and where the windscreen should be, Higgins jumped to his feet, not a scratch on him, and he started doing this jig. "I'm fine, I'm fine. I've got nine lives, babes, nine lives," he kept repeating, cackling like a madman. "Get in the fucking car," is all I could say as I went about reversing the motor out of the wall. Half the brickwork came with me as I managed to get the thing back on the road and off we went. The car was a wreck and all Higgins could say was, "Yeah, yeah babes, let's go out for a drink," like a lunatic. It was madness.

I drove about two miles home and it was carnage all the way. The windscreen wipers were all bent and chewed up, hitting me and Higgins in the face. He kept bashing them away, laughing like a nutter, repeating, "I've been saved, I've been saved, there must be a reason, it's a miracle" until finally we pulled up at my house. I pushed the button on the electronic garage doors, floored the engine and, next thing, BANG, the engine fell out of the bottom of the car.

Steam was coming out of everywhere, petrol was all over the driveway and this car was completely wrecked. Higgins didn't even notice. "Where are we going for a drink? We need to celebrate my new life," and so on, like a stuck record. What Higgins hadn't realised was that if that engine had dropped out at any point after the crash and before my driveway, the three of us were goners. No doubt about it. We'd have tipped up, crashed and that would've been that – curtains.

After that, we got inside the house. Higgins just wouldn't shut up but all I could think about was the police. Then I realised – the tax disc was still attached to that windscreen and the Old Bill would soon know whose car trashed half of Surrey. Higgins was still running around the house loving it, while I rang a cabbie mate to help me out. It was about now that I realised I had the circle of the steering wheel imprinted on my chest where I'd obviously banged into it after the crash. That's how serious it was. There's me checking for broken ribs and there's Alex running up and down the stairs shouting "I'm alive James, I'm alive."

Anyway, my cabbie mate and me went and retrieved the windscreen and the tax disc and we were safe. Not my proudest moment but it happened. I thought the shit night had finished there but Alex had other ideas.

"I want to play you right now for £300," he said, convinced that flying through a glass windscreen and getting up without a scratch on him was some sort of sign from God. "Are you fucking mad?" I asked him. "We could've been in the morgue and you want to play for money. Are you really all there?"

I'd had enough by now.

"Let's play, let's play, it's the best time," he kept saying but I wanted him out by then. "Get out of that fucking door before I hit you," I shouted at him and he delivered a big tongue lashing before swanning off out into the night. That was one of many times we came close to blows, even though we never did actually touch each other.

It got worse. At the time, I wasn't talking to my neighbour because he wanted to cut this big old lovely tree down that hung over his property but I'd told him no chance and he had the right hump with me.

HIGGINS

Higgins knew this but that didn't stop him from walking round there and knocking him up at whatever time in the morning it now was.

"It is Alex Higgins here, I need help. Jimmy White has just tried to assault me," he said to this neighbour, who was just about to cross me off his Christmas card list forever. "I need a lift to Reading for a tournament tomorrow, and I need one this instant."

Higgins expected this neighbour, who couldn't stand me, to take him all the way to Reading, in the pissing rain at stupid o'clock. And the maddest thing is that the neighbour did it! Higgins could charm and persuade anyone to help him when he needed to. I spoke to him four days later and it was like nothing had happened.

He claimed that his past as a jockey meant he knew how to fall through the windscreen and that he was under control at all times. As for our argument and me telling him to get out of the house – he had completely forgotten it. That's how it always was with Alex, the next day he was back to his usual self, no offence taken.

●●●●●●●

When we played each other we both played to the crowd. If I won a tournament he would be on the phone praising a great shot and I did it the same. We never praised each other for being consistent or ruthless or anything like that – the compliments only came if we played a mad shot or had won a frame in a stupid way. It's just the way we were. No wonder we got on like a house on fire.

But I was his only friend in snooker. Everybody else was terrified of him and fair play to them, they were entitled to be. He was a bomb ready to go off and you never knew how long the fuse was. He was a man who used to go on the piss with blokes like Oliver Reed and Keith Moon; how on earth could most people be expected to relax around a man as crazy as that? When he felt like enjoying himself and really going for it, there was no stopping him.

One time we were in Australia for the Winfield Masters and me and Higgins fancied a bit of exercise, for once. We decided to go for a game of golf but when we got there it was pissing down with rain and we couldn't go out on the course. All our equipment and clubs and clothes were given to us free of charge, we didn't have to pay any green fees or nothing so it would've been a really great day apart from the rain.

Me and Higgins – being me and Higgins – decided to have a little drink or two as we watched the rain pour down.

We had three hours to kill before the taxi back to the hotel and we were getting bored in the clubhouse so some refreshments seemed to be the best idea. Glass of champagne followed glass of champagne, chased down with vodka and we were on one, big time.

The three hours passed by and on our way out of the clubhouse – the game long abandoned by now – I saw the bill for our afternoon's fun:

Hire of golf clubs $0
Hire of golf cart $0
Green fees $0
Balls $0
Bar Bill $847

The pair of us had been thirstier than I thought...

But that was exactly what he was like.

Your best friend at the bar one minute, a lunatic the next.

You used to see Davis looking terrified whenever Alex was around. He wasn't usually violent with other players because he was far more ruthless with his tongue than his fists. One day, Virgo, while he was chairman of the WPBSA, was seen running in the opposite direction after Higgins had lost a match against Tony Meo. Virgo had known Higgins longer than most of us and grew up playing in the tough clubs of Salford so wasn't to be messed with, but even he didn't want anything to do with him when he lost.

He was the chairman of our sport and he was trying to avoid one of his own players. That tells you all you need to know about how crazed Higgins could be if he lost or if life was not going exactly as he wanted it.

Occasionally, Higgins's verbal lashing turned physical and that is when he really messed up.

At the 1986 UK Championship, he nutted the tournament director, Paul Hatherall. It was crazy, unreal. He had some sort of conversation with Paul downstairs about a drug test or something and then Higgins just lost it. He threw the head and caught Paul. That was a terrible thing to do. That was one of the worst things he ever did. I know he regretted it instantly because he loved the game and didn't want to bring it into disrepute that much. He got done for £12,000 and was banned for quite a few tournaments – something that hurt him a lot more than the fine itself. It summed Alex up. The perfect gentleman one minute and a total nutcase the next.

As his form declined and he lost the ability to produce the

magic shots like he used to, his behaviour got worse until I was just about the last person in the snooker world who had a kind word for him.

He couldn't help himself and his behaviour was just getting worse, especially by 1990 when he messed up big time.

First of all, during the Snooker World Cup while representing Northern Ireland, he threatened to have Dennis Taylor shot – and also made an obscene comment about one of his family members – because Higgins believed Taylor was trying to stash away £6,000 for the highest break of the tournament. Higgins wanted any bonus prize money to be shared amongst the team and thought Dennis would keep the £6,000 for himself. That was total bullshit. That was totally wrong. There was still plenty of time left in the World Cup when Dennis made that break, so there was no guarantee his break would even win it. Even if it had, Dennis had more class than that and wasn't even trying to take all the money for himself so Higgins was completely wrong and totally and utterly out of order.

He continued to go downhill, on and off the table, after that and copped a one-year ban at the World Championship for punching a press officer in the stomach. He just couldn't get to grips with the fact his game was not what it was. It was sad to see.

Unfortunately, it was going to get a lot sadder.

In the last 10 or 15 years of his life I saw things go badly wrong for him and it broke all of our hearts. He had massive problems. He felt that the WPBSA were after him, he felt that everybody was shortchanging him and ripping him off and he became totally obsessed with money, no matter how small an amount.

HIGGINS

I was his best mate but I wasn't blind to his faults.

Higgins had an awful decline. Over the years he just withdrew into himself and the bookies and when he was diagnosed with throat cancer in 1998 I was devastated.

Let's be honest, it wasn't the biggest shock in the world because of the lifestyle we'd led but you still don't want to hear news like that.

Many people thought the cancer would kill Higgins but they underestimated his strength and his survival instinct. He went through hell to get cured, endless treatments that left him knackered, underweight and looking terrible. Every time I saw him I got more upset about the way he looked, how thin he was getting, how much the old Higgins would hate the way the new Higgins appeared. His hair went thin, he lost all his teeth and his clothes just hung off him.

Nobody wants to see their best mate end up like that. "Don't be worrying about me," he would say, his voice just a tiny whisper because his throat hurt so much. "I will be just fine."

He was right as well, in a way, because he beat the cancer. However, he just could not shake the pain that his treatment had caused.

By far and away the worst thing was the fact his teeth had all fallen out. That meant he spent the last 10 years of his life unable to eat anything proper. He was never a big eater – a sandwich would last him a day-and-a-half – and his sisters did all they could to buy him food, sorting him a flat in Belfast and trying to make him look after himself.

But he just wouldn't have it.

The thing with Higgins was that he just wasn't equipped to handle the real world. Paying bills, paying tax, eating properly, whatever; it just never entered his head. He'd shuffle from venue to venue with a couple of carrier bags worth of clothes, the Racing Post and his snooker cue. That was it. He was 14 years older than me but it was me who sometimes felt like the older brother. The kid from South London, bursting with the street education I'd picked up in Zan's, taking care of this bloke from Belfast who lived life by a completely different set of rules to anyone I've ever met.

Higgins ranted and raved about the snooker world, calling the WPBSA all the names under the sun and claiming they owed him thousands. In one way you could understand his frustration because he'd taken snooker to new heights of fame and fortune but he went about it the wrong way and made enemies when he should've been trying to make friends. I wanted to play the system for everything it had, Higgins wanted to fuck the system – and that was the biggest difference between us.

He did have a point though because without Higgins, the game would still have been an underground sport, played in pubs and clubs but ignored by the wider world. He'd single-handedly given it some glamour and thrill and he now felt he was owed for what he'd done for the sport. He just couldn't get why he wasn't a millionaire, living in a big house with a swimming pool but the reason for that was simple – gambling.

However much Higgins loved snooker, it only ever took second place to his first love, horse racing.

As a young kid, he had come over from Belfast to try and make it as a jockey and he worked at some stables in Berkshire. He absolutely worshipped horses and horse racing and, of course, with horse racing comes gambling and that's why he was always skint. Towards the end of his life he was still gambling whatever he could get his hands on but, again, there was no telling him. I've lost millions myself in the bookies so I'm the last one to say anything but it was the gambling that was his major problem because he became so focused on it that he forgot to look after himself, he forgot to eat, he forgot to give a shit about anything other than the next race or the next meeting.

We all tried to help him in our own way.

His sisters were fantastic with him, putting food in his fridge and constantly telling him to take his medication but Higgins would find these herbal remedies and would read medical textbooks and make up his own treatments, which he then forgot to take anyway. He was deaf and blind to all of us, especially over food. He would live on the odd bowl of soup or a bit of cake plus a sip or two of Guinness in his local pub, The Royal Bar, on the corner of Donegal Road and Sandy Row, just a minute or so from where he'd grown up. He'd shuffle around the pub, left alone by the regulars and looked after by the bar staff, who knew how frail he was, while he spent whatever cash he could find in the bookies.

As I've already mentioned, I thought the best way to save Higgins was to try and get him back on a snooker table and he was given a chance to do that through the Snooker Legends tour. He could've come back on tour, back on the road and back with his old mates. It would've been the best thing for him but Higgins, above everything else, was his own man and he just didn't want to. When I would sign up for exhibitions I would tell promoters that I could also get Higgins as well and they couldn't sign on the dotted line quick enough – he was still a big, big star, even if he didn't realise that himself. I remember going to see him and telling him that this was the chance he'd been waiting for. "Alex, get some practice in so you don't feel uncomfortable," I said. "This will earn you some money and help you out." But he wouldn't listen. He would come to do the odd exhibition and then only practise that morning, hoping against hope that it would just come back to him. Snooker doesn't work like that, not even for a genius.

When we booked him for exhibitions you couldn't get him out of the betting shop in time and then he couldn't play like he wanted to because he hadn't practised so he'd get the needle and lose his temper and it was shocking and horrible to witness.

To watch your hero and, more importantly, your best mate, in situations like that, really upset me. Higgins never realised how many lives he touched, how many friends he should've had and could've had.

His one exhibition with Snooker Legends, when he played Cliff Thorburn, broke my heart. Cliff was out of touch and Higgins, as you know, was dreadful – it took them hours to play about four frames. There was not much entertainment and Higgins was so skinny he could barely push the ball around the table. We all did our best to cheer Higgins up and get him through but he couldn't get the magic back. It upset Cliff that much that he had tears in his eyes afterwards, stunned at how frail Alex had become.

Years before, Cliff had punched Higgins in a bar after his mouth ran away with him. He'd also beaten him in the World Championship final and for a long time there'd been no love lost between them. And yet now here we were with Cliff as devastated as the rest of us.

Higgins still had an ability to hit the headlines – even though on one occasion it was my fault.

HIGGINS

I'm going to confess something now. In 2007, before we got involved with Snooker Legends, Higgins punched a referee, Terry Riley, during an exhibition game.

And, for once, he wasn't really to blame.

I was playing against him in Spennymoor, County Durham. This match was going along nicely and it was the last frame of the night. I was about 100 in front but Higgins wanted to pot the remaining balls on the table.

As he was leaning over the green, I turned to Terry and said, "He's touched the blue." He hadn't done and I don't know why I said it, we'd had a few to drink that night so I'm blaming that. The referee then went, "Foul five, Jimmy White." Higgins turned around, asked him what he said and then just punched him.

The referee – quite rightly – wasn't having that and got Higgins around the throat before this sea of people start coming out of the crowd for us. I'm shitting myself by now and next thing, it's mayhem but Higgins and the referee were then separated and we had to get out of there.

Talksport were trying to get hold of us, trying to work out where we were legging it to as we tried to keep our heads down. It was a close call and it was like the Wild West days of old when you'd run to the car with your cue in one hand and your case in the other, legging it for your lives. Needless to say, Higgins loved it.

•••••••

By 2010 a few of us decided that some drastic action was needed. Higgins desperately needed some teeth otherwise there was no chance he would ever put on any weight. We set up the Save Alex Higgins Fund and put on a big fundraiser at the Yang Sing restaurant in Manchester so he could go abroad to have his tooth implants.

Coronation Street actors Ryan Thomas and Jack Shepherd turned up, as did Virgo, Tony Knowles and the soul singer Dougie James also performed. We were all truly shocked by his appearance that night but being back in the limelight lifted his spirits. Just like the old days, being the centre of attention was the perfect medicine for Higgins.

He was so stick-thin that we didn't think he had the strength to get up and say a few words but the spotlight on him soon changed all that. On the night we raised £20,000, thanks to a donated Ronnie Wood guitar and a few other bits.

"Jimmy, can I have the money tonight?" was what he asked me. We were scared he wanted it straight for the bookies.

We didn't know then that the money raised that night wouldn't be paying for new teeth – they would be paying for his funeral.

Catching up with Higgins that night in Manchester was fantastic. All the old stories came out, we had a lot of laughs and there was a lot of love for him in the room. At one point, God knows how, he got up and did some karaoke and ended up dancing, his suit jacket about four sizes too big for him by now. The room was bouncing as The Hurricane entertained his public again.

He was really poorly with pneumonia but he was determined to beat it. "I will sort this out. I will get better, get some teeth and then come back on tour," he told me. 'Thank God,' I thought. 'Finally I'll get my old mate back and we can earn some money and sort him out.'

HIGGINS

Higgins looked me in the eye and that old sparkle looked like it was coming back. He wanted a new cue and he wanted to get back on the road to do what he was born to do, entertain the fans.

He was happiest with a cue in his hand and he adored the audience. He didn't want century breaks or trophies, he wanted the love of the people – and I still think that getting him patched up with a bit more weight on him would've seen him back on the road.

But he never, ever listened – not to me, his sisters, his doctors or anybody else. All he cared about was the bookies and in the end it became the difference between life and death.

●●●●●●●

At the time Ann was putting the key in her brother Sandy's front door, I was in Pattaya in Thailand. Me and Ken Doherty were out on Walking Street, having a few beers and enjoying ourselves when the news came through.

I knew Alex was struggling but when I answered my phone I don't think I've experienced shock like it. Jason Francis, from Snooker Legends, had been given a tip-off from somebody at the BBC in Belfast and he had to break the news to me. "Jimmy, Alex is dead," was all he said. I just couldn't take it in, I couldn't absorb it at first. I ended up talking to Jason about how I was cueing and about my exhibition the night after – just normal snooker chat because my mind wouldn't let me believe it.

"Jimmy, get some rest," Jason said. "And look after yourself." I eventually put my mobile in my pocket, it finally hit me and I staggered to the kerb and sat down. I sat by the side of the road for about two hours, crying my eyes out, hardly able to catch my breath.

How could Alex be dead? He'd beaten fucking cancer – how had he now died?

It turned out that malnutrition was given as the official cause. I was so fucking angry. I'm still angry now. Who in the Western world dies of malnutrition in 2010? What is that all about? It was such a waste of an amazing bloke. Why wouldn't he listen to us all? Why wouldn't he help himself? The frustration of that lasts to this day. I suppose I just miss my mate.

We flew back from Thailand for his funeral – something I was dreading.

It was, obviously, a horrible day but also very uplifting and touching. The funeral was held at St. Anne's Cathedral in Belfast and the streets were lined with about 3,000 people, all clapping and cheering and showing exactly how much Higgins meant to them.

Before the public service there was a private ceremony, attended by close family because they wanted a bit of privacy to say their goodbyes outside of the church because it was packed.

After that, we all took turns as pallbearers, even though I was still in shock, and we carried his coffin onto a big, beautiful, horse-drawn carriage that took him to St. Anne's.

The most touching sight for me was the sight of this mural that had been painted near the flats where his body had been found.

In the space of just a week, this huge painting had been done in black and grey, paying its own tribute to Higgins. We followed behind this black carriage and the crowd were lovely with us, cheering us on and clapping.

HIGGINS

Northern Ireland is one of the warmest and friendliest places on the planet and Belfast did itself proud that day.

Lauren, Alex's daughter got up and read out a beautiful poem while the Dean of Belfast, Houston McKelvey, read out a tribute written by me.

The plan was for me to get up there and read it but on the day I was just too upset, too gutted, to be able to do Alex justice with my own voice.

I like to think though that it represented my love and respect and admiration for the man.

The wake after the funeral was packed with snooker players. Irishmen made up most of the funeral party as Eugene Hughes, Patsy Fagan, Stephen Murphy, Ken Doherty and Joe Swail were among the mourners and John Virgo, Willie Thorne, Stephen Hendry and Tony Meo were also there, sharing stories and banter and telling tales about what life was like living with The Hurricane.

Nobody in Alex's life really understood what made him tick, me included.

He could be your best friend or your worst enemy, within seconds of each other. He was a walking, talking contradiction. The clever, humble man who loved reading books, knocking off The Daily Telegraph crossword in 10 minutes flat and teaching himself new things but who couldn't see that gambling was the stupidest thing ever; the maniac who was always there for you when you needed him most; the reckless husband who loved his kids more than anything in the world; a man with a split personality that was never diagnosed but was there for all to see.

He had all these faults but, ultimately, every snooker player at his funeral and every snooker player in the world today owes him so much. He made the game what it was and what it is today.

Watching and playing him was a huge thrill and privilege and getting to know him was a pleasure and an honour.

I miss him massively and, so does the snooker world; a world that he changed forever with his genius and showmanship.

Rest In Peace mate.

13

Second Wind

I stand over the cushion, chalking my cue, buying myself some time. I scan the table and there are 12 reds left, as well as the colours, and I could do with all of them. I'm playing Stephen Maguire at the Paul Hunter Classic in Furth, Germany. I've beaten Ahmed Saif 4-1 in my first game, including a century break in the last frame to seal it.

After that win, I return to the players' lounge, puffing on an e-cigarette, sipping a coffee and catching up with the other players, laughing and taking the piss until the television screens next to the toilets let me know that my table is free to face Stephen.

I put my cheese and ham sandwich back in its clingfilm and I walk past security, round past the cue stall and memorabilia shop and down onto the main table. Me and Stephen are live on Eurosport and although I'm soon 3-1 down, he's just potted a brown and then gone too straight on the next red and jawed it.

The cue-ball is tight up against the black and the only available red is up against the cushion. I play a delicate shot but the red stays up and I return to my seat.

Stephen is too good a player not to make the most of this chance and he seizes on it, making a break of 59. I get out of my chair and concede the frame and the match.

He beats me 4-1 to go into the last 32 of the tournament. My cue gets broken down and goes back into my case; the name 'Whirlwind' embroidered on it, I sign a handful of autographs and stop for photographs with three young fans on the way back through the crowd.

Thanks folks.

Yeah, not quite my day. I'll be back; see you all soon.

On another day, I could've won that but Stephen kept me in my seat for too long. Oh well, there's always another tournament around the corner.

Another quick coffee, dash of milk and a sweetener please, another toot on the e-cigarette and I then race for the complimentary players' bus – there's one every 30 minutes and I don't want to have to hang around waiting – I pick my seat, cue case in hand, and head back to the Mercure hotel for some dinner – steak tonight, I think – and a large, cold bottle of water.

I've got a 7am flight tomorrow morning, plus a two-hour transit in Zurich before I get back to Heathrow so I won't be up late tonight.

I've got Tommy Tiger on the phone every hour as well, asking *if I've sorted him tickets for Chelsea out yet. I'm on it son, I'm on it.*

I'm 52 years old.

Welcome to the life of James Warren White.

My ambition today remains as simple as the day I started taking snooker seriously.

I want to be world champion. I want to hear the Crucible go crazy as that final black disappears.

David Vine is no longer with us and Ted Lowe won't be able to call the final frames either but I want to lift that trophy as my kids run on, as happy and as delighted as I am.

Snooker has given me a dream life – it would be nice for it to have the dream ending.

But, look, I'm a realist. I know that is probably never going to happen. I know that the standard of the game is higher than ever, I'm not getting any younger and the growth of the game in China is going to mean that the next breed of players coming through are going to be even more focused and disciplined than the current lot; if that's possible.

The facts are the facts. I've not qualified for the Crucible since 2006 and, I won't lie, that has been difficult at times. When your professional life has been so wrapped up in one tournament – and you become so well-known for it – it's hard when you stop getting invited to the party.

I've been unlucky and lost in the last qualifying round a few times but I feel more confident at the moment. Hopefully this year I will be fresh for the qualifiers and I will make it even if it's not getting any easier. I'm not done yet.

If I stepped out of myself and looked at me then I'd give me no chance of winning the World Championship either but I know what I'm capable of.

It's not boxing or football. There is no age limit to snooker and, crucially, I absolutely love practising. That is a real pleasure for me these days. It didn't always feel like that but I love practising in Epsom, or in Riley's in Southampton, and I hope it stays like that.

The day I stop enjoying practising will probably be the day I decide to hang the cue up but that isn't here yet and I don't really ever see it coming.

I still think I've got the game to do it. I need to cement a little bit more form and confidence and win a tournament or two but I know that if I can get to the Crucible and put together two weeks of good snooker then it could still be mine. It's only six fucking matches.

It's a bit like when Tom Watson almost won The Open the other year – I still believe that if I get everything right, hold everything together and get some luck then anything is possible.

At the moment, I'm hanging onto a place in the top 64 by a thread and in recent times it's looked like I could lose my tour card altogether – something that would've shattered me.

I've not been helped by some severe pain in my right foot that has badly affected my performances recently and I know I'm in a constant battle to stay on the tour as a result. Thirty years of leaning over a snooker table has led to a condition called plantar fasciitis which affects the tendon in your foot. Some people call it 'Policeman's Heel' because you get it after spending a lot of time on your feet – no snooker player has ever made a penny while sat down – and it can be really painful. I ended up having an operation in 2013 to try and relieve the pain but it's still not

100 per cent and when your fluency around the table is as badly affected as mine's been recently, it does knock your game and your confidence.

When I think about it all, the more settled, clean and sober my life has become, the quicker my fall down the rankings has been but I wouldn't change now. I wouldn't go back to the old ways, not for anything.

I wouldn't say I'm the happiest I've ever been at the moment because I'm just me, just Jimmy. I've never really been unhappy. Life's given me some tough moments, the same as everyone, including you, reading this – but I've never been an over-thinker or a depressed kind of guy. What I definitely am though is calmer. Long gone are the days of gambling, of drinking too much, of snorting and smoking the worst drug on the planet. These days all I want to do is practise, see my kids and grand-kids, entertain my fans and win snooker matches.

I've mentioned my drugs problem in this book because I want it to be a massive warning to people out there. The Devil's Dandruff is wicked and it will kill you. I hope the public will be sympathetic to why I've come out with all this. I could easily have brushed it under the carpet but I know, first hand, what drugs can do to your mind, body and soul. I saw it wreck my world title chances and I saw it almost kill me.

If I stop one person from being tempted then that's good enough for me.

•••••••

People ask me if losing six World Championship finals both-ers me and I can honestly say that I don't give them a second thought. Would I do things differently if I had my time again?

What do you think?

Of course I would. I'd prepare properly, I'd stick with one manager, I'd get an early night and I'd realise that the talent I had back then wouldn't and couldn't last forever and I'd also stay as far away from cocaine as possible.

It was the coke that really cost me.

And it cost me 10 world titles.

However, you can't live your life thinking like that or you would simply go mad; your head would explode with regrets and worries and what-ifs. That's not for me. If you don't take the positives out of life than what's the point of even getting out of bed in the morning?

And the positives for me are massive.

In 2007, I was playing in an exhibition in Southampton and afterwards I went to a nightclub with some mates.

As I was buying a round of drinks at the bar, I looked across and saw a girl out with her mate. Her name was Kelly.

Kelly had absolutely zero interest in me that night. She didn't care one little bit and wasn't in the mood to be chatted up by me. I stuck with it though, talking to her and her mate, buying them both drinks and trying my best to impress her.

Fortunately enough, I had won her mate round and as they went to get their coats and leave, her pal whispered to me where Kelly worked.

After that, I knew I had to try and chase it up – but she still wasn't having any of it.

I started pursuing her, in a very old-fashioned way, getting in touch quite a bit, trying to flirt with her and impress her. I did this for months but I knew I was getting nowhere and then, just as I was about to give up for good, she rang me to see how I was and whether I did fancy going out for that drink after all.

"I'll take you to London to see a show," I told her. We went to watch 'Jersey Boys' in the West End and we had a nice dinner before I drove her back to Southampton afterwards, like the perfect gentleman.

We saw each other a couple of times the week after and we've been together ever since.

She is a woman who I adore and she's very good for me. When you have someone you love, like I do Kelly, it stops you from chasing women and making a prat of yourself. There could be two top models fighting over me – although I doubt they'd be fighting! – but I wouldn't look twice and I wouldn't ever dream of straying.

If I'd met her years ago I might've strayed but I've changed since then and I love her to bits. She has played a massive part in me enjoying a slower pace of life.

Kelly lives in Southampton, so I split my time between there and Surrey.

Having a steady and loving relationship has changed me for the better but, saying that, I'm still very proud of what me and Maureen managed because my five kids are the most important, special people in my world. She's been a fantastic mother to my children and you can hardly stay angry for long with someone who's done that, can you?

Lauren, my eldest, is a fantastic mum and wife and I'm super proud of her.

Lauren always loved looking after her sisters and brother because she's a lot older than the others and she looks after me too these days by keeping my finances in good order.

I trusted too many people in the past and ended up bankrupt but she trusts nobody and makes sure everything is okay.

Ashleigh picks and chooses what she wants to do with her life and she's still not quite sure what that is yet but there ain't nothing wrong with that. She's the real brainy one and she could do anything she puts her mind to – she's just deciding what it is.

Georgia recently became a mum to little Bobby so is totally occupied with that but the entire family adore him to bits while Breeze is my youngest daughter and she's very hard working and knows what she wants from life. She gets married soon and she's looking forward to the big white wedding that we've gone halves on. She's no freeloader and insisted on that. We're going to have a massive do and I'm probably going to dance very badly and have a great night.

Tommy, my boy, is at boarding school, which he loves. He's doing very well and he's been there two years. He wasn't sure if he wanted to go or not at first but after living the life I've lived, I insisted that books and studying came first. I sounded like Mr Beatty actually...

"Give it a week," I told him. "See how you get on. I bet you'll love it." After that week he came back home with a black eye and loads of bruises from rugby. He was black and blue but he had a massive grin on his face and he was sold on the idea.

In my day, a black eye would've been priceless; I could've played on that, worked the angles on it – making up a story and a bit of a tale, trying to find a way to get some advantage from it. But Tommy? Nothing. Not a word. He's such a totally opposite lad to what I was like, he's his own man and very respectful.

SECOND WIND

Despite everything else, the fights and the kick-offs and the bullshit and all the drama, me and Maureen have managed to produce five kids who have all turned into wonderful, intelligent, confident people and the older I get, the more I admire and love them all.

Also, now my kids are having kids themselves, you get to enjoy it all over again. When you get called 'Grandad' you feel old but when you pick up your grandchild, the years fall off you again. To me, I'm the luckiest man I know.

As for snooker and the state of the modern game, I personally think there's never been a better time to be a professional snooker player.

When Barry Hearn took over the sport in 2009, it was in decline and anyone who says otherwise is just kidding themselves. There wasn't enough tournament prize money, media attention or glamour about the sport.

Before anything else, snooker is entertainment and the punters pay their money or tune in on telly because they want to watch exciting, dramatic and entertaining play but there was none of that then.

It was as if the game had just settled for being second-best but Barry has come in, given it the same treatment he's given the darts, and we're booming again.

There are loads and loads of tournaments around the world. You can pick and choose which ones you want to play in so you don't get burnt out and you can soon race up the rankings. In the '80s, it would take you forever to go from, say, 20 in the world to the top eight but if you go on a consistent run these days you can really climb the ladder quickly and that is very attractive to the young kids coming through.

There are so many new players around and I don't even recognise half of them. When I say young, I mean teenage lads and blokes in their early 20s who've been drilled at snooker since they could hold a cue.

They've been brought up in disciplined snooker clubs – normally in Asia, where the game is bigger than ever – and they arrive in England and they're ready to smash you off the table in no time at all.

Zan's it ain't.

In fact, now that Tony Meo no longer plays, I reckon there's only me and Davis left who know what an old-school snooker hall even looks like.

That's progress, I suppose.

These kids have come along and if you don't get in there and do the business straightaway and stamp down your authority then you get murdered, it's as simple as that. You have to have perfect shot selection and attack when there's value. I used to attack for the sake of it, because I loved it, but I'd attack when there was no value to my shots whereas these days I hang back, make sure I leave nothing on and then really cash in when there's plenty of value around the black.

The level of talent at the top of the game is frightening. O'Sullivan remains streets ahead of the rest and can win what he wants, when he wants.

He is the one modern player I'd pay to see play but there are others who are not far behind him.

Judd Trump has been labelled as the 'new Jimmy White' because of his attacking, quick play and he can really kick on in the next few years, Neil Robertson loves going for his shots and entertaining the crowd, Mark Selby did fantastically to beat O'Sullivan to the world title and he also has the skills and temperament to be at the top of his game for a long, long time.

I also love watching John Higgins play – he's had problems with his cue and whatever else recently but he's a class act – and Ding Junhui could also be a world champion if he could control his nerves. I sometimes get the feeling that when he's playing in China it all gets a bit much for him. He is so in demand over there and the spotlight is on him constantly and I think he sometimes struggles with that.

•••••••

One area that Barry has done a particularly good job at is punishing those who've deserved it when it comes to match-fixing.

In 1985, just as I was preparing to defend my Masters title at Wembley, I was in my dressing room and there was a knock at the door. I opened it and this geezer had somehow got backstage.

I could tell straightaway that there was something not quite right about him. Something shifty.

He walked into my dressing room, put a suitcase on the table, opened it and let me know his thoughts.

The suitcase was full of used £20 notes.

"That's all yours," this bloke said. "If you let Willie Thorne beat you 5-2, that is yours to keep. There's £35,000 in there." He tried to say it in a jokey way, as if we were big mates and that what he was asking me to do wasn't fucking evil. I wasn't having any of it.

"Keep the money," I said, trying to keep it lighthearted. "If I lost to Willie, people would think I was bent anyway."

No disrespect to Willie but I was head and shoulders above him as a player by then so the public would've known something was up if I'd lost.

I'd never go bent; not then, not now, not ever.

I didn't report it at the time and I regret that. I should've gone to the police or the authorities and told them what had happened but I was very young and life was just a joke then.

I told my dad though and he went crazy. "Jimmy, you've got to get them thrown out," he said, really pissed off, which was saying a lot as Dad was always so relaxed. Looking back, he was right – I should've done something about it.

Ten years later, just as I was recovering from my cancer scare, I had cause to question another strange series of events. It was when I had to play Peter Francisco in the World Championship. Betting was suspended before the game even started after unusual betting patterns were detected. Apparently, large amounts of money were going on me to win 10-2.

As a result, the WPBSA had a meeting. Their chairman at the time was the late world champion John Spencer. He was assigned to watch the game.

I remember I was really knackered during that match after a mad, mad, bender which wouldn't have put me in the best shape to hit top form. Peter appeared nervous and shifty, he wouldn't look anyone in the eye. I soon found myself with a strong lead in the game.

Eventually, John took me to one side. "Jimmy, let him win a frame," he said. "That means those bets are all cancelled." But I couldn't do that, it just didn't feel right. "I understand what you mean John and maybe I should but the punters in the arena don't deserve it."

SECOND WIND

It took a lot back then to make me serious or angry about stuff but I wasn't happy at all with the situation.

There was an investigation after the match and Peter was eventually banned for five years for bringing the game into disrepute, though he wasn't found guilty of match fixing.

Anyone who does go bent deserves nothing from the game. I'm old-school when it comes to that – throw the book at them. When Stephen Lee was found guilty in 2008 and 2009, he was still one of the best players in the world.

O'Sullivan hadn't played much that year and Lee raced through the rankings and won about £270,000 so why he needed to do what he did is something I can't get my head around at all.

In Lee's case, the size of the scandal involving him and where he is now is the only lesson a young player needs when they get tempted by bookmakers.

Lee had the lot, the big house, the cars, the happy family and so on but now his reputation is destroyed and he's apparently living on benefits.

Is it worth it? Was it worth it?

No fucking chance.

But he's only got himself to blame. Anyone who goes bent deserves to have their career ruined, as simple as that. He had one of the most beautiful cue actions in the game and he was so hard to beat.

Now he's barely allowed to pick up a cue. It is heartbreaking to see.

People can say whatever they like about me – and some probably will after reading this book – but I've always won and lost with good humour, grace and, if I do say so myself, a bit of class. I'd never even think about throwing away that reputation just for a few quid.

If I heard that there'd been a certain amount of money going on someone, I reckon I would recognise in the way they play. I'm not saying that I would always be right but I think I would know having been in the game so long. The right people spotted that Stephen wasn't playing normally, so it's not something you're going to get away with for long.

The man on the street, a postman or whatever, has one bet a week for, say, £30 and if he's backing someone who's gone bent, how is that fair? Especially since the man on the street is the person who made snooker what it is. No ifs, no buts, no three strikes and you're out.

If you're found guilty, you're gone – it's the only way it can be and the only way it should be.

• • • • • • •

China is undoubtedly where the future of the game lies and although all the players love the attention, the tournaments and the fun of travelling over there, one thing that will upset me – and pretty much every single person on the tour – is if the World Championship was to move over there.

And, I'm afraid, I think it's going to happen one day.

I just can't see how the game won't be drawn further and further across to Asia because of how big its boom over there has been. You sometimes forget how big China is and how many people live and breathe the game over there, so how's this for a number? At any one time, night or day, two million people are playing a frame of snooker somewhere in China!

SECOND WIND

Two million! How the hell does the game ignore a country with that kind of love and devotion to the sport.

Barry Hearn has come out publicly and said the World Championship will stay in Sheffield and I trust him on his word on that but he won't be the boss forever, so I think it's a no-brainer that one day we will all be travelling over there, rather than the Crucible.

That would be heartbreaking for me because Sheffield is where the sport belongs and where the sport's had its greatest moments. If the World Championship hadn't have moved there then who knows what state the sport would be in by now? The Crucible deserves respect and deserves its place in the sport.

And so what about me today then?

Where is my life at?

What keeps me going?

I'll put it like this. A couple of years back, I decided it was time to celebrate the life and the luck I've had with a testimonial for my 50th birthday.

For a long time, it looked like I wouldn't even get to 50 so that was an achievement in itself!

The idea was the day would raise a few quid but me, being me, barely made a penny from it because I went all out and booked The Grosvenor Hotel in London.

If you're going to have a party – have a proper one. I learnt that while sat in Victor Yo's front room, gawping up at all these Bunny Girls, 35 years ago.

We did two events, a daytime exhibition between me and O'Sullivan – who gave up his time for free – and then an evening party with Ronnie Wood, Mick Taylor, Bill Wyman and Mick Hucknall playing a concert so everybody could have a dance and a laugh. Barry Hearn got on board with the idea and sold tables and it was a fantastic night. The band Ronnie put together was different class, even if I had to foot the bill for all their rehearsal costs!

As it got close to midnight I looked around this room, full of my snooker mates, my family, Kelly by my side while three Rolling Stones had the dance floor packed out and I thought to myself 'Jimmy son, you've not done too bad have you?' and I was right; I hadn't and I haven't.

The Grosvenor is a long, long way from Dodgy Bob and Enoch Powell, from Bernard Manning and The Invitation but, underneath it all, the boy from The Duke and from Tooting is still in there, still excited about the sound the cue-ball makes when you've hit it sweetly, still thrilled by winning and practising and getting out of a tricky snooker and being part of the tour, still enjoying the same sport that I fell head over heels for all those years ago.

In all honesty, would I, at 52, really get up at 5am, queue in airports around the world with my oversized luggage, fly all over the place and live on hotel meals if I didn't still love the game?

I could've been a commentator by now – there's a possibility for the future – or I could've gone into snooker management – and used myself as an example of how not to do it – but I'm still out there, still trying, still chasing the dream.

Snooker is who I am, it's in my bones, and it's been the one constant in a life lived hard, fast and funny and a life that's thrilled millions of others as much as it's thrilled me.

That's good enough for me.

I'll take that all day long.

SECOND WIND

Would it be nice to say I was a six-time world champion?
Yeah, of course it would.
But do I regret the way life's turned out? Not for a second.
I never have. I never will.
For as long as I can take a cloth off a table, stick on some lights and set up a frame of snooker, I know I'll be happy – the Tooting kid who lived his dream, forever in Zan's, forever The Whirlwind.

Statistics

Date of birth: May 2nd 1962
Turned professional: 1980
Professional centuries: 331
Career prize money: £4.7m
Most frequently played opponent: Steve Davis
Highest professional break: 147
Most centuries in a season: 25 (1991/92)

Amateur tournament wins

English Amateur Championship: 1979
World Amateur Championship: 1980

Professional tournament wins

British Open: 1987, 1992
Canadian Masters: 1988
Carlsberg Challenge: 1984, 1985
Classic: 1986, 1991
European Challenge: 1991
European League: 1993
European Open: 1992
Grand Prix: 1986, 1992
Hong Kong Masters: 1988
Irish Masters: 1985, 1986
Malaysian Masters: 1986
Masters: 1984

Matchroom League: 1993
New Zealand Masters: 1984
Northern Ireland Classic: 1981
Players Championship: 2004
Pontins Professional: 1999
Pot Black: 1986
Scottish Masters: 1981
Thailand Masters: 1984
UK Championship: 1992
World Masters Men's Singles: 1991
World Matchplay: 1989, 1990
World Seniors Championship: 2010

Stats up until October 2014

Index

INDEX

INDEX

INDEX

J I M M Y

WHITE

SECOND WIND
MY AUTOBIOGRAPHY